A Short Guide to

WRITING ABOUT LITERATURE

A Short Guide to
WRITING ABOUT LITERATURE

SECOND EDITION

SYLVAN BARNET   *Tufts University*

LITTLE, BROWN AND COMPANY   *Boston*

FIRST PRINTING

Printed simultaneously in Canada by
Little, Brown & Company (Canada) Limited

PRINTED IN THE UNITED STATES OF AMERICA

Acknowledgments

The author gratefully acknowledges permission to use excerpts from works by the following authors:

ADAMS, ROBERT M. (p. 92). Reprinted from "Ibsen on the Contrary," in *Modern Drama,* edited by Anthony Caputi (New York: W. W. Norton & Co., Inc., 1966), by permission of the author.

BATESON, F. W. (pp. 132–33). Reprinted from *English Poetry* by F. W. Bateson by permission of Barnes & Noble, Inc., and Longman Group Limited.

BROWN, JOHN RUSSELL (p. 102). Reprinted from *Shakespeare's Plays in Performance* by John Russell Brown by permission of St. Martin's Press, Inc., and Macmillan & Co., Ltd.

CIARDI, JOHN (pp. 149–58). "Robert Frost: The Way to the Poem" from *Dialogue with an Audience* by John Ciardi. Copyright © 1958 by John Ciardi. Published by J. B. Lippincott Company.

COGHILL, NEVILL (pp. 37, 38). "Wags, Clowns and Jesters," in *More Talking of Shakespeare,* edited by John Garrett. (London: Longmans, Green & Co., Ltd.; and New York: Theatre Arts Books.) © 1959 by Longmans, Green & Co., Ltd. Reprinted by permission of Theatre Arts Books.

DAICHES, DAVID (p. 74). Paraphrase of pp. 73–83 of *The Novel and the Modern World* by David Daiches, printed by permission of the University of Chicago Press.

DREW, ELIZABETH (pp. 35, 36). Reprinted from *The Novel: A Modern Guide to Fifteen English Masterpieces* by Elizabeth Drew. Copyright © 1963 by Elizabeth Drew and used by permission of the publisher, Dell Publishing Co., Inc.

ELIOT, T. S. (p. 30). Lines from "Little Gidding" from *Four Quartets* by T. S. Eliot are reprinted by permission of Harcourt Brace Jovanovich, Inc., and Faber and Faber Ltd.

FAULKNER, WILLIAM (pp. 179–87). "A Rose for Emily," copyright 1958 by William Faulkner, reprinted from *Collected Stories of William Faulkner,* by permission of Random House, Inc.

FERGUSSON, FRANCIS (p. 93). Reprinted from *The Human Image in Dramatic Literature* by Francis Fergusson by permission of Columbia University Press. Copyright 1952, Columbia University Press.

FRIEDMAN, NORMAN (p. 38). Reprinted from "Point of View in Fiction," *PMLA,* 70 (1955), 1184, by permission of the Modern Language Association.

FROST, ROBERT (pp. 149–50). "Stopping by Woods on a Snowy Evening" (in John Ciardi, "Robert Frost: The Way to the Poem," pp. 149–58), from *Complete Poems of Robert Frost*. Copyright 1923 by Holt, Rinehart and Winston, Inc. Copyright 1951 by Robert Frost. Reprinted by permission of Holt, Rinehart and Winston, Inc.

FRYE, NORTHROP (pp. 27–28). Reprinted from *The Well-tempered Critic* by Northrop Frye, copyright © 1963 by Indiana University Press, by permission of the publisher.

GREEN, MARTIN (pp. 30, 59–60). Reprinted from *Re-appraisals* by Martin Green by permission of W. W. Norton & Company, Inc. Copyright © 1965, 1963 by Martin Green.

HERBERT, ROBERT L. (pp. 4–5). Reprinted from the International Fine Arts Exhibition catalog by permission of the author and The National Gallery of Canada (Ottawa).

JARRELL, RANDALL (p. 7). "The Death of the Ball Turret Gunner," from *The Complete Poems* by Randall Jarrell, copyright © 1945, 1969 by Mrs. Randall Jarrell. Reprinted by permission of Farrar, Straus & Giroux, Inc.

JOYCE JAMES (pp. 55–56). From "Araby" from *Dubliners* by James Joyce. Originally published by B. W. Huebsch, Inc., in 1916. All rights reserved. Reprinted by permission of The Viking Press, Inc.

KAUFFMANN, STANLEY (pp. 174–77). *"Wild Strawberries"* — April 27, 1959 — copyright © 1959 by Stanley Kauffmann, reprinted from *A World on Film* by Stanley Kauffmann by permission of Harper & Row, Publishers.

KILDAY, GREGG (pp. 171–74). "The Moviegoer: *Women in Love*" reprinted from the *Harvard Crimson* by permission of Gregg Kilday and the *Harvard Crimson*.

KRUTCH, JOSEPH WOOD (pp. 111–115). Reprinted from *"Modernism"* in *Modern Drama* by Joseph Wood Krutch by permission of Marcelle Krutch.

LODGE, DAVID (pp. 79–83). Reprinted from *Language of Fiction* (pp. 148–152) by David Lodge by permission of Columbia University Press and Routledge & Kegan Paul Ltd. Copyright 1966, Columbia University Press.

McCARTHY, MARY (p. 60). Reprinted from "Settling the Colonel's Hash" from *On the Contrary* by Mary McCarthy by permission of Farrar, Straus & Giroux, Inc.

MUIR, KENNETH. Quote on pp. 104–105 reprinted from *Shakespeare: The Great Tragedies* (London: Longmans, Green & Co., Ltd., 1961) by Kenneth Muir by permission of the author. Essay on pp. 109–111, "Hamlet's Foil," reprinted from *Shakespeare: Hamlet* by Kenneth Muir by permission of Edward Arnold (Publishers) Ltd.

NEMEROV, HOWARD (pp. 58–59). Reprinted from *Poetry and Fiction: Essays* by Howard Nemerov by permission of Rutgers University Press.

SEWALL, RICHARD B. (p. 38). Reprinted from *The Vision of Tragedy* by Richard B. Sewall by permission of Yale University Press.

TRILLING, LIONEL (p. 28). From *The Liberal Imagination* by Lionel Trilling. Copyright 1940 by Lionel Trilling. Reprinted by permission of The Viking Press, Inc.

VAN DOREN, MARK (pp. 145–49). From *Introduction to Poetry* by Mark Van Doren. Copyright 1951 by William Sloan Associates, Inc. Copyright © 1966 by Mark Van Doren. Reprinted by permission of Hill and Wang, Inc.

VAN GHENT, DOROTHY (pp. 57–58, 72, 73). Reprinted from *The English Novel* by Dorothy Van Ghent by permission of Holt, Rinehart and Winston, Inc.

PREFACE

This book is about writing, especially writing about literature. It does not try to cover all of the topics included in the usual rhetoric: it offers no instruction in the use of the apostrophe, no list of commonly misspelled words, no rules governing the positions of modifiers. I have assumed that these mechanical things have already been covered. This book does offer specific suggestions designed to help the student write effectively about literature.

The first chapter, "Writing about Literature," considers the nature of critical writing, treats matters of explication and analysis, and then discusses the problems of choosing a topic and of organizing the material. The chapter ends with a brief summary of the process of writing a critical essay.

The second chapter, "Style and Format," is a fairly short and direct approach to the elements of clear writing. It treats such matters as denotation, connotation, subordination, paragraphs, and so forth, and provides a number of specific illustrations, taken from good writers. The latter part of the chapter is devoted to manuscript form, quotations, footnotes, and bibliography.

The third, fourth, fifth, and sixth chapters introduce the reader to various approaches used in writing about fiction, drama, poetry and film. These chapters also include sample essays and a number of illustrative paragraphs that should help the reader to see what good writing is and to understand the sorts of problems good writers deal with.

Each of these last four chapters includes, about midway, an essay by a student, and each concludes with two essays by published essayists. The topics and approaches vary widely. No instructor wants his students to imitate any specific essayist, but again it is useful to have samples of adequate prose and examples of some of the things people do when they write about literature. These essays, along with the earlier material on writing and documentation, may provide the student with helpful guides to writing his own readable prose and to developing his own approaches to writing about literature and film.

I hope that the preceding remarks tell the reader all that he wants to know about the scope of the book, but some further words must be added. Dr. Johnson said that "there is not so poor a book in the world that would not be a prodigious effort were it wrought out entirely by a single mind, without the aid of previous investigators." I cannot name all of the previous investigators who have helped to shape my ideas, but I must acknowledge my indebtedness to publishers and authors for permission to reprint copyrighted material, to Martin B. Friedman for several suggestions, to Morton Berman and William Burto for letting me use passages from our *Introduction to Literature,* and to students for providing me with thousands of essays to think about. I wish also to thank those persons who offered valuable assistance by reading the manuscript, especially Jonathan Baumbach, Richard Beal, Morton Berman, William Burto, Charles Christensen, David Giele, Albert Gilman, Eileen Mason, Ann Parker, and Warren Stone. Finally, I want to record my indebtedness to the late Hyder Edward Rollins, who was the first to show me that the commonest errors in writing about literature are easily corrected when one is alerted to look for them.

S. B.

CONTENTS

PART TWO

A Short Guide to

WRITING ABOUT LITERATURE

PART ONE

1

WRITING ABOUT LITERATURE

THE NATURE OF CRITICAL WRITING

In everyday talk the commonest meaning of **criticism** is something like "finding fault," and to be critical is to be censorious. But a critic can see excellences as well as faults. Because we turn to criticism with the hope that the critic has seen something we have missed, the most valuable criticism is not that which shakes its finger at faults but that which calls our attention to interesting things going on in the work of art. Here are two statements, the first by John Dryden (1631–1700), the second by W. H. Auden (b. 1907), suggesting that criticism is most useful when it calls our attention to things worth attending to.

> They wholly mistake the nature of criticism who think its business is principally to find fault. Criticism, as it was first instituted by Aristotle, was meant a standard of judging well; the chiefest part of which is, to observe those excellencies which should delight a reasonable reader.
>
> *Essays*, ed. W. P. Ker (Oxford, 1926), I, 179

What is the function of a critic? So far as I am concerned, he can do me one or more of the following services:

1. Introduce me to authors or works of which I was hitherto unaware.

2. Convince me that I have undervalued an author or a work because I had not read them carefully enough.

3. Show me relations between works of different ages and cultures which I could never have seen for myself because I do not know enough and never shall.

4. Give a "reading" of a work which increases my understanding of it.

5. Throw light upon the process of artistic "Making."

6. Throw light upon the relation of art to life, to science, economics, ethics, religion, etc.

The Dyer's Hand (New York, 1963), pp. 8–9

The emphasis on observing, showing, illuminating, suggests that the function of critical writing is not very different from the commonest view of the function of imaginative writing. Here is Joseph Conrad in his preface to *The Nigger of the "Narcissus"*:

> My task which I am trying to achieve is, by the power of the written word, to make you hear, to make you feel — it is, before all, to make you *see*. That — and no more, and it is everything.

Let us begin with a very brief essay, one not about literature but about painting. In *The Gleaners* Jean-François Millet tried to show us certain things, and now an essayist tries to show us — tries to make us see — what Millet was doing and how he did it. The following short essay is a note in the catalog issued in conjunction with the art exhibition at the Canadian World's Fair, Expo 67.

JEAN-FRANÇOIS MILLET. 1814–1875

The Gleaners. c. 1857

Jean-François Millet, born of well-to-do Norman peasants, began his artistic training in Cherbourg. In 1837 he moved to Paris where he lived until 1849, except for a few extended visits to Normandy. With the sounds of the Revolution of 1848 still rumbling, he moved to Barbizon on the edge of the Forest of Fontainebleau, already noted as a resort of landscape painters, and there he spent the rest of his life. One of the major painters of what came to be called the Barbizon School, Millet began to celebrate the labours of the peasant, granting him a heroic dignity which expressed the aspirations of 1848. Millet's identification with the new social ideals was a result not of overtly radical views, but of his instinctive humanitarianism and his rediscovery in actual peasant life of the eternal rural world of the Bible and of Virgil, his favourite reading since youth. By elevating to a new prominence the life of the common people, the revolutionary era released the stimulus which enabled him to continue this essential pursuit of his art and of his life.

The Gleaners, exhibited in the Salon of 1857, presents the very poorest of the peasants who are fated to bend their backs to gather with clubbed fingers the wisps of overlooked grain. That they seem so entirely wedded to the soil results from the perfect harmony of Millet's fatalistic view of man with the images which he created by a careful disposition of lines, colours and shapes. The three women are alone in the bronzed stubble of the foreground, far removed from the bustling activity of the harvesters in the distance, the riches of whose labours have left behind a few gleanings. Millet has weighted his figures ponderously downward, the busy harvest scene is literally above them, and the high horizon line which the taller woman's cap

Oil. 32⅞ × 43¾ in. Musée du Louvre, Paris.

just touches emphasizes their earth-bound role suggesting that the sky is a barrier which presses down upon them, and not a source of release.

The humility of primeval labour is shown, too, in the creation of primitive archetypes rather than of individuals. Introspection such as that seen in Velazquez' *Water Carrier of Seville*, in which the three men are distinct individuals, is denied by suppressing the gleaners' features, and where the precise, fingered gestures of La Tour's *Saint Jerome* bring his intellectual work toward his sensate mind, Millet gives his women club-like hands which reach away from their bent bodies toward the earth.

It was, paradoxically, the urban-industrial revolution in the nineteenth century which prompted a return to images of the pre-industrial, ageless labours of man. For all their differences, both Degas and Van Gogh were to share these concerns later, and even Gauguin was to find in the fishermen of the South Seas that humble being, untainted by the modern city, who is given such memorable form in Millet's *Gleaners*.

Robert L. Herbert

In this essay there is, of course, evaluation or judgment as well as interpretation or understanding. First, the writer assumes it is worth his effort to talk about Millet's picture. Second, he explicitly praises some qualities ("perfect harmony," "memorable form"), but mostly the evaluation is implicit in and subordinate to the description of what the writer sees. He sees things and calls them to our attention as worthy of note. He points out the earth-bound nature of the women, the difference between their hands and those of Saint Jerome (in another picture that was in the exhibition), the influence of the Bible and of Virgil, etc. It is clear that he values the picture, and he states some of the reasons he values it; but he is not worried about whether Millet is a better artist than Velazquez, or whether this is Millet's best painting. He is content to help us see what is going on in the picture.

Let us look for a moment at the **organization** or plan of this essay. In his effort to help us see what is going on, the author keeps his eye on his subject. His opening paragraph includes a few details (e.g., the fact that Millet was trained in Cherbourg) that are not strictly relevant to his main point (the vision embodied in the picture), but these must be included because the essay is not only a critical analysis of the picture but an informative headnote in a catalog of an exhibition of works by more than a hundred artists. Even in this preliminary paragraph he moves quickly to the details closely related to the main business: Millet's peasant origin, his early association with landscape painters, his humanitarianism, and his reading of the Bible and Virgil. The second paragraph takes a close look at some aspects of the picture (the women's hands, their position in the foreground, the harvesters above and behind them, the oppressive sky), and the third paragraph makes illuminating comparisons with two other paintings. The last paragraph, like most good concluding paragraphs, while recapitulating the main point (the depiction of ageless labors), enlarges the vision by including references to Millet's younger contemporaries who shared his vision. Notice that this new material does not leave us looking forward to another paragraph but neatly opens up, or enriches, the matter and then turns it back to Millet. (For additional remarks on introductory and concluding paragraphs, see pp. 36–38.)

A work of literature, like a painting, is a work of art. It is an object that embodies thoughts and feelings, and study of it can increase our understanding of exactly what it is. An enormous body of literature is worth our study, and a wide range of kinds of literary study is designed to bring us into a closer relation with the work. Any writing that helps a reader to understand a literary work can properly be called literary criticism. Sometimes the critic will study the author's sources, seeking to show us — say, by a comparison between Plutarch's *Lives* and Shakespeare's *Julius Caesar* — some of the special qualities in the literary work. Sometimes he will study the author's biography, seeking to show us, for example, that Tennessee Williams's *The Glass Menagerie* draws heavily upon his childhood experiences. Sometimes he will study the anthropological and socio-logical background of the work, seeking to show us that a Greek tragedy owes its form to earlier rituals, that A *Midsummer Night's Dream* is indebted to May Day customs, or that the word "thou" in Shakespeare's sonnets has a very different force from the word "you." But undergraduates are not ordinarily expected to have the familiarity with little-known material to do much in these directions except perhaps the first — source study. Usually undergraduates are asked to exert a trained intelligence in explicating (literally, unfold-ing or spreading out) or in analyzing (literally, separating into parts in order to understand functions and relationships) a work or a part of a work. These activities are not sterile exercises: they are attempts to get on to paper — for one's own sake and for the sake of others — a sense of what a reader sees when he responds to a literary work of art.

Two Common Approaches: Explication and Analysis

Explication is ordinarily a line-by-line or episode-by-episode com-mentary on what is going on. (It takes some skill to work one's way along without saying "In line one . . . , in the second line . . . , in the third line. . . ." One must sometimes manfully say something like "The next stanza begins with . . . and then introduces. . . ." And, of course, one can discuss the second line before the first line if that seems to be the best way of handling the passage.) An ex-plication is not a paraphrase, a rewording — though it may include paraphrase — but a commentary revealing the meaning of the work. To this end it calls attention, as it proceeds, to the connotations of words, the function of rhymes, the shifts in point of view, the de-velopment of contrasts, and any other contributions to the meaning. Take, for example, this short poem by Randall Jarrell, published in 1945.

The Death of the Ball Turret Gunner

From my mother's sleep I fell into the State,
And I hunched in its belly till my wet fur froze.
Six miles from earth, loosed from its dream of life,
I woke to black flak and the nightmare fighters.
When I died they washed me out of the turret with a hose.

One student's explication runs thus:

Reading the first line aloud, one pauses slightly after

"sleep," dividing the line in half. The halves make a sharp

contrast. The point of transition in this line is "I fell,"
a helpless movement from the mother to the State, from sleep
to the State. The mother and the State make an evident
contrast, and so do "sleep" and "the State," which resemble
each other in their initial sound and in their position at
the end of a half-line but which have such different associations, sleep being comforting and the State being associated with totalitarianism. "The country" or "the land"
might be comforting and nourishing, but "the State" has no
such warm suggestions. We will soon see in the poem that
life in the "belly" of the State is a mindless and cold
death-like life which ends with an abrupt and brutal physical death. A mother, even in her "sleep," naturally pro-
tects and nourishes the child in her warm womb; the State
unnaturally continues to cramp the man in its icy belly.
He "hunched in its belly" until his "wet fur froze." Though
the only specified antecedent of "its" is the State, we
gather from the title that "its" refers also to the airplane
in whose womb-like ball turret he led his confined existence
and died. The airplane and the State are brought together
in the word "its," for both are seen as confining and destructive machines, and both are implicitly contrasted to
the mother, whose womb nourishes. Given the title, the fur
probably literally refers to the fur lining of the jackets
that fliers wore in World War II, but it also metaphorically
suggests the sub-human or animal-like existence he led while
confined by this unfeeling foster parent, the State-air-
plane. His unnatural existence is further emphasized by the

fact that, in the airplane, he was "Six miles from earth."
From such an existence, far removed from the "dream of life"
that people hope for, and still hunched in the fetal position in the turret, he was born again, that is, he awoke to
(or became aware of) not a rich fulfillment of the dream but
a horrible reality that can only be described as a nightmare
--a terrifying experience that is the perversion of the life
that men dream of. Possibly "woke to black flak" imitates,
in its staccato k's at the ends of words, the sound of the
gunfire that simultaneously awakened and killed him. His
awakening or birth is to a nightmarish reality and death.
It is not surprising, but it is certainly horrifying, that
in this world of an impersonal State that numbs and destroys
life the remnants of his body are unceremoniously flushed
out of the turret with a hose. This is the third horrible
release: the first was from the mother into the State; the
second was from the belly of the State into the belly of the
airplane; and now in shreds from the belly of the airplane
into nothing. That this entire life-history is told rather
flatly, with no note of protest, of course increases the
horror. The simplicity of the last line, a straightforward
literal statement, more effectively brings out the horror of
the experience than an anguished cry or an angry protest
could do. Notice, also, that the first sentence is two
lines long, and so is the second sentence. But this third
and last sentence is only one line long, its relative brevity perhaps helping to communicate the idea that the speaker's life was cut off sooner than it might have been.

An explication need not proceed mechanically line by line, but as a whole it usually moves through the poem from the beginning to the end. A difficulty, of course, is that any given line may take on additional meanings by virtue of what comes later. The first line in Jarrell's poem says nothing of the mother's womb, but in the context of the second line, with its reference to the State's "belly," and in the context of the remaining lines, which see the turret as a womb, it is fair in retrospect to see a suggestion of the mother's womb in the first line.

Because the language of a literary work is denser (richer in associations or connotations) than the language of discursive prose such as this paragraph, explication is much concerned with bringing to the surface the meanings that are in the words but that may not be immediately apparent. Explication, in short, seeks to make explicit the implicit. Other sample explications, or fragments of explications, appear in Chapters 3, 4, and 5.

Analysis, a breaking of the work into parts, or the study of one or more parts, is more common than explication in the study of works longer than a page or two; though, of course, if one has world enough and time, one can set out to explicate all of *Moby-Dick* or *Paradise Lost*. (More likely, one will explicate a page in *Moby-Dick*, or a verse paragraph in *Paradise Lost*.) An analysis may, for example, consider only the functions of the setting in *The Adventures of Huckleberry Finn* or of the narrator's voice in *Paradise Lost*. Although Chapters 3, 4, and 5 contain numerous specimens of analytic criticism, a sample analysis may be useful here.

Suppose one wants to write about the role of the clown in *Othello*. After thinking about the play and consulting the jottings made while thinking and rereading, one decides that the essay's underlying argument, or thesis — the clown *has* a role — breaks down into, say, five parts or paragraphs. (Of course, it takes a good deal of thinking before one sees that the notes can be reasonably arranged into these groups.) The topic ideas — the ideas that will be developed in a series of paragraphs — might be these:

1. The role of the clown in *Othello* is small but significant.

2. His first appearance, with musicians beneath Othello's window in III.i, is moderately funny on the surface.

3. This scene is more than funny; it provides relief, and yet it is related to the tragic motif.

4. In his second appearance, in III.iv, he puns on the word "lie," a word central to the play.

5. The study of a relatively small detail can suggest the complexity of what goes on in Shakespeare's plays.

When properly amplified (*not* padded, but set forth with convincing detail), the essay might run thus:

The Clown in *Othello*

Of the several dozen characters in *Othello*, the clown is among the least notable. He appears in only two scenes, speaking only about thirty lines. Nothing really depends upon him. If he is cut out, Iago will still succeed in duping Othello into murdering Desdemona, and Othello will still commit suicide in the fifth act. Yet the clown is in the play, and he presumably pulls his weight.

He first appears in III.i, bandying words with the musicians whom Cassio has brought to play beneath Othello's window. Like most of Shakespeare's other clowns, this one engages in bawdy repartee. Although a modern audience does not understand the jokes until they are explained in footnotes, and then does not find them funny, presumably the Elizabethan audience understood and enjoyed the jokes and was grateful for the humor. The joke about wind instruments — "And thereby hangs a tale" — with its pun on "tail" is given the most space, leading to the paradox about "music that may not be heard." [1] But even if we assume that the scene was once funny, we may still wonder what it is doing in the play.

It does quite a bit. First, it provides relief from the preceding tension: Cassio has been deprived of his office, and Iago's plot to use Cassio as a means to destroy Othello is well under way. A few lines after the clown's scene, Cassio will raise the tension again by unwittingly furthering Iago's plot. But the comic business is not mere relief; it contains the metaphor of music that was introduced when Othello had good-humoredly hoped that the kisses he shared with Desdemona would be their greatest discords (II.i.196). In an aside Iago had said, "O, you are well tuned now! / But I'll set down the pegs that make this music" (II.i.198–99); that is, he had vowed to loosen the strings (the lovers are conceived of as two stringed instruments in harmony) in order to produce discord or disharmony. We earlier saw him introduce discord into Brabantio's house when he shouted bawdy warnings and more recently when he caused the "dreadful bell" to sound the alarm. Now, in the scene with the clown, we hear music spoken of in bawdy terms in line 19 ("put up your pipes in your bag"). The bawdiness is underlined by "for love's sake" (line 13), ordinarily an expression roughly equivalent merely to "for goodness' sake," but here with a second sexual meaning: this pipe music is banished "for love's sake" because it would inter-

---

[1] Lines 6–15. All quotations from *Othello* are taken from the Signet Classic Edition, ed. Alvin Kernan (New York, 1963).

rupt the consummation of Othello's and Desdemona's marriage. Finally, in this scene there is yet another connection between the clown's jests and the tragic plot. When Cassio says, "Dost thou hear me, mine honest friend?" the clown punningly replies, "No. I hear not your honest friend. I hear you" (line 21). "Honest friend" looks back to Cassio, who has proved to be an unreliable friend and whose attempt now to regain Othello's friendship through the musicians is less than honest. Moreover, "honest friend" looks ahead to III.iii, when Iago will villainously play the role of honest friend.

The clown's second and last appearance, at the beginning of III.iv, follows the terrifying scene in which Iago, feigning to be Othello's friend, poisons Othello's mind and rouses him to murderous thoughts. Again the clown provides relief by his punning, and again the punning is relevant to the tragic plot. Desdemona asks him (line 1) where "Cassio lies" — that is, where Cassio lives or lodges — and the clown pretends to take the word in the sense of "tells untruths": "I dare not say he lies anywhere. . . . He's a soldier, and for me to say a soldier lies, 'tis stabbing" (lines 3–6). "Lie" and "lies" are mentioned seven times in this brief encounter which is the prelude to a series of tragic lies later in the scene: Emilia lies when she says she does not know where Desdemona's handkerchief is; Othello lies when he says he is untroubled; Desdemona lies when she says she has not lost the handkerchief. Iago, of course, has already lied and will continue to lie. No less important, the clown's insistent use of "lie" is the prelude to the appearance of the word in the next scene, when Othello bitterly puns on the sexual meaning (IV.i.36–37): "Lie with her? Lie on her? — We say lie on her when they belie her. Lie with her!" Desdemona, of course, has been belied; she and Cassio did not lie together.

We need not worry about whether or not Shakespeare was conscious of the threads that tie the clown to the tragic plot. Possibly he was not; possibly his mind unconsciously introduced the bawdy references to music after the figure of Othello and Desdemona as "well tuned." Possibly, too, the clown's puns on "lie" were thought to be no more than jokes to provide a light moment between scenes of great tension. But these jokes do in fact connect with other things in the play, making their contribution, however small, to the tragedy of *Othello*. It is not surprising that in *Othello*, as in any other work of genius, a complexity of artistry and a subtlety of meaning pervade even the smallest details.

Although Chapter 2 offers some detailed suggestions about writing, we can pause a moment here to call attention to several principles.

1. The introductory paragraph, with its reference to all of the characters, begins with a relatively wide view and then moves in on its subject, the clown. By the end of the paragraph the exact topic — "What does the clown do?" — is introduced.

2. The next three paragraphs, the body of the essay, discuss the clown's role in his two scenes; his first appearance is, reasonably, considered first.

3. Some brief and relevant quotations are used. They give the reader the necessary details, and they do not interrupt the flow of the argument as long quotations are likely to do.

4. The writer assumes that the reader has read the work being discussed; therefore, he does not fill his essay with a tedious synopsis. But aware that the reader has not memorized the work, the writer gives him helpful reminders, as in "He first appears in III.i, bandying words with the musicians whom Cassio has brought. . . ."

5. The writer has opinions, but he keeps himself in the background, for the most part revealing the work rather than himself.

6. The present tense is used in narrating the action of a play or a piece of fiction, as in "He first appears in III.i . . . ," and in "When Cassio says. . . ." Of course, earlier actions normally require the present perfect ("Cassio has already revealed his plan"), later actions the future, but in narrating what *is* happening use the present.

7. The concluding paragraph has a structure more or less the reverse of the introductory paragraph. It moves from the clown in *Othello* to art in general, setting the particular topic in a framework.

Only points 2 and 4 can be thought of as rules: an essay must be organized and must not synopsize unnecessarily. The other points are not rules but rather are time-tested procedures that may be of help.

Finding a Manageable Topic

1. If a topic is assigned, write on it.

2. If you are to choose a topic, choose one that can be treated thoroughly within the allotted space. Unless you have an enormous amount of time for reflection and revision, you cannot write a meaningful essay of five hundred or even a thousand words on "Character in Nabokov's *Ada*," on "Figurative Language in *Othello*," or on "Symbolism in *Moby-Dick*." If you have read the work thoughtfully, you ought to be able to find a much smaller topic, one that you can think hard about for the relatively few hours that you have and that you can discuss in detail within the limits of the paper. A "smaller" topic need not be a dull or trivial topic; treated properly, it may illuminate the entire work, or, to change the metaphor, it may serve as a mine-shaft that gives entry to the work. "Hamlet's Relationship to Horatio," carefully thought about, will in five hundred or a thousand words tell a reader more (and will have taught its author more) than will "Hamlet as a Tragic Hero." Similarly, "Huck Finn's Imagination" is a better topic than "The Character of Huck Finn," and "The

Meanings of 'Economy' in *Walden*" a better topic than "The Meaning of *Walden*."

How do you find a topic? An idea may hit you suddenly; as you are reading you find yourself jotting in the margin, "Contrast with Joyce's treatment of disillusionment," "too heavy irony," or "ugh." Or an idea may come slowly on rereading. Perhaps you gradually become aware of the frequency of "really" in *The Catcher in the Rye*, and you notice that Holden Caulfield, who is regularly given to saying things such as "if you really want to know" and "I really mean it," at one point explicitly comments on the nature of reality. You work on this and begin to relate it to his abundant discussions of phoneys, and you emerge, perhaps, with the **thesis,** or argument, or proposition, that in Holden's mouth "really" is not merely the filler it seems to be but is a clue to his quest for the real in a world of appearances or phoneys. If you have thought about the topic, converted it into a thesis, and stripped it of irrelevancies, you should be able to formulate it in a few words. This formula, or something like it, can be your title. There is nothing wrong with a title as direct as "Holden's Use of 'Really' "; although it is scarcely exciting, it is informative. Beware of cute titles, especially those that do not give the reader a good idea of what will follow such as "Really" or "A Boy's Word." "The Real Holden and Reality" is about as far as one can go.

One other example of a thesis may be useful here: Mark Van Doren's analysis of Wordsworth's "The Solitary Reaper" (Chapter 5) is held together by his proposition (p. 146) that the poem is admirable "yet each stanza is inferior to the one before it." Van Doren does not simply talk at random about the poem; he has an argument and he presents it. Notice, too, that Van Doren announces his thesis in his first paragraph. An essayist may have fretted for hours before finding his thesis, but he ought to let the reader know the gist of it early in the essay. The title, the first paragraph, or both are usually appropriate places.

Every literary work affords its own topics, and every essayist must set forth his own thesis, but a few useful generalizations may be made. You can often find a thesis by asking one of two questions:

1. What is this doing? That is, why is this scene in the novel or play? Why is the clown in *Othello?* Why are these lines unrhymed? Why is this stanza form employed?

2. How was this done? That is, how did the author make this character funny or dignified or pathetic? How did he communicate the idea that this character is a bore without boring me? Why do I find this poem witty?

The chapters on fiction, drama, poetry, and film try to provide the relevant critical vocabulary; they also try to do two other things: suggest the sorts of problems critics write about, and offer paragraphs that can serve as models of critical writing. After reading the chapter on fiction, for example, you should have not only some idea of what plot, symbolism, setting, etc., are but also some idea of how to write about them. It is primarily from those chapters and from your instructor that you should get help in developing your sense of appropriate topics, but a few examples are offered here. For the sake of clarity, these topics are stated baldly. They are rough beginnings and need to be shaped into theses. Consider the difference between "Hamlet's Relationship to Horatio" (an unshaped topic) and the thesis you might work out: Although Hamlet admires Horatio's stoic temperament and values his companionship, Hamlet's temperament is more heroic.

Sample Topics in Fiction

PLOT
"Death as a Device to Link Episodes in *Huckleberry Finn*"
"The Appropriateness of the Ending of *Lord of the Flies*"

THEME
"The Female as Victim in Melville's 'The Tartarus of Maids' "
"Absurdity in Camus's *The Plague*"
"Paralysis in Joyce's *Dubliners*"
"Imagery as a Revelation of Theme in . . ."

CHARACTER (Sometimes a mere character sketch may be acceptable; more often one will study character to see how it contributes to the theme or — pp. 104–105 — how it helps to define another character.)
"Ch'en and Kyo: A Contrast between a Terrorist and a Revolutionary in Malraux's *Man's Fate*"
"What Holden Caulfield Is *Really* Like"
"Stephen Dedalus: Prig or Artist?"
"The Function of the Three Mates in *Moby-Dick*"
"The Distinctive Language of Huck Finn"
"Dilsey and Joe Christmas: The Poles of Faulkner's Conception of the Role of Black Americans"

FORESHADOWING (Really an aspect of Plot and Character.)
"Suspense and Surprise in . . ."
"Early Tragic Overtones in *Moby-Dick*"
"The Humor of the Unexpected"

SETTING

"The Function of the Setting in . . ."
"Contrasts in the Settings in . . ."

SYMBOLISM

"The Meaning of the White Whale"
"Walls in *Bartleby*"
"The River in *Huckleberry Finn*"
"The Sun in Camus's *The Stranger*"

POINT OF VIEW

"Objectivity in 'The Killers' "
"Editorializing in *Tess of the D'Urbervilles*"
"The Unreliable Narrator in . . ."

Sample Topics in Drama

When writing about a play, you may find a topic similar to one of those given above. But in addition to those centering on theme, character, foreshadowing, setting, and symbolism, you may find the following examples useful.

IRONY

"Unconscious Irony in *Macbeth*"
"Conscious Irony in *Major Barbara*"

TRAGEDY

"King Oedipus: Tragic Hero or Pathetic Victim?"
"A Comparison between King Oedipus and Willy Loman"
"Willy Loman and Arthur Miller's Theory of Tragedy"
"Sartre's *No Exit*: A Tragedy without a Tragic Hero"

COMEDY

"The Comic in the Tragic: Beckett's *Waiting for Godot*"
"The Two Jesters in *As You Like It*"
"The Comic Portrayal of Villainy in . . ."
"The Comic Treatment of a Class Society in Shaw's
   Pygmalion"
"Tragic Implications in *Major Barbara*"

PLOT

"The Relevance of the Subplot in *King Lear*"
"Coincidence in *Ghosts*"
"The Turning Point in . . ."
"Flashbacks in *Death of a Salesman*"

GESTURES

"Comic Mannerisms in . . ."
"Appropriate Gestures for Hamlet in the Prayer Scene"

Sample Topics in Poetry

VOICE

"The Unawareness of Egotism: The Duke in 'My Last
  Duchess' "
"The New England Voice in Frost's Poems"
"Prufrock's Ironic Self-Depreciation"

DICTION

"The Use of Colloquialisms in Frost"
"Shifts in Diction in Allen Ginsberg"

FIGURATIVE LANGUAGE

"Scientific Imagery as a Vehicle for Passion"
"Metaphors of the Theater in Yeats's 'Lapis Lazuli' "
"Organic Metaphors in a Poem by Whitman"

SYMBOLISM

"Frost's Woods and Stars"
"The City in Robert Lowell's Poetry"

STRUCTURE

"Logic and Illogic in . . ."
"Paradox in . . ."
"The Movement from Anger to Resignation in . . ."
"The Development of the Theme, Stanza by Stanza, in . . ."

IRONY

"Understatement as a Means of Protest in American
  Folk Ballads"
"Understatement in . . ."

PATTERNS OF SOUND

"Rhyme and Reason in . . ."
"The Significance of Metrical Variations in . . ."
"The Not-So-Free Verse of 'When Lilacs Last in the Dooryard
  Bloom'd' "

Topics for essays on film often resemble those for essays on fiction
and drama, but because there are special problems discussion of the
matter is postponed until Chapter 6, "Writing About Film."

CONSIDERING THE EVIDENCE

Once you have your topic ("The Clown in *Othello*") and have
shaped it into a thesis ("The clown is relevant"), be certain that you
have all the evidence. Usually this means that you should study the
context of the material you are discussing. An excerpt from A. E.

Housman serves as a famous instance of the failure to keep the context in mind. Housman wrote of a line in Milton's *Arcades:*

> But in these six simple words of Milton —
>
> Nymphs and shepherds, dance no more —
>
> what is it that can draw tears, as I know it can, to the eyes of more readers than one? What in the world is there to cry about? Why have the mere words the physical effect of pathos when the sense of the passage is blithe and gay? I can only say, because they are poetry, and find their way to something in man which is obscure and latent, something older than the present organization of his nature.
>
> *The Name and Nature of Poetry* (New York, 1933), p. 45

This tells us something about Housman but nothing about the line in *Arcades;* in its context the line is not a command to stop dancing but only to stop dancing "By sandy Ladon's lillied banks" and to come to "A better soil."

Similarly, if, for example, your topic is images of light and dark, take account of *all* of the images of this sort. Some may not fit the pattern you discern in the vast majority, but fairness and self-protection require that you call attention to the exceptions and indicate why they do not destroy your thesis. Before you argue that because Holden distrusts the adult world, "old" is his ultimate word of condemnation, remember that he speaks of "old Phoebe" and of "old Thomas Hardy," both of whom he values greatly. Before you argue that the style of *Romeo and Juliet* is highly formal, remember that it includes such lines as "Where's Potpan, that he helps not to take away? He shift a trencher! He scrape a trencher!" (There *is* a good deal of highly formal writing in the play, and an essay can be written on it, but the essayist should be aware that the play has other styles too.) Before you argue that the imagery in *Romeo and Juliet* associates the lovers with light and death with dark, remember that not every image of light and dark works this way. At the beginning of the play several extended passages associate the infatuated Romeo with darkness. The discrepancy can be explained; it must be explained.

Two additional relevant concerns: (1) know what the words mean, and (2) know the limitations of the reprint you are using. The first point is obvious. Pay attention to footnotes if they are given; look up words and allusions that are obscure to you, and, if the piece is not recent, consider the possibility that a word that looks familiar but that makes little sense may have an older and different meaning. When Alexander Pope says that he will "catch the manners living as they rise," "manners" denotes not etiquette but kinds or psychological types, an obsolete usage except in such a phrase as

"What manner of man is he?" The second point, the limitations of your text, may or may not be relevant, depending on the nature of the assignment. If the instructor tells you to stay with the page in front of you, work from that. But if you are given more freedom, you may find it advisable to know something about the reprint you are working from. Some editors provide a "Note on the Text," telling you whether they are reprinting the first or the last edition, listing their emendations, etc. By reading the editor's textual note you may learn, for example, that although he has printed the first two lines of Shakespeare's "Sonnet 146" thus:

> Poor soul, the center of my sinful earth,
> Thrall to these rebel pow'rs that thee array,

the only authoritative text (1609) — the text from which all other texts are derived — did not print "Thrall to," but accidentally reprinted "my sinful earth." "Thrall to" is merely an editor's guess; among other guesses are "Fooled by," "Leagued with," and "Rebuke." Any other two syllables that will make sense are equally valid guesses. Clearly it is unwise to build an interpretation that rests heavily on any of these guesses. A final example illustrates the point: Henry James revised his novels for the New York Edition; therefore, before you write about his development from the early novels to the late ones, make sure that you have read the early novels and not late revisions of them.

ORGANIZING THE MATERIAL

After locating a topic, converting it into a thesis, and weighing the evidence, a writer has the job of organizing the material into a coherent whole, a series of paragraphs that steadily builds up an effective argument. Notice that the paragraphs in the essay on *Othello* (pp. 11–12) cannot be shuffled about without a loss in clarity. The idea of discussing the earlier scene before the later scene is reasonable; indeed, if the discussions of the two scenes were reversed, the writer would have to have a good reason for violating the play's chronology. He might have such a reason. If he felt that the second scene was much slighter, he might take it up first, explaining that it is best to get this less important scene out of the way before turning to the heart of the matter, the clown's first scene. Again, to avoid an anticlimax, the writer might reverse the chronological order if there were evidence in the work that ran counter to his thesis — but had to be shown — and this evidence came chronologically after the evidence supporting his thesis.

Something should be said about an essay organized around a

comparison or a **contrast,** say, between the settings in two novels, between two characters in a novel, or between the symbolism in two poems. Probably the student's first thought, after making some jottings, is to discuss one half of the comparison and then to go on to the second half. Instructors and textbooks usually condemn such an organization, arguing that the essay breaks into two parts and that the second part involves a good deal of repetition of categories set up in the first part. Usually they recommend that the student organize his thoughts differently, somewhat along these lines:

1. First similarity
   a. first work (or character, or characteristic)
   b. second work
2. Second similarity
   a. first work
   b. second work
3. First difference
   a. first work
   b. second work
4. Second difference
   a. first work
   b. second work

and so on, for as many additional differences as seem relevant. For example, if one wishes to compare *Huckleberry Finn* with *The Catcher in the Rye,* one may organize the material thus:

1. First similarity (the narrator and his quest)
   a. Huck
   b. Holden
2. Second similarity (the corrupt world surrounding the narrator)
   a. society in *Huckleberry Finn*
   b. society in *The Catcher*
3. First difference (degree to which the narrator fulfills his quest and escapes from society)
   a. Huck's plan to "light out" to the frontier
   b. Holden's breakdown

Here is another way of organizing a comparison and contrast:

1. First point: the narrator and his quest
   a. similarities between Huck and Holden
   b. differences between Huck and Holden
2. Second point: the corrupt world
   a. similarities between the worlds in *Huck* and *The Catcher*
   b. differences between the worlds in *Huck* and *The Catcher*

3. Third point: degree of success
   a. similarities between Huck and Holden
   b. differences between Huck and Holden

But a comparison need not employ either of these structures. There is even the danger that an essay employing either of them may not come into focus until the essayist stands back from his seven-layer cake and announces, in his concluding paragraph, that the odd layers taste better. In one's preparatory thinking, one may want to make comparisons in pairs (Good-natured humor: the clown in *Othello*, the clownish grave-digger in *Hamlet*; Social satire: the clown in *Othello*, the grave-digger in *Hamlet*; Relevance to main theme: . . . ; Length of role: . . . ; Comments by other characters: . . .), but one must come to some conclusions about what these add up to before writing the final version. This final version should not duplicate the thought processes; rather, it should be organized so as to make the point clearly and effectively. After reflection, one may believe that although there are superficial similarities between the clown in *Othello* and the clownish grave-digger in *Hamlet*, there are essential differences; then in the finished essay one probably will not wish to obscure the main point by jumping back and forth from play to play, working through a series of similarities and differences. It may be better to discuss the clown in *Othello* and then to point out that, although the grave-digger in *Hamlet* resembles him in A, B, and C, the grave-digger also has other functions (D, E, and F) and is of greater consequence to *Hamlet* than the clown is to *Othello*. Some repetition in the second half of the essay (e.g., "The grave-digger's puns come even faster than the clown's. . . .") will serve to bind the two halves into a meaningful whole, making clear the degree of similarity or difference. The point of the essay presumably is not to list pairs of similarities or differences, but to illuminate a work, or works, by making thoughtful comparisons. In a long essay one cannot postpone until page 30 a discussion of the other half of the comparison, but in an essay of, say, less than ten pages nothing is wrong with setting forth one half of the comparison and then, in light of it, the other half. The essay will break into two unrelated parts if the second half makes no use of the first, or if it fails to modify the first half, but not if the second half looks back to the first half and calls attention to differences that the new material reveals. A student ought to learn how to write an essay with interwoven comparisons, but he ought also to know that there is another way to write a comparison.

The following summary, paragraph by paragraph, of Stanley Kauffmann's comparison of film versions of Joyce's *Ulysses* and *Finnegans Wake* gives an idea of how a comparison can be treated. Kauffmann's essay, published in the *New American Review* #2, is, of course, filled with concrete details that here are omitted, but the gist of the eleven paragraphs is as follows:

1. Because subjectivity fascinates film-makers, it is natural that Joyce's two great novels of subjectivity would be filmed. One film is good, the other poor.

2. The poor film is *Ulysses*, a book that summarizes a vast amount of life.

3. The film of *Ulysses* has two motifs: tolerance and sexual candor. But these are only minor parts of the novel.

4. The film cannot be said to be faithful to the novel. True, it adds almost nothing; but it omits an enormous amount.

5. Some things of course simply cannot be filmed, so let us look at what is present rather than what is absent in the film. The opening is good, but . . . , and . . . , and . . . are poor.

6. In general, the acting is poor.

7. On the other hand, the film of *Finnegans Wake* is pretty successful, capturing the effect of a dream.

8. Though a bit long, and with some of the faults of the film of *Ulysses*, the film of *Finnegans Wake* is interesting, imaginative, and inventive.

9. The director uses subtitles, an effective device because Joyce's words (often puns) are "visual objects."

10. The actors effectively convey in their lines the sense of a dream.

11. The film captures the mythic quality that the film of *Ulysses* fails to capture.

Finally, the point of a comparison is to call attention to the unique features of something by holding it up against something similar but significantly different. If the differences are great and apparent, a comparison is a waste of effort. ("Blueberries are different from elephants. Blueberries do not have trunks. And elephants do not grow on bushes.") Indeed, a comparison between essentially and evidently unlike things can only obscure, for by making the comparison the writer implies there are significant similarities, and the reader can only wonder why he does not see them. The essays that do break into two halves are essays that make uninstructive comparisons: the first half tells the reader about five qualities in Dickens, the second half tells the reader about five different qualities in Dylan Thomas.

COMMUNICATING JUDGMENTS

Because a critical essay is a judicious attempt to help a reader see what is going on in a work, or in a part of a work, the voice of the explicator or analyst sounds, on first hearing, impartial; but good explication and good analysis include — at least implicitly — evaluation. The critic may say not only that the setting changes (a neutral expression) but also that "the novelist aptly shifts the setting" or "unconvincingly describes . . ." or "effectively juxtaposes. . . ." These evaluations he supports with evidence. He has feelings about the work under discussion, and he reveals them, not by continually saying "I feel" and "this moves me," but by calling attention to the degree of success or failure he perceives. Nothing is wrong with occasionally using "I," and noticeable avoidances of it — passives, "this writer," and the like — suggest an offensive sham-modesty; but too much talk of "I" makes a writer sound like an egomaniac.

One final remark on communicating judgments: write sincerely. Sincerity alone will not get an A, for it must be united with intelligence, diligence, and skill. But any attempt to neglect your own thoughtful responses and replace them with fabrications designed to please an instructor will surely fail. The words that clearly communicate your responses are hard enough to find; the words that express your hunch about what your instructor expects your responses to be are impossible to find.

A Review: How to Write an Effective Essay

Everyone must work out his own procedures and rituals, but the following suggestions may provide some help.

1. Read the work carefully.

2. Choose a worthwhile and compassable subject, something that you think merits your time and is not so big that your handling of it must be superficial. As you work, give shape to your topic, narrowing it, for example, from "The Character of Hester Prynne" to "The Effects of Alienation on Hester Prynne."

3. Reread the work, taking notes (preferably on 3 x 5 cards, writing on one side only) of all relevant matters. As you read, reflect on your reading and record your reflections. If you have an idea, jot it down; don't assume that you will remember it when you get around to writing your essay.

4. Sort out your cards into some kind of reasonable divisions, and reject cards irrelevant to your topic. As you work you may discover a better way to group your notes. If so, start reorganizing. If you are writing an explication, the order probably is essentially the order of the lines or of the episodes, but if you are writing an analysis you may wish to organize your essay from the lesser material to the greater (to avoid anticlimax) or from the simple to the complex (to insure intelligibility). If, for example, you are discussing the roles of three char-

acters in a story, it may be best to build up to the one of the three that you think the most important. If you are comparing two characters, it may be best to move from the most obvious contrasts to the least obvious. When you have arranged your notes into a meaningful sequence of packets, you have approximately divided your material into paragraphs.

5. Jot down an outline, indicating the topic idea of each paragraph, and under each topic idea jot down the supporting details that give it substance. This outline ought to tell you pretty much how good your ideas are. (Suggestions for introductory and concluding paragraphs are given on pp. 36–38.)

6. Reread the work, looking for additional material that strengthens or weakens your main point; take account of it in your notes and in your outline.

7. With your outline in front of you, write a draft, checking your notes for fuller details, such as supporting quotations. If, as you work, you find that some points in your outline are no longer relevant, eliminate them; but make sure that the argument flows from one point to the next. As you write, your ideas will doubtless become clearer; some may prove to be poor ideas. (One rarely knows exactly what his ideas are until he has set them down on paper. As the little girl said, in answer to the suggestion that she should think before she spoke, "How do I know what I think until I say it?") Not until you have written a draft do you really have a strong sense of how good your essay may be.

8. After a suitable interval, preferably a few days, read the draft with a view toward revising it, not with a view toward congratulating yourself. As you read, correct infelicities of style (e.g., awkward repetitions that make you sound simple-minded, inflated language that makes you sound pompous), add supporting detail where the argument is undeveloped (a paragraph of only one or two sentences is usually an undeveloped paragraph), and ruthlessly delete irrelevancies however interesting and well written they may be. But remember that a deletion probably requires some adjustment in the preceding and subsequent material. Make sure that the opening and concluding paragraphs are effective, and that between these paragraphs the argument, aided by transitions, runs smoothly. The details should be relevant, the organization reasonable, the argument clear. Check all quotations for accuracy. If there is time, put the revision aside, reread it in a day or two, and revise it again, especially with a view toward shortening it.

9. Type a clean copy, following the principles (concerning margins, pagination, footnotes, etc.) set forth in the next chapter. If you have borrowed any ideas, be sure to give credit (usually in foot-

notes) to your sources. Remember that plagiarism is not limited to the unacknowledged borrowing of words; a borrowed idea, even when put into your own words, requires acknowledgment.

10. Proofread and neatly make corrections as explained on page 40, item 8.

In short, (*a*) is the writing true (do you have a point that you state accurately), and (*b*) is the writing good (do your words and your organization clearly and effectively convey your meaning)? All of this adds up to Mrs. Beeton's famous recipe: "First catch your hare, then cook it."

2

STYLE AND FORMAT

Writing is hard work (Lewis Carroll's school in *Alice's Adventures in Wonderland* taught reeling and writhing), and there is no point in fooling ourselves into believing that it is all a matter of inspiration. There is ample evidence that many of the poems, stories, and plays that seem (as we read them) to flow so effortlessly were in fact the product of innumerable revisions. "Hard labor for life" was Conrad's view of his career as a writer. There is no guarantee that effort will pay off, but failure to expend effort is sure to result in writing that will strike the reader as slovenly, not worth reading. If duty compels the reader to stay with it, he will read it with increasing displeasure; if it is really bad, he will be baffled as well as displeased. It won't do to comfort yourself with the thought that you have been misunderstood. You may know what you *meant to say*, but your reader is the judge of what indeed you *have said*. As Coleridge puts it, writers must not only know what they mean, but must know "what the words mean by which they attempt to convey their meaning."

Big books have been written on the elements of good writing, but the best way to learn to write is to do your best, revise it a few days later, hand it in, and then study the annotations an experienced reader puts on your essay. In revising the offending passages, you will learn what your weaknesses are. After drafting your next essay, put it aside for a day or so; when you reread it, preferably aloud, you may find much that offends. If the argument does not flow, check to see whether your organization is reasonable and whether you have made adequate transitions. Do not hesitate to delete interesting but irrelevant material that obscures the argument. Make the necessary revisions and repeat the process if there is time. Revision is indispensable if you wish to avoid (in Maugham's words) "the impression of writing with the stub of a blunt pencil."

Still, a few principles can be briefly set forth here. On Dr. Johnson's belief that men do not so much need to be taught as they need to be reminded, these principles are brief imperatives rather than detailed instructions.

Get the Right Word

Denotation. Be sure the word you choose has the right denotation (explicit meaning). Do not say "tragic" when you mean "pathetic," "sarcastic" when you mean "ironic," "free verse" when you mean "blank verse," "disinterested" when you mean "uninterested."

Connotation. Be sure the word you choose has the right connotation (association, implication). Here are three examples of words with the wrong connotations for their contexts: "The heroic spirit is not dead. It still *lurks* in the hearts of men." ("Lurks" suggests a furtiveness inappropriate to the heroic spirit. Something like "lives" or "dwells" is needed.) "Close study will *expose* the strength of Albee's style." ("Reveal" would be better than "expose" here; "expose" suggests that some weakness will be brought to light, as in "Close study will expose the flimsiness of the motivation.") "Although Creon suffers, his suffering is not great enough to *relegate* him to the role of tragic hero." (In place of "relegate," we need something like "elevate" or "exalt.")

Concreteness. Catch the richness, complexity, and uniqueness of things. Do not write "Here one sees his lack of emotion" if you really mean "Here one sees his indifference" or "his iciness" or "his impartiality" or whatever the exact condition is. Instead of "The clown's part in *Othello* is very small," write "The clown appears in only two scenes in *Othello*" or "The clown in *Othello* speaks only thirty lines." ("Very," as in "very small" or "very big," is almost never the right word. A role is rarely "very big"; it "dominates" or "overshadows" or "is second only to. . . .")

In addition to using the concrete word and the appropriate detail, use illustrative **examples.** Northrop Frye, writing about the perception of rhythm, illustrates his point.

> Ideally, our literary education should begin, not with prose, but with such things as "this little pig went to market" — with verse rhythm reinforced by physical assault. The infant who gets bounced on somebody's knee to the rhythm of "Ride a cock horse" does not need a footnote telling him that Banbury Cross is twenty miles northeast of Oxford. He does not need the information that "cross" and "horse" make (at least in the pronunciation he is most likely to

hear) not a rhyme but an assonance. . . . All he needs is to get bounced.

The Well-tempered Critic
(Bloomington, Indiana, 1963), p. 25

Frye does not say our literary education should begin with "simple rhymes" or with "verse popular with children." He says "with such things as 'this little pig went to market,' " and then he goes on to add "Ride a cock horse." We know exactly what he means. Notice, too, that we do not need a third example. Be detailed, but know when to stop.

Your reader is likely to be brighter and more demanding than Lady Pliant, who in a seventeenth-century play says to a would-be seducer, "You are very alluring — and say so many fine Things, and nothing is so moving to me as a fine Thing." "Fine Things," of course, are what is wanted, but only exact words and apt illustrations will convince an intelligent reader that he is hearing fine things.

Levels of usage. Although the dividing lines cannot always be drawn easily, tradition recognizes three levels: formal, informal, and vulgar or popular, though sometimes "popular" is used to designate a level between informal and vulgar. **Formal writing** — at its highest or most formal — presumes considerable importance in the writer, the audience, and the topic. A noted figure, say a respected literary critic, examining an influential book and addressing the world of thoughtful readers, may use a highly formal style, as Lionel Trilling does here in a criticism of V. L. Parrington's *Main Currents in American Literature*.

> To throw out Poe because he cannot be conveniently fitted into a theory of American culture, to speak of him as a biological sport and as a mind apart from the main current, to find his gloom to be merely personal and eccentric, "only the atrabilious wretchedness of a dipsomaniac," as Hawthorne's was "no more than the skeptical questioning of life by a nature that knew no fierce storms," to judge Melville's response to American life to be less noble than that of Bryant or of Greeley, to speak of Henry James as an escapist, as an artist similar to Whistler, a man characteristically afraid of stress — this is not merely to be mistaken in aesthetic judgment; rather it is to examine without attention and from the point of view of a limited and essentially arrogant conception of reality the documents which are in some respects the most suggestive testimony to what America was and is, and of course to get no answer from them.
>
> *The Liberal Imagination* (New York, 1950), p. 21

Consider also the beginning of the Gettysburg Address; unless you are the President of the United States dedicating a national cemetery during a civil war, it is best not to speak of "Four score and seven years." "Eighty-seven" will have to do. Of course, formal English includes many simple words ("four," "and," "seven"), but it is notable for its use of relatively uncommon words, such as "score" and "hallow," and its long sentences, balanced or antithetical, which suspend their meaning until the end. Notice that in Trilling's sentence the structure is this: "To throw . . . , to speak . . . , to find . . . , to judge . . . , to speak . . . ," and we still do not have an independent clause. Two-thirds of the way through, with "this is not merely to be mistaken," the previous words come into focus, but the meaning is still incomplete. To do such-and-such "is not merely to be mistaken," but what *is* it to be? At last we are told: "It is to examine without attention . . . and . . . to get no answer. . . ."

A formal sentence need not be long. Here is a fairly short formal sentence by W. H. Auden: "Owing to its superior power as a mnemonic, verse is superior to prose as a medium for didactic instruction." In another frame of mind Auden might have written something less formal, along these lines: "Because it stays more easily in the memory, verse is better than prose for teaching." This revision of Auden's sentence can be called **informal,** but it is high on the scale, the language of an educated man writing courteously to an audience he conceives of as his peers. It is the level of almost all serious writing about literature. A low informal version might be: "Poetry sticks in the mind better than prose; so if you want to teach something, poetry is better." This is the language any of us might use in our most casual moments; it is almost never the language used in writing about literature.

Below low informal is the **vulgar** language of near-illiterates who do not write essays on literature: "Poems stays in me mind like words don't. Poems teach good." People who do write essays on literature should not treat their subject and their reader as though they were members of the family with whom they may horse around. (This last sentence, already too informal by virtue of "horse around," could be made even more offensive: "They shouldn't fool around with what they're talking about and with their reader like they're horsing around with the kids.") In between high formal and vulgar English is the language educated people use when writing with some respect for their subject and for their audience. Don't be stuffy and don't be coarse. Be serious but not solemn. There is rarely any need to write that in *Measure for Measure* Claudio is "incarcerated" or that Claudio is "thrown in the clink." "Imprisoned" will probably do the job best. Nor will it do to "finagle" with an inappropriate expression by putting it in "quotes." As the previous sentence indicates, the quotation marks do not make such expressions acceptable, only more obvious and more offensive. The quotation marks tell the reader that the writer knows he is using the wrong word but is unwilling to find the right word. If for some reason a relatively low word is the right one, use it and don't apologize with quotation marks (for instance, the use of "fiddle-faddle" without quotation marks on p. 92).

In short, in "every phrase / And sentence that is right," as T. S. Eliot says in *Four Quartets*,

> every word is at home,
> Taking its place to support the others,
> The word neither diffident nor ostentatious,
> An easy commerce of the old and the new,
> The common word exact without vulgarity,
> The formal word precise but not pedantic,
> The complete consort dancing together.

Repetition and variation. Although some repetitions — say, of words like "surely" or "it is noteworthy" — reveal a tic that ought to be cured by revision, don't be afraid to repeat a word if it is the best word. The following paragraph repeats "interesting," "paradox," "Salinger," "what makes," and "book"; notice also "feel" and "feeling."

> The reception given to *Franny and Zooey* in America has illustrated again the interesting paradox of Salinger's reputation there; great public enthusiasm, of the *Time* magazine and Best Seller List kind, accompanied by a repressive coolness in the critical journals. What makes this a paradox is that the book's themes are among the most ambitiously highbrow, and its craftsmanship most uncompromisingly virtuoso. What makes it an interesting one is that those who are most patronising about the book are those who most resemble its characters; people whose ideas and language in their best moments resemble Zooey's. But they feel they ought not to enjoy the book. There is a very strong feeling in American literary circles that Salinger and love of Salinger must be discouraged.
>
> Martin Green, *Re-appraisals* (New York, 1965), p. 197

Repetition, a device necessary for continuity and clarity, holds the paragraph together. There are, of course, variations: "*Franny and Zooey*" becomes "the book," and then instead of "the book's" we get "its." Similarly, "those who" becomes "people," which in turn becomes "they." Such substitutions, which neither confuse nor distract, keep the paragraph from sounding like a broken phonograph record.

Pronouns are handy substitutes, and they ought to be used, but other substitutes need not always be sought. An ungrounded fear of repetition often produces a vice known as elegant variation: having mentioned *Franny and Zooey*, an essayist next speaks of "the previously mentioned work," then of "the tale," and finally of "this work of our author." This is far worse than repetition; it strikes the reader as silly. Pointless variation of this sort, however, is not to be confused with a variation that communicates additional useful information, such as "these two stories about the Glass family"; this variation is entirely legitimate, indeed necessary, for it furthers the discussion. But elegant variation can be worse than silly; it can be confusing, as in "My first *theme* dealt with plot, but this *essay* deals with character." The reader wonders if the writer means to suggest that an essay is different from a theme.

Notice in these lucid sentences by Helen Gardner the effective repetition of "end" and "beginning."

> *Othello* has this in common with the tragedy of fortune, that the end in no way blots out from the imagination the glory of the beginning. But the end here does not merely by its darkness throw up into relief the brightness that was. On the contrary, beginning and end chime against each other. In both the value of life and love is affirmed.
>
> The Noble Moor (Oxford, 1956), p. 203

The substitution of "conclusion" or "last scene" for the second "end" would be worse than pointless; it would destroy Miss Gardner's point that there is *identity* or correspondence between beginning and end.

But do not repeat a word if it is being used in a different sense. Get a different word. Here are two examples of the fault: "This *theme* deals with the *theme* of the novel." (The first "theme" means "essay"; the second means "underlying idea," "motif.") "Caesar's *character* is complex. The comic *characters* too have some complexity." (The first "character" means "personality"; the second means "persons," "figures in the play.")

The sound of sense. Avoid awkward repetitions of sound, as in "The story is marked by a remarkable mystery," "The reason the season is Spring . . . ," "Circe certainly . . . ," "This is seen in the scene in which. . . ." These irrelevant echoes call undue attention to the words. But wordplay can be effective when it contributes to meaning. Miss Gardner's statement that in the beginning and the end of *Othello* "the value of life and love is affirmed," makes effective use of the similarity in sound between "life" and "love." Her implication is that these two things that sound alike are indeed closely related, an idea that reinforces her contention that the beginning and the end of the play are in a way identical.

Write Effective Sentences

Economy. Say everything relevant, but say it in the fewest words possible. The wordy sentence, "There are a few vague parts in the story that give it a mysterious quality," can be written more economically as "A few vague parts in the story give it a mysterious quality." (Nothing has been lost by the deletion of "There are" and "that.") Even more economical is: "A few vague parts add mystery to the story." The original version says nothing that the second version does not say, and says nothing that the third version — nine words against fifteen — does not say. If you find the right nouns and verbs, you can often delete adjectives and adverbs. (Compare "a mysterious quality" with "mystery.") Another example of wordiness is: "Sophocles's tragic play *Antigone* is mistitled because Creon is the tragic hero, and the play should be named for him." These twenty words can be reduced, with no loss of meaning, to nine words: "Sophocles's *Antigone* is mistitled; Creon is the tragic hero." Something is wrong with a sentence if you can delete words and not sense the loss. Examples of locutions that need trimming are "rising crescendo," "red in color," and "illiterates who cannot read." But in cutting out dead wood, do not cut out supporting detail. Supporting detail is wordiness only when the details are so numerous and obvious that they offend the reader's intelligence.

Overpredication commonly is wordy. Do not write "A novel that is ill-constructed seldom pleases a reader," but rather "An ill-constructed novel seldom pleases a reader." Beware especially of "that . . . that," as in "A novel that is ill-constructed seldom pleases a public that is discerning." A better sentence is: "An ill-constructed novel seldom pleases a discerning public." A writer has a piece of information he wishes to convey. Does it deserve a word, a phrase, or a clause? If he has written, "A novel that is ill-constructed seldom pleases a public that is discerning," rereading ought to show him that he has given two clauses to material that can be said in two words.

The **passive voice** (the subject is the object of the action) is a common source of wordiness. Do not say "This story was written by Melville"; instead, say "Melville wrote this story." The revision is one-third shorter, and it says everything that the longer version says. Sometimes, of course, the passive voice, although less vigorous, may be preferable to the active voice. Changing "The novel was received in silence" to "Readers neglected the novel" makes the readers' response more active than it was. The passive catches the passivity of the response. Furthermore, the revision makes "Readers" the subject, but the true subject is (as in the original) the novel.

Parallels. Use parallels to clarify relationships. Few of us are likely to compose such deathless parallels as "I came, I saw, I conquered," or "of the people, by the people, for the people," but we can see to it that in our writing coordinate expressions correspond in their grammatical form. A parallel such as "He liked to read and to write" (instead of "He liked reading and to write") makes its point neatly. No such neatness appears in "Joyce wrote poems, excellent stories, and novels"; the reader is left wondering what value the poems and novels have. If one of the items has a modifier, usually all should have modifiers. Notice how the omission of "the noble" in the following sentence would leave a distracting gap: "If the wicked Shylock cannot enter the fairy story world of Belmont, neither can the noble Antony." Other examples of parallels are: "Mendoza longs to be an Englishman and to marry the girl he loves" (not "Mendoza longs to be an Englishman and for the girl he loves"); "He talked about metaphors, similes, and symbols" (not "He talked about metaphors, similes, and about symbols"). If one wishes to emphasize the leisureliness of the talk, one might put it thus: "He talked about metaphors, about similes, and about symbols." (The repetition of "about" in this version is not wordiness; because it emphasizes the leisureliness, it does some work in the sentence.) Notice, in the next example, how Miss Gardner's parallels ("in the," "in his," "in his," "in the") lend conviction: "The significance of *Othello* is not to be found in the hero's nobility alone, in his capacity to know ecstasy, in his vision of the world, and in the terrible act to which he is driven by his anguish at the loss of that vision. It lies also in the fact that the vision was true."

Subordination. Make sure that the level of subordination is appropriate to the logical importance of the detail. Make the less important element subordinate to the more important. Notice how in the following example the first clause, which summarizes the writer's previous sentences, is a dependent clause; the new material is made emphatic by being put into two independent clauses. "As soon as the Irish Literary Theatre was assured of a nationalist backing, it started to dissociate itself from any political aim, and the long struggle with the public began." The second and third clauses in this sentence, linked by "and," are coordinate, that is, of equal importance. We have already discussed parallels ("I came, I saw, I conquered") and pointed out that parallel or coordinate elements should appear so grammatically in the sentence. The following line gives time and eternity equal treatment: "Time was against him; eternity was for him." The quotation is a **compound sentence** — composed of two or more clauses that can stand as independent sentences but that are connected with a coordinating conjunction such as *and, but, for, nor, yet,* and *if;* or with a correlative conjunction such as *not only . . . but also;* or with a conjunctive adverb such as *also,* or *however;* or with a colon, semicolon, or (rarely) a comma. But a **complex sentence** (an independent clause and one or more subordinate clauses) does not give equal treatment to each clause; whatever is outside of the independent idea is subordinate. In the sentence, "Aided by Miss Horniman's money, Yeats dreamed of a poetic drama concentrating on romantic and historical plays," the author puts Yeats' dream in the independent clause and subordinates the relatively unimportant Miss Horniman. Had the author wished to give Miss Horniman more prominence, the passage might have run: "Yeats dreamed of a poetic drama concentrating on romantic and historical plays, and this dream was subsidized by Miss Horniman." Here, at least, Miss Horniman stands in an independent clause, linked to the previous independent clause by *and*. (Notice, however, that even in the revision Miss Horniman is not very prominent because the subject of the second independent clause is still Yeats's dream — "this dream.") If the author had wanted to make her yet more prominent, he might have written "While Yeats dreamed of a poetic drama concentrating on romantic and historical plays, Miss Horniman provided the means by which the dream might be realized." In short, though simple sentences and compound sentences have their place, they make everything of equal importance. Since everything is not of equal importance, you must often write complex sentences, subordinating some things to other things.

Write Unified and Coherent Paragraphs

Unity. A unified paragraph is a group of sentences (rarely a single sentence) on a single idea. The idea may have several twists or subdivisions, but all of the parts — the sentences — should form a whole that can be summarized in one sentence. A paragraph is, to put the matter a little differently, one of the major points supporting your thesis. If your essay is some five hundred words long — about two double-spaced typewritten pages — you probably will not break it down into more than four or five parts or paragraphs. Each paragraph has a unifying idea, which may appear as a **topic sentence**. Most commonly, the topic sentence is the first sentence in the paragraph, forecasting what is to come in the rest of the paragraph. Less commonly, it is the last sentence in the paragraph, summarizing the points that the paragraph's earlier sentences have made. Least commonly — but thoroughly acceptably — the topic sentence may appear nowhere in the paragraph, in which case the paragraph has a **topic idea** — an idea that holds the sentences of the paragraph together although it has not been explicitly stated. Whether explicit or implicit, an idea must unite the sentences of the paragraph. If your paragraph has only one or two sentences, the chances are that you have not adequately developed its idea.

A paragraph can make several points, but the points must be related, and the nature of the relationship must be indicated so that there is, in effect, a single unifying point to the paragraph. Here is a paragraph, unusually brief, that may seem to make two points but that, in fact, holds them together with a topic idea. The author is Edmund Wilson.

> James Joyce's *Ulysses* was an attempt to present directly the thoughts and feelings of a group of Dubliners through the whole course of a summer day. *Finnegans Wake* is a complementary attempt to render the dream fantasies and the half-unconscious sensations experienced by a single person in the course of a night's sleep.
>
> *The Wound and The Bow* (New York, 1947), p. 243

Wilson's topic idea is that *Finnegans Wake* complements *Ulysses*. Notice, by the way, that the sentence about *Finnegans Wake* concludes the paragraph. Not surprisingly, Wilson's essay is about this book, and the structure of the paragraph allows him to get into his subject.

Below is another paragraph that may seem to have more than one subject (Richardson and Fielding were contemporaries; they were alike in some ways; they were different in others), but again the paragraph is unified by a topic idea (although Richardson and Fielding were contemporaries and were alike in some ways, they differed in important ways).

> The names of Richardson and Fielding are always coupled in any discussion of the novel, and with good reason. They were contemporaries, writing in the same cultural climate (*Tom Jones* was published in 1749, a year after *Clarissa*). Both had genius and both were widely recognized immediately. Yet they are utterly different in their tastes and temperaments, and therefore in their visions of city and country, of men and women, and even of good and evil.
>
> Elizabeth Drew, *The Novel* (New York, 1963), p. 59

This paragraph, like Edmund Wilson's, closes in on its subject.

The beginning and especially the end of a paragraph are usually the most emphatic parts. A beginning may offer a generalization that the rest of the paragraph supports. Or the early part may offer details, preparing for the generalization in the later part of the paragraph. Or the paragraph may move from cause to effect. Although no rule can cover all paragraphs (except that all must make a point in an orderly way), one can hardly go wrong in making the first sentence of every paragraph either a transition from the previous paragraph or a statement of the paragraph's topic. Here is a sentence that makes a transition and also states the topic: "Not only narrative poems but also meditative poems may have a kind of plot." This sentence gets the reader from plot in narrative poetry (which the writer has been talking about) to plot in meditative poetry (which the writer goes on to talk about).

Coherence. If a paragraph has not only unity but also a structure, then it has coherence, its parts fit together. Make sure that each sentence is properly related to the preceding one. Nothing is wrong with such obvious **transitions** as "moreover," "however," "but," "for example," "this tendency," "in the next chapter," etc.; but of course (1) these transitions should not start every sentence (they can be buried thus: "Lowell, moreover, . . ."), and (2) they need not appear anywhere in the sentence. The point is not that transitions must be explicit, but that the argument must proceed clearly. The gist of a paragraph might run thus: "Speaking broadly, there were in the Renaissance two comic traditions. . . . The first. . . . The second. . . . The chief difference. . . . But both traditions. . . ." Here is a paragraph by Elizabeth Drew discussing one aspect of *Great Expectations*. The structure is basically chronological, but notice too the effective use of a parallel as a linking device within the last sentence. (The links are italicized.)

> Some of the most poignant scenes in the book are the *opening ones*, which describe the atmosphere in which Pip grows up. *He is introduced* as "a small bundle of shivers" alone in the graveyard, *which is followed* by the terrifying intrusion of the world of active violence and fear as the convict seizes him. *Then we see* the household at the forge, where he is made to feel guilty and ashamed of his very existence; the Christmas party at which he is baited and bullied by his elders; his treatment at the hands of the hypocritical Pumblechook; his introduction to Estella, who reveals to him that he is coarse and common. *Dickens knows* that in children "there is nothing so finely perceived and so finely felt, as injustice," and looking back on his childhood, *Pip too knows* that truth: "Within myself, I had sustained, from my babyhood, a perpetual conflict with injustice."   *The Novel*, p. 197

Introductory and concluding paragraphs. It is impossible to lay down rules for writing introductory and concluding paragraphs. The best way to see how they should be handled is to pay attention to them when you read essays, but a few tips may be useful.

When writing an introductory paragraph, try to say something interesting. Do not paraphrase your title in your first sentence: "This theme will study the function of the clown in *Othello*." But, at the same time, do not be so eager to say something interesting that you say something irrelevant ("The clowning in *Hamlet* is complex"), or something melodramatic or grandiose ("All the world loves a clown"). Often you can make use of a quotation, either from the work or from a critic; but because the device is a bit too easy, it should be employed only occasionally and with discrimination. You cannot go wrong in suggesting your thesis in your opening paragraph, moving from a rather broad view to a narrower one. For example, the introductory paragraph of the essay on *Othello* (p. 11) begins with a sweeping view of the entire dramatis personae of *Othello*, narrows to a view of the clown, and ends with the clear suggestion that the essay will study the work that the clown does in the play. An introductory paragraph can be conceived of as a funnel, wide at the top and narrowing into what will be the body of the essay. Nevill Coghill begins an essay called "Wags, Clowns and Jesters" thus:

> Among the less exalted orders of the Shakespearian populace there are three that tend to shade off into a kind of class, whose main functions, mannerisms and idiosyncrasies are easy to recognize, though they tend to merge and mingle, or at least to overlap: they are the Wags, the Clowns and the Jesters.
>
> *More Talking of Shakespeare*, ed. John Garrett
> (London, 1959), p. 1

One other kind of introduction is tricky and should be used cautiously. Sometimes an introductory paragraph delicately misleads the audience; the second paragraph reverses the train of thought and leads into the main issue. Here is an example by Joseph Wood Krutch, from *"Modernism" in Modern Drama.* Only the first part of the second paragraph is given below, but from it you can see what direction Krutch is taking.

> One evening in 1892, the first of Oscar Wilde's four successful comedies had in London its first performance. It is said that after the last curtain the audience rose to cheer — and it had good reason to do so. Not in several generations had a new play so sparkled with fresh and copious wit of a curiously original kind.
>
> By now the play itself, *Lady Windermere's Fan*, seems thin and faded. To be successfully revived, as it was a few seasons ago in the United States, it has to be presented as "a period piece" — which means that the audience is invited to laugh at as well as with it. . . .
>
> (Ithaca, N.Y., 1953), p. 43

With conclusions, as with introductory paragraphs, try to say something interesting. It is not of the slightest interest to say "Thus we see . . . [here the writer echoes his title and his first paragraph]." There is some justification for a summary at the end of a long paper because the reader may have half forgotten some of the ideas presented thirty pages earlier, but a paper that can easily be held in the mind needs something different. A good concluding paragraph does more than provide an echo of what the writer has already said. It rounds out the previous discussion, normally with a few sentences that summarize (without the obviousness of "We may now summarize"), but it also may draw an inference that has not previously been expressed. To draw such an inference is not to introduce a new idea — a concluding paragraph is hardly the place for a new idea — but is to see the previous material in a fresh perspective. A good concluding paragraph closes the issue while enriching it. Notice how the three examples given below all wrap things up and, at the same time, open out by suggesting a larger frame of reference.

The first example is the concluding paragraph of Nevill Coghill's "Wags, Clowns and Jesters."

> "A shrewd knave and an unhappy" is Lafeu's wise comment on Lavache. He is an extreme example of what one finds in so many of Shakespeare's creations — there is more to them than they actually need for the plays in which they appear — they spill over into life.

The second example is the conclusion to Norman Friedman's "Point of View in Fiction" (*PMLA*, 70 (1955), 1160–84). In this fairly long discussion of the development of a critical concept, Friedman catalogs various points of view and then spends several pages arguing that the choice of a point of view is crucial if certain effects are to be attained. The omniscient narrator of a novel who comments on all that happens, Friedman suggests, is a sort of free verse of fiction, and an author may willingly sacrifice this freedom for a narrower point of view if he wishes to make certain effects. Friedman concludes:

> All this is merely to say, in effect, that when an author surrenders in fiction, he does so in order to conquer; he gives up certain privileges and imposes certain limits in order the more effectively to render his story-illusion, which constitutes artistic truth in fiction. And it is in the service of this truth that he spends his creative life.

Notice that Friedman devotes the early part of his pargaraph to a summary of what has preceded, and then in the latter part he puts his argument in a new perspective. One more example of a concluding paragraph that restates the old and looks toward the new comes from Richard B. Sewall's discussion of *The Scarlet Letter*.

> Henry James said that Hawthorne had "a cat-like faculty of seeing in the dark"; but he never saw through the dark to radiant light. What light his vision reveals is like the fitful sunshine of Hester's and Dimmesdale's meeting in the forest — the tragic opposite of Emerson's triumphant gleaming sun that "shines also today."
>
> *The Vision of Tragedy* (New Haven, 1959), p. 91

Write Emphatically

All that has been said about getting the right word, about effective sentences, and about paragraphs is related to the matter of

emphasis. But we can add a few points here. The first rule (it will be modified in a moment) is: Be emphatic. But do not attempt to achieve emphasis, as Queen Victoria did, by a *style* consisting *chiefly* of *italics* and *exclamation* marks!!! Nor can you rely on expressions such as "very important," "definitely significant," and "really beautiful." The proper way to be emphatic is to find the right word, to use appropriate detail, to subordinate the lesser points, and to develop your ideas reasonably. The beginning and the end of a sentence (and of a paragraph) are emphatic positions; of these two positions, the end is usually the more emphatic. Here is a sentence that properly moves to an emphatic end: "Having been ill-treated by Hamlet and having lost her father, Ophelia goes mad." If the halves are reversed, the sentence peters out: "Ophelia goes mad because she has been ill-treated by Hamlet and she has lost her father." Still, even this version is better than the shapeless "Having been ill-treated by Hamlet, Ophelia goes mad, partly too because she has lost her father." The important point, that she goes mad, is dissipated by the lame addition of words about her father. In short, avoid anticlimaxes such as "Macbeth's deed is reprehensible and serious."

But the usual advice, build to emphatic ends, needs modification. Do not write something that sounds like an advertisement for *The Blood of Dracula:* "In her eyes DESIRE! In her veins — the blood of a MONSTER!!!" Be emphatic but courteous; do not shout.

One further caution: It is all very well to speak in a courteously low voice, but do not be so timid that you whisper assertions in a negative form. Think twice before you let something like this remain in your manuscript: "Melville is not unsuccessful in his depiction of the pathos of madness." The writer seems reluctant to come out and say "Melville succeeds in depicting the pathos of madness." If this statement needs qualification (e.g., Melville succeeds only in such-and-such a chapter or only intermittently), give the qualifications, but do not think that the weaseling "not unsuccessful" is adequate. It is not unlikely that the reader will not be pleased, which means that it is likely he will be displeased.

SOME REMARKS ABOUT MANUSCRIPT FORM
Basic Manuscript Form

Much of what follows is nothing more than common sense.

1. Use 8½ × 11 paper of good weight. Keep as lightweight a carbon copy as you wish, but hand in a sturdy original.

2. Double-space, typing (with a reasonably fresh ribbon) on one side of the page only. (If you submit a handwritten copy, use lined paper and write on every other line if the lines are closely spaced.)

3. Leave an adequate margin — an inch or an inch and a half — at top, bottom, and sides.

4. Number the pages consecutively, using Arabic numerals in the upper right-hand corner.

5. Put your name and class or course number in the upper left-hand corner of the first page. It is a good idea to put your name in the upper left corner of each page so that your essay can be easily reassembled if somehow a page gets separated.

6. Center the title of your essay below the top margin of the first page. Begin the first word of the title with a capital, and capitalize each subsequent word except articles, conjunctions, and prepositions, thus: The Diabolic and Celestial Images in *The Scarlet Letter*.

7. Begin the essay an inch or two below the title.

8. Your extensive revisions should have been made in your drafts, but minor last-minute revisions may be made on the finished copy. Proofreading may catch some typographical errors, and you may notice some small weaknesses. Additions should be made *above* the line, with a caret below the line at the appropriate place. Indicate deletions by drawing a horizontal line through the word or words you wish to delete. Delete a single letter by drawing a vertical line through it. Use a vertical line, too, to separate words that should not have been run together.

Quotations and Quotation Marks

1. Distinguish between short and long quotations, and treat each appropriately. Short quotations (usually defined as less than three lines of poetry or five lines of prose) are enclosed within quotation marks and run into the text (rather than set off, without quotation marks). Examples:

> LeRoi Jones's "Preface to a Twenty Volume Suicide Note" ends with a glimpse of the speaker's daughter peeking into her "clasped hands," either playfully or madly.

> Pope's *Essay on Criticism* begins informally with a contraction, but the couplets nevertheless have an authoritative ring: " 'Tis hard to say, if greater want of skill / Appear in writing or in judging ill."

Notice that in the second example a slash (diagonal line, virgule) is used to indicate the end of a line of verse other than the last line quoted. The slash is, of course, not used if the poetry is set off, indented, and printed as verse, thus:

> Pope's *Essay on Criticism* begins informally with a contraction, but the couplets nevertheless have an authoritative ring:
>
>> 'Tis hard to say, if greater want of skill
>> Appear in writing or in judging ill;

But of the two less dangerous is the offense
To tire our patience than mislead our sense.

Material that is set off (usually three or more lines of verse, five or more lines of prose) is not enclosed within quotation marks. To set it off, triple-space before and after the quotation and single-space the quotation. (Some manuals of style call for double-spacing, some for indenting prose quotations. But whichever procedure you adopt, be consistent.) Be sparing in your use of long quotations. Do not bore the reader with material that can be effectively reduced either by paraphrase or by cutting. If you cut, indicate ellipses as explained below under 3.

2. The quotation must fit grammatically into your sentence.

Not: Near the end of the play Othello remembers that he "have done the state some service."

Corrected: Near the end of the play Othello remembers that he has "done the state some service."

3. The quotation must be exact. Any material that you add must be in square brackets, thus:

When Pope says that Belinda is "the rival of his [i.e., the sun's] beams," he uses comic hyperbole.

Stephen Dedalus sees the ball as a "greasy leather orb [that] flew like a heavy bird through the grey light."

If you wish to omit material from within a quotation, indicate the ellipsis by three spaced periods. If a sentence ends in an omission, add a closed-up period and then three spaced periods to indicate the omission. The following example is based on a quotation from the sentences immediately above this one:

The manual says that "if you . . . omit material from within a quotation, [you must] indicate the ellipsis. . . . If a sentence ends in an omission, add a closed-up period and then three spaced periods. . . ."

Notice that although material preceded "If you," periods are not needed to indicate the omission because "If you" began a sentence in the original. Customarily initial and terminal omissions are indicated only when they are part of the sentence you are quoting. Even such omissions need not be indicated when the quoted material is obviously incomplete — when, for instance, it is a word or phrase. (See the first example in this section, which quotes Pope's phrase "the rival of his beams.") Notice, too, that although quotations must be given word for word, the initial capitalization can be adapted, as here where "If" is reduced to "if."

When a line or more of verse is omitted from a passage that is set off, the three spaced periods are printed on a separate line.

4. Identify the speaker or writer of the quotation, so that the reader is not left with a sense of uncertainty. Usually this identification precedes the quoted material (e.g., "Smith says . . .") in accordance with the principle of letting the reader know where he is going, but occasionally it may follow the quotation, especially if it will provide something of a pleasant surprise. For example, in a discussion of T. S. Eliot's poetry, you might quote a hostile comment on one of the poems and then reveal that Eliot himself was the speaker.

5. Commas and periods go inside of the quotation marks; other marks of punctuation (e.g., semicolons, colons, and dashes) go outside. Question marks and exclamation points go inside if they are part of the quotation, outside if they are your own.

> Amanda ironically says to her daughter, "How old are you, Laura?" Is it possible to fail to hear Laura's weariness in her reply, "Mother, you know my age"?

6. Use *single* quotation marks for material contained within a quotation that itself is within quotation marks, thus:

> T. S. Eliot says, "Mr. Richards observes that 'poetry is capable of saving us.' "

7. Use quotation marks around titles of short works, that is, for titles of chapters in books and for stories, essays, and poems that might not be published by themselves. Unpublished works, even book-length dissertations, are also enclosed in quotation marks. Use *italics* (indicated by underlining) for books, that is, for novels, periodicals, collections of essays, plays, and long poems such as *The Rime of the Ancient Mariner* and *Paradise Lost*.

Footnotes

Kinds of footnotes. Footnotes are of two sorts: (1) they may give the sources of quotations, facts, and opinions used; or (2) they may give additional comment that would interrupt the flow of the argument in the body of the paper. This second type perhaps requires amplification. A writer may wish to indicate that he is familiar with an opinion contrary to the one he is offering, but he may not wish to digress upon it during the course of his argument. A footnote lets him refer to it and indicate why he is not considering it. Or a footnote may contain full statistical data that support his point but that would seem unnecessarily detailed and even tedious in the body of the paper.

What to footnote. Honesty requires that you acknowledge your indebtedness for material, not only when you quote directly from a work, but also when you appropriate an idea that is not common knowledge. Not to acknowledge such borrowing is plagiarism. If in doubt as to whether or not to give credit in a footnote, give credit. But you ought to develop a sense of what is considered common knowledge. The date of first publication of *The Scarlet Letter* can be considered common knowledge. Few can give it when asked, but it can be found out from innumerable sources, and no one need get the credit for providing you with the date. Similarly, the idea that Hamlet delays is a matter of common knowledge. But if you are impressed by So-and-so's argument that Claudius has been much maligned, you should give credit to So-and-so.

Reducing the number of footnotes. Keep the number of footnotes down to an honest minimum, partly by including the documentation within the body of the paper where reasonable and partly by not cluttering up the bottoms of the pages with references to material that is common knowledge. If you give frequent quotations from Shakespeare, in the footnote to the first quotation specify which edition you are using and then mention that all subsequent quotations from Shakespeare are from this edition. After each subsequent quotation, put parentheses including act, scene, and line (III.ii.178); if you are quoting from various plays, be sure to include the title of the play in the parentheses. If the quotation is run into the text, close the quotation, give the parenthetic material, and then add the final period. Example:

> The idea that a tragic hero has exhausted all of his life's possibilities is revealed in *Macbeth*, when Malcolm says, "Macbeth / Is ripe for shaking" (IV.iii.237–38).

If the quotation is set off, end the quotation with a period, double space, and below the last words of the quotation add the parenthetic material. This parenthetic identification, in the body of the paper, does everything that a footnote would do.

The second kind of footnote, which gives additional commentary, should be used sparingly. There are times when supporting details may be appropriately relegated to a footnote, but if the thing is worth saying, it is usually worth saying in the body of the paper. Do not get into the habit of affixing either trivia or miniature essays to the bottom of each page of your essay.

Footnote numbers. Number the notes consecutively throughout the essay or chapter.

Footnote position. Although some instructors allow students to group all of the notes at the rear of the essay, most instructors believe that the best place for a footnote is at the bottom of the appropriate page. If in your draft you type your footnotes on one page, when typing your final copy you can easily gauge how much space the footnotes for any given page will require. Micrometric carbon paper (carbon paper with a protruding margin which bears the line numbers from 64, at the top, down to 1, at the bottom) is a great help.

Footnote style. To indicate that there is a footnote, put a raised Arabic numeral after the final punctuation of the sentence, unless clarity requires it earlier. (In a sentence about Black, Smith, and Jones you may need a footnote for each and a corresponding numeral after each name instead of one at the end of the sentence, but usually a single reference at the end will do. The single footnote might explain that Black says such and such in his book entitled ————, Smith says such and such in his book entitled ————, and Jones say such and such in his book entitled ————.) At the bottom of the page triple-space before giving the first footnote. Then indent five spaces, raise the typewriter carriage half a line, and type the Arabic numeral. Return the carriage to the regular position and type the footnote, single-spacing it. If it runs more than one line, the subsequent lines are flush with the left margin, but each new note begins with an indentation of five spaces. Each note begins with an indented and raised numeral, then a capital letter, and ends with terminal punctuation. Double-space between footnotes.

First reference to a book. Examples:

[1]X. J. Kennedy, <u>An Introduction to Poetry</u>, 2nd ed. (Boston, 1971), p. 41.

[2]D. H. Lawrence, <u>Studies in Classic American Literature</u> (New York, 1966), pp. 87-88.

[3]<u>The Letters of John Keats, 1814-1821</u>, ed. Hyder Edward Rollins (Cambridge, Mass., 1958), II, 129.

1. Although normally only the city is given, if the city is obscure or might be confused with another city of the same name — as Cambridge, Massachusetts, with Cambridge, England — add the necessary amplification, abbreviating if possible.

2. When both volume and page are given (see footnote 3 above), the volume is given in Roman numerals, the page in Arabic numerals. "Vol." and "p." are not used.

3. Notice that the name of an editor or translator is given after the title, with an appropriate abbreviation, as in footnotes 3, 4, 5, 6.

⁴Alexander Pope, <u>Epistles to Several Persons</u>, ed. F. W. Bateson, 2nd ed. (New Haven, 1961), p. 17.

⁵Paul Ginestier, <u>The Poet and the Machine</u>, trans. Martin B. Friedman (Chapel Hill, 1961), p. 28.

⁶Albert Gilman and Roger Brown, "Personality and Style in Concord," <u>Transcendentalism and Its Legacy</u>, ed. Myron Simon and Thornton H. Parsons (Ann Arbor, 1966), pp. 103–104.

4. Give the author's name as it appears on the title page; give the title as it appears on the title page, but a very long title may be shortened thus: *A New and Complete Concordance . . . to . . . Shakespeare;* you need not give a subtitle; underline the title of the book, to indicate italics, whatever the typography of the original; if an article, conjunction, or preposition begins the title, capitalize it, but do not capitalize these parts of speech in other places in the title.

5. Although the name of the publisher is not usually given, some instructors require it, thus:

⁷Robert Gittings, <u>John Keats</u> (Boston: Little, Brown and Co., 1969), p. 98.

6. If the author's name has been given in the body of the page (e.g., in such a sentence as "D. H. Lawrence says that Hawthorne . . ."), do not repeat his name in the footnote. Merely begin with the title. If the author's name and the title have both been given in the body ("D. H. Lawrence says, in *Studies in Classic American Literature,* that Hawthorne . . ."), repeat neither his name nor the title in the footnote. In this case, the footnote would begin with the opening of the parenthesis before the place of publication, thus:

⁸(New York, 1966), p. 17.

First reference to a journal. Footnote 9 below is for a journal paginated consecutively throughout the year; footnote 10 is for a journal that paginates each issue individually. A journal paginated separately requires the month or week or day as well as the year. Current practice favors omitting the volume number for popular weeklies (see footnote 11) and for newspapers, in which case the full date is given without parentheses.

[9]John Oliver Perry, "The Relationship of Disparate Voices in Poems," _Essays in Criticism_, 15 (1965), 49.

[10]Donald Gallup, "T. S. Eliot and Ezra Pound: Collaborators in Letters," _Atlantic_, 225 (June 1970), 49-62.

[11]Bernard McCabe, "Taking Dickens Seriously," _Commonweal_, May 14, 1965, pp. 244-47.

The author's name and the title of the article are given as they appear in the journal, the title of the article in quotation marks and the title of the journal in italics (i.e., underlined). Until recently the volume was given with capital Roman numerals, the page or pages with Arabic numerals, but current practice uses Arabic numerals for both the volume and the pages.

If a book review has a title, the review may be treated as an article. If, however, the title is merely that of the book reviewed, the following form is commonly used:

[12]Robert H. West, rev. of Robert Rentoul Reed, Jr., _The Occult on the Tudor and Stuart Stage_ (Boston, 1965), _Shakespeare Quarterly_, 21 (1970), 86-87.

Subsequent references. If you quote a second time (or third or fourth) from a work, use a short form. The most versatile short form is simply the author's last name and the page number, thus:

[13]Perry, p. 51.

You can even dispense with the author's name if you have mentioned him in the sentence to which the footnote is keyed. That is, if you have said, "Perry goes on to say . . . ," the footnote need only be:

[14]P. 52.

If, however, you have made reference to two works by the author, you must indicate by a short title which work you are referring to, thus:

[15]Lawrence, _Studies_, p. 34.

Or, if your sentence mentions that you are quoting Lawrence, the footnote may be:

[16]_Studies_, p. 34.

If you have said something like "Lawrence, in _Studies in Classical American Literature_, argues . . . ," the reference may be merely:

In short, a subsequent reference should be as brief as clarity allows. The form *ibid.* (for *ibidem,* in the same place), indicating that the material being footnoted comes from the same place as the material of the previous footnote, is no longer commonly used. *Op. cit.* (for *opere citato,* in the work cited) and *loc. cit.* (for *loco citato,* in the place cited), equally unnecessary, have almost disappeared. Identification by author, or by author and short title if necessary, is preferable. A reminder: as p. 43 suggests, if you are going to quote frequently from one source, it will be best to say in your first reference to this source that subsequent quotations from this work will be indicated by parentheses within the body of the paper.

References to introductions and to reprinted essays. You may want to footnote some material that is printed along with a reprint of a work of literature. If, for example, you use Robert B. Heilman's edition of Shakespeare's *The Taming of the Shrew,* and you say "Robert B. Heilman points out . . . ," your footnote will look like this:

[18]Introduction to William Shakespeare, The Taming of the Shrew (New York, 1966), p. xxv.

Heilman's edition of the play includes, as a sort of appendix, several previously published commentaries. If you want to quote from one of them, the monstrous footnote to the quotation might run:

[19]Maynard Mack, "Engagement and Detachment in Shakespeare's Plays," in Essays on Shakespeare and Elizabethan Drama in Honor of Hardin Craig, ed. Richard Hosley (Columbia, Missouri, 1962), rptd. in William Shakespeare, The Taming of the Shrew, ed. Robert B. Heilman (New York, 1966), p. 213.

Secondhand references. If you are quoting, say, A. S. F. Gow, but have derived the quotation not from Gow's book but from a book or article that quotes from it, your footnote should indicate both the place where the original quotation may be found and the place where you found it.

[20]A. S. F. Gow, A. E. Housman: A Sketch (New York, 1936), p. 43, quoted in Gilbert Highet, The Classical Tradition (New York, 1949), p. 497.

In this example, Highet's *Classical Tradition* is the book that has been read. If Highet had not given the date or page of Gow's book, and if you have not followed up Highet's lead and looked at Gow's book, your footnote would give only as much information as could be gathered from Highet.

Bibliography

A bibliography is a list of the works cited in the piece of writing or, less often, a list of all of the relevant writing. (There is rarely much point in the second sort; if you have made no use of a particular book or article, why list it?) Normally a bibliography is given only in a long manuscript such as a research paper or a book, but instructors may require a bibliography even for a short paper if they wish to see at a glance the material that the student has used. In this case, a heading such as "Works Consulted" or "Works Cited" is less pretentious than "Bibliography."

Because a bibliography is arranged alphabetically by author, the author's last name is given first. If a work is by more than one author, it is given under the first author's name; his last name is given first, but the other author's or authors' names follow the normal order of first name first. (See the entry under "Wimsatt" below.) Anonymous works are sometimes grouped at the beginning, arranged alphabetically under the first word of the title (or the second word, if the first word is an article), but the recent tendency has been to list them at the appropriate alphabetical place, giving the initial article, if any, but alphabetizing under the next word. Thus, an anonymous article entitled "A View of Faulkner" would retain the "A" but would be alphabetized under V.

In addition to giving the last name first, a bibliographic entry differs from a footnote in putting a period after the author's name; in putting a period after the title of a book and after the number of volumes if more than one; and in not enclosing in parentheses the place and date of publication of a book. Moreover a bibliographic entry for a book gives the name of the publisher between the place and the date: the place is followed by a colon, the publisher's name, a comma, the date, and finally a period. And, of course, a bibliographic entry does not include page references for books, though it includes the page numbers that an essay in a book or in a journal spans. Begin flush with the left-hand margin; if the entry runs over the line, indent the subsequent lines of the entry a few spaces. Double-space between entries. Below are a few samples.

Bush, Douglas. "Wordsworth: A Minority Report,"
 Wordsworth: Centenary Studies, ed. Gilbert T. Dunklin.
 Princeton: Princeton University Press, 1951, pp. 3-22.

Fixler, Michael. "The Affinities between J.-K. Huysmans and
 the 'Rosicrucian' Stories of W. B. Yeats," PMLA, 74
 (1959), 464-69.

Frye, Northrop. <u>Fables of Identity: Studies in Poetic Mythology</u>. New York: Harcourt, Brace & World, 1963.

_____. <u>Fools of Time: Studies in Shakespearian Tragedy</u>. Toronto: University of Toronto Press, 1967.

The horizontal line indicates that the author is the same as in the previous item; multiple titles by one author are arranged alphabetically, as here where *Fables* precedes *Fools*.

Gogol, Nikolai. <u>Dead Souls</u>, trans. Andrew MacAndrew. New York: New American Library, 1961.

Lang, Andrew. "Ballads," <u>Encyclopaedia Britannica</u>, 11th ed., III, 264-67.

MacCaffrey, Isabel Gamble. Intro. to John Milton, <u>Samson Agonistes and the Shorter Poems</u>. New York: New American Library, 1966.

This entry suggests that the student made use of the introduction, rather than the main body, of the book; if the body of the book were used, the book would be alphabetized under M for Milton, and the form would resemble that of the next item, with "ed. Isabel Gamble MacCaffrey" following the title.

Pope, Alexander. <u>The Correspondence of Alexander Pope</u>, ed. George Sherburn. 5 vols. Oxford: Clarendon Press, 1956.

Vendler, Helen. Rev. of <u>Essays on Style</u>, ed. Roger Fowler. <u>Essays in Criticism</u>, 16 (1966), 457-63.

<u>Victorian Poetry and Poetics</u>, 2nd ed., ed. Walter E. Houghton and G. Robert Stange. Boston: Houghton Mifflin, 1968.

Wimsatt, W. K., Jr., and Cleanth Brooks. <u>Literary Criticism: A Short History</u>. New York: Alfred A. Knopf, 1957.

A final warning:

If you do not master these easy principles, watch out. Montaigne suggests that if a student is stupid or lazy "his tutor should strangle him, if there are no witnesses, or else he should be apprenticed to a pastry-cook in some good town."

PART TWO

PART TWO

3

FICTION

It is usual to say that a narrative — a story, whether a short story or a novel — has an **introduction,** a **complication,** and a **resolution;** that is, it gets under way, some difficulty or problem or complexity arises (usually a **conflict** of opposed wills or forces), and there is some sort of untying or settling-up — or, better, settling-down.* These terms can be illustrated most simply in a familiar piece, O. Henry's "The Gift of the Magi." We are introduced to a young wife who has only (in addition to a husband) $1.87 and long hair; her husband has only (in addition to a wife) a treasured gold watch. It is the day before Christmas, and gifts must be bought. What to do? As everyone knows, she sells her hair to a wig-maker to buy a watch-fob, only to find that her husband has bought her a set of combs by selling his watch. So (here is the resolution), these "two foolish children in a flat who most unwisely sacrificed for each other the greatest treasures of their house," smile and set about making dinner. Lest we mistake the author's tone — though his **verbal irony** is unmistakable, for his words clearly mean approximately the opposite of what they say — he adds that "these two were the wisest."

It is usual to say that "The Gift of the Magi" has a clever **plot.** And it does, if by a plot one means something like "a curious hap-

---

* A short story, of course, is not a novel synopsized. A **short story** usually reveals only a single character at a moment of crisis, whereas a **novel** usually traces the development of an individual or a group through cumulative experiences. If the short story is very short, an essayist has a fairly good chance of elucidating the whole, or writing about all of the aspects that seem important to him. But an essayist who writes about a longer story or a novel will have to be content with treating either a few pages or one thread that runs through the work. The last paragraph of this chapter sketches two critical approaches to long fiction.

pening." It sets forth a cute idea, and no one who reads it ever forgets the idea — the surprising ending. But in one usage of the word plot, "The Gift of the Magi" has scarcely a plot at all. In E. M. Forster's terms, it is only a story (something alleged to have happened), not a plot (happenings that are causally connected). Forster illustrates his distinction thus:

> A plot is also a narrative of events, the emphasis falling on causality. "The king died and then the queen died," is a story. "The king died, and then the queen died of grief" is a plot. The time-sequence is preserved, but the sense of causality overshadows it.
>
> *Aspects of the Novel* (New York), p. 86

In O. Henry's tale, the impact comes from the coincidence of two trains of events (she sells her hair to buy a fob, he sells his watch to buy combs) rather than from the working out of the implications of a deed.

Some fiction has a good deal of physical action — wanderings, strange encounters, births, and deaths. But there is also fiction in which little seems to happen. These apparently plotless stories, however, usually involve a mental action — a significant perception, a decision, a failure of the will — and the process of this mental action is the plot.

The sense of causality, valued so highly by Forster, is in part rooted in **character.** Things happen, in most good fiction, at least partly because the people have certain personalities or characters and, given their natures, because they respond plausibly to other personalities. As we get to know more about their drives and goals, we enjoy seeing the writer complete the portraits, finally presenting us with a coherent and credible picture of men in action. In this view, plot and character are inseparable. Plot is not simply a series of happenings, but happenings that come out of character, that reveal character, and that influence character. Henry James puts it thus: "What is character but the determination of incident? What is incident but the illustration of character?" But, of course, not only what a character does helps to define him. The narrator often describes him, and the character's words and dress reveal aspects of him. David Lodge's analysis (pp. 79–83) of a page from Dickens's *Hard Times* astutely points out the devices Dickens uses to help us understand what Gradgrind is like.

You may be asked merely to set forth a character sketch, describing some person in the story or novel. In preparing such a sketch take into consideration (1) what the character says (but remember that what he says need not be taken at face value; he may be a hypocrite, or self-deceived, or biased), (2) what he does, (3) what others say about him, and (4) what others *do* (their actions may help to indicate what your character could do but does not do). Usually, however, you will be asked to do more than sketch a character. Probably you will discuss his function, or contrast him with other characters, or trace the development of his personality. (One of the most difficult topics, the character of the narrator, will be discussed later in the chapter, under the heading "point of view.") You probably will still want to keep in mind the four suggestions for getting at a character, but you will also want to go further, relating your findings to additional matters of the sort we will now examine.

The writer of fiction provides a coherent world in which the details work together. The **foreshadowing** that would eliminate surprise, or at least greatly reduce it, and thus destroy a story that has nothing else to offer, is a powerful tool in the hands of the writer of serious fiction. Even in such a story as Faulkner's "A Rose for Emily," where we are surprised to learn near the end that Miss Emily has slept beside the decaying corpse of her dead lover, from the outset we expect something strange; that is, we are not surprised by the surprise, only by its precise nature. The first sentence of the story tells us that after Miss Emily's funeral (the narrator begins at the end) the townspeople cross her threshold "out of curiosity to see the inside of her house, which no one save an old manservant . . . had seen in at least ten years." As the story progresses, we see Miss Emily prohibiting people from entering the house, we hear that after a certain point no one ever sees Homer Barron again, that "the front door remained closed," and (a few paragraphs before the end of the story) that the townspeople "knew that there was one room in that region above the stairs which no one had seen in forty years." The paragraph preceding the revelation that "the man himself lay in bed" is devoted to a description of Homer's dust-covered clothing and toilet articles. In short, however much we are unprepared for the precise revelation, we are prepared for some strange thing in the house; and, given Miss Emily's purchase of poison and Homer's disappearance, we have some idea of what will be revealed.

Joyce's "Araby" is another example of a story in which the beginning is a preparation for all that follows. Consider the first two paragraphs.

> North Richmond Street, being blind, was a quiet street except at the hour when the Christian Brothers' school set the boys free. An uninhabited house of two storeys stood at the blind end, detached from its neighbours in a square ground. The other houses of the street, conscious of decent lives within them, gazed at one another with brown imperturbable faces.
>
> The former tenant of our house, a priest, had died in the back

drawing-room. Air, musty from having been long enclosed, hung in all the rooms, and the waste room behind the kitchen was littered with old useless papers. Among these I found a few paper-covered books, the pages of which were curled and damp: *The Abbot*, by Walter Scott, *The Devout Communicant* and *The Memoirs of* V*idocq*. I liked the last best because its leaves were yellow. The wild garden behind the house contained a central apple-tree and a few straggling bushes under one of which I found the late tenant's rusty bicycle-pump. He had been a very charitable priest; in his will he had left all his money to institutions and the furniture of his house to his sister.

A dead-end ("blind") street contains "imperturbable" houses, including an uninhabited one. The former tenant of the house that the narrator lived in was a priest who died in the back drawing-room, leaving, among other things, musty air, yellowing books, and a rusty bicycle pump. If we have read with any care, we find that Joyce indeed gives us in these paragraphs a vision of the paralysis of Ireland that he elsewhere speaks of. As we read further in the story, we are not surprised to learn that the boy for a while manufactured quasi-religious experiences (religion being dead — remember the priest and his rusty bicycle pump). In his ears, shop-boys sing "litanies," his girl friend's name springs to his lips "in strange prayers," and his vision of her is a "chalice" which he carries "safely through a throng of foes." He plans to visit a bazaar, and he promises to bring her a gift; but after he has with some difficulty arrived at the bazaar, he is vastly disappointed by the trivial conversation of the attendants, by the counting of the day's receipts (money-changers in the temple), and by the darkness ("the upper part of the hall was now completely dark"). The last line of the story runs thus: "Gazing up into the darkness I saw myself as a creature driven and derided by vanity; and my eyes burned with anguish and anger." Everything in the story coheres; the dead-end street, the dead priest, the rusty pump — all are perfect preludes to this story about a boy's recognition of the nothingness that surrounds him. (The "vanity" that drives and derides him is not only the egotism that moved him to think he could bring the girl a fitting gift but also the nothingness that is spoken of in the biblical "Vanity of vanities, all is vanity.")

An essay on foreshadowing will almost surely work through the evidence chronologically, though of course the initial paragraph may discuss the end and indicate that the remainder of the essay will be concerned with tracing the way in which the author prepares the reader for this end and simultaneously maintains the right amount of suspense. If the suspense is too slight, we stop reading, not caring what comes next. If it is too great, we are perhaps reading a story in which the interest depends entirely on some strange happening rather than a story with sufficiently universal application to make it worthy of a second reading. The essay may study the way in which details gain in meaning as the reader gets further into the story. Or it may study the author's failure to keep his details relevant and coherent, his tendency to introduce material for its momentary value at the expense of the larger design. An essay on an uneven story may do both: it may show that although there are unfortunate irrelevancies, there is also considerable skill in arousing and interestingly fulfilling the reader's expectations. If the essayist feels that the story is fundamentally successful, the organization of his thoughts may reflect his feelings. After an initial paragraph in which he states his overall position, he may discuss the failures and then go on, at greater length, to discuss the strengths, thus ending strongly on his main point. If he feels that the story is essentially a failure, he may first briefly discuss its merits and then go on to his main point, the unsatisfactory nature of the story. To reverse this procedure, clearly, would be to leave the reader with an impression contrary to the essayist's thesis.

Foreshadowing normally makes use of **setting.** The setting or environment in the first two paragraphs of Joyce's "Araby" is not mere geography, not mere locale: it provides an **atmosphere,** an air that the characters breathe, a world in which they move. Broadly speaking, setting includes not only the physical surroundings but the point or points in time. The background against which we see the characters and the happenings may be specified as morning or evening, spring or fall, and this temporal setting in a good story will probably be highly relevant; it will probably be part of the story's meaning, perhaps providing an ironic contrast or perhaps exerting an influence on the characters.

Some comments on familiar examples from Thomas Hardy's novels may clarify the significance of setting. In *Tess of the D'Urbervilles* we are told of a place called Flintcomb Ash, where "the whole field was in color a desolate drab; it was a complexion without features, as if a face, from chin to brow, should be only an expanse of skin. The sky wore, in another color, the same likeness; a white vacuity of expression with the lineaments gone." Or, near the end of the novel, when, just before her arrest, Tess lies upon a great stone slab at Stonehenge, she is associated with all the victims of history and prehistory. Dorothy Van Ghent calls attention to the role that the earth plays in *Tess*. There are

> the long stretches of earth that have to be trudged in order that a person may get from one place to another, the slowness of the business, the irreducible reality of it (for one has only one's feet), its

grimness of soul-wearying fatigue and shelterlessness and doubtful issue at the other end of the journey where nobody may be at home.

The English Novel (New York, 1953), p. 201

Mrs. Van Ghent goes on to say, in discussing *The Mayor of Casterbridge*:

> The Roman ruins round about the town of Casterbridge are a rather . . . complicated metaphor, for they are works of man that have fallen into earth; they speak mutely of the anonymity of human effort in historical as well as in geological times; their presence suggests also the classic pattern of the Mayor's tragedy, the ancient repetitiveness of self-destruction; and they provide thus a kind of guarantee or confirming signature of the heroism of the doomed human enterprise. p. 202

David Lodge, on pages 79–81, points out that Dickens's "plain, bare, monotonous vault of a schoolroom," the domain of the schoolmaster Gradgrind, is a kind of extension of Gradgrind himself, who has a "square wall of a forehead," an "inflexible" voice, and a "square coat." In short, in a good piece of fiction the setting is not merely "colorful" but relevant.

In "Composition and Fate in the Short Novel," using Thomas Mann's "Death in Venice" as an illustration, Howard Nemerov distinguishes between two kinds of relevance in literature:

> One kind has to do with the temporal succession of events, as though the single point of the idea must be viewed in an added dimension as a straight line; in order to tell how a distinguished German author dies in Venice we must get him to Venice, keep him there, and supply a disease for him to die of. He will doubtless see many things, and think many things, on his journey — what things? We need another kind of relevance, having to do with association, symbol, metaphor, as well as with probable and realistic observation; while the distinguished author is in Venice it occurs to him, waking, that his situation is like that discussed in the *Phaedrus*, and dreaming, that his situation is like that of King Pentheus in *The Bacchae* of Euripides.
>
> *Poetry and Fiction: Essays*
> (New Brunswick, 1963), pp. 241–42

Without this first kind of relevance, of course, there is no story; without the second kind it is a different story. The story we value has both kinds. Nemerov continues with his illustration from "Death in Venice":

> When Aschenbach dies, there by the shore, we are told that the weather was autumnal, the beach deserted and not even very clean; suddenly we are given this: "A camera on a tripod stood at the edge of the water, apparently abandoned; its black cloth snapped in the

freshening wind." That is all, our attention is given to Tadzio, Aschenbach's death soon follows, the camera is never mentioned again.

Crudely speaking, this camera is unnecessary and no one could possibly have noticed anything missing had the author decided against its inclusion; yet in a musical, compositional sense it exquisitely touches the center of the story and creates a resonance which makes us for a moment aware of the entire inner space of the action, of all things relevant and their relations to one another.

Our sense of this is mostly beyond exposition, as symbolic things have a way of being; but some of its elements may be mentioned. About the camera by the sea there is, first, a poignant desolation, the emptiness of vast spaces, and in its pictorial quality it resembles one of the earliest images in the story, when Aschenbach, standing by the cemetery, looks away down the empty streets: "not a wagon in sight, either on the paved Ungererstrasse, with its gleaming tramlines stretching off towards Schwabing, nor on the Föhring highway." Both pictures are by Di Chirico. The camera's black cloth reminds us of the gondola, "black as nothing else on earth except a coffin," and the repeated insistence on black in that description; also of the "labor in darkness" which brings forth the work of art. For we perceive that the camera stands to the sea as, throughout this story, the artist has stood to experience, in a morally heroic yet at the same time dubious or ridiculous or even impossible relation of form to all possibility, and that at the summer's end, in the freshening wind, the camera is abandoned. It would be near forgivable, so full of Greek mysteries is this work, if we thought the tripod itself remotely Delphic.

p. 243

It is not enough, of course, to weave a pattern of references, a chain of images. (An essay that merely catalogs references to blackness in "Death in Venice" will not be of much interest.) The writer's story must be about something; and his language is the net that catches it, the device whereby he makes something we value, something which says something about human experience. This intangible he gives us has been called "felt life" and "felt reality." Here is a paragraph by another critic, Martin Green, sharply criticizing Hawthorne for naming experiences rather than catching them. Green begins by quoting from Hawthorne's "Young Goodman Brown."

"On he flew among the black pines, brandishing his staff with frenzied gestures, now giving vent to an inspiration of horrid blasphemy, and now shouting forth such laughter as set all the echoes of the forest laughing like demons around him." Nothing there evokes the experience of blasphemy. Everything evokes memories of fanciful fiction. "Another verse of the hymn arose, a low and mournful strain, such as the pious love, but joined to words which expressed all that our natures can conceive of sin, and darkly hinted at far more." This is the language of empty exaggeration; after all that our natures can conceive comes "far more." "Young Goodman Brown" is not an allegory because it allegorizes nothing. There is no experience embodied in its language, and consequently no reason to construct elaborate meanings for its oddities.

Re-appraisals (New York, 1965), pp. 73-74

Green may be wrong, but notice how he makes his point: he begins with a quotation from the story, offers his criticism, and then offers another quotation that allows him to restate his criticism. He concludes the paragraph with yet another and broader restatement.

An "experience," of course, is not a happening through which the author necessarily passed; rather, it is a thought, an emotion, a vision that is meaningful and is embodied in the piece of fiction for all to read. Inevitably the writer uses symbols (the blackness, the camera, and the beach on which Nemerov comments). Symbols are neither puzzles nor colorful details but are among the concrete embodiments that give the story whatever accuracy it has. Joyce's dead-end street, dead priest, apple tree (suggestive of the Garden of Eden, now fallen?), and rusty bicycle pump all help to define very precisely the condition of a thoroughly believable Dublin. Mary McCarthy, in an essay on symbolism, points out that symbols are not odd things stuck into a story but are things that properly belong in the world of the story. She effectively illustrates her point with an example from Tolstoy's *Anna Karenina*.

> . . . Toward the beginning of the novel, Anna meets the man who will be her lover, Vronsky, on the Moscow-St. Petersburg express; as they meet, there has been an accident; a workman has been killed by the train. This is the beginning of Anna's doom, which is completed when she throws herself under a train and is killed; and the last we see of Vronsky is in a train, with a toothache; he is off to the wars. The train is necessary to the plot of the novel, and I believe it is also symbolic, both of the iron forces of material progress that Tolstoy hated so and that played a part in Anna's moral destruction, and also of those iron laws of necessity and consequence that govern human action when it remains on the sensual level.
>
> One can read the whole novel, however, without being conscious that the train is a symbol; we do not have to "interpret" to feel the import of doom and loneliness in the train's whistle — the same import we ourselves can feel when we hear a train whistle blow in the country, even today.

On the Contrary (New York, 1962), p. 236

The symbols, to repeat, are a part of the world of the story, contributing to its sense of immediacy or reality as well as radiating suggestions or (to use Henry James's figure) casting long shadows. In Hardy's *Jude the Obscure*, for example, the pigeons that Jude and Sue are forced to sell are symbols of Jude's and Sue's caged existence, but they are also pigeons that Jude and Sue are forced to sell. Furthermore, other references to birds in the novel function similarly, as do the passages dealing with the trapped rabbit. Birds and rabbits are a part of Jude's world, meaningful on the realistic level but resonant too. An essayist who discusses symbolism in a piece of fiction will probably want to examine the degree to which the symbols are integral and interrelated.

Below is a fine essay by a student, pointing out that the repeated references to darkness in Joyce's *Dubliners* are an important part of the meaning of the book. The title and the first paragraph of the essay give the reader an idea of what will follow. The next paragraph discusses the first story in the book, and the third paragraph discusses the last story (the essayist wisely avoids plodding through fifteen stories; by choosing the first and the last stories he implies that all the stories share the motif). The next paragraph sets forth the general implications of darkness, and it is followed by a fairly detailed paragraph analyzing the motif in one story. In the concluding paragraph the essayist concedes that the references to darkness are literal as well as symbolic, but he quietly insists that the symbolic implications are there, too.

Darkness in Dubliners

The fifteen short stories in Joyce's collection called Dubliners are not simply fifteen separate stories, or even fifteen stories united only by being about people in the city for which the book is named. The unity is greater than physical locale; there is a unity of theme, which Joyce himself said was "paralysis,"[1] and this sense of paralysis is conveyed not only by what the characters do--or, more often, what they do not do--but also by Joyce's insistence on the dark sky, or the darkness inside a room, in most of the stories. Darkness, especially of night, seems to surround

---

[1] Letter to the publisher, quoted in Harry Levin, *James Joyce* (London, 1944), p. 29.

the characters, hindering them from any advance and representing their mental condition.

Most of the stories are set in a dark street or a dark
room. For example, the very first story, "The Sisters,"
begins as follows:

> There was no hope for him this time: it was the third
> stroke. Night after night I had passed the house (it
> was vacation time) and studied the lighted square of
> the window: and night after night I had found it
> lighted in the same way, faintly and evenly.

As the story continues, we find that a priest has at last
died. The narrator visits the house "after sunset" (a time
of day that itself suggests the death of the day) and he
learns that the dead priest "was quite resigned" and "was
a disappointed man." Near the end of the story we learn that
the priest was mentally sick, and was once found "sitting up
by himself in the dark in his confession-box." In short,
the priest's mind was darkened, and this is revealed in the
episode of the confession-box and in the several references
to night, a time when men do not usually work or make progress. Death and darkness are associated, and Dublin seems
to be a dying city.

If we jump, for a moment, across the entire book, to
some sentences in the last paragraph of the last story, "The
Dead," we find remarkable connections with the first story.
Again it is night, and again we get references to a dim
light surrounded by darkness. This time a man is in his
bedroom, looking out of a window on a snowy night. The
final paragraph includes such expressions as "He watched

sleepily the flakes, silver and dark, falling obliquely against the lamplight," "journey westward," "the dark central plain," "their last end," "falling," "buried," and "the living and the dead." In this story the whole of Dublin is wrapped in night and in a cover of snow, and the chief character falls asleep. Here as in the first story about the dead priest, the literal time of day—night—contributes to the sense of death or paralysis. The people in Dublin seem to live in darkness—that is, in frustration and spiritual emptiness.

In almost all the stories, the darkness is made the more ominous by feeble lights that seem to try to overcome it but of course fail to do so. In the first story, for example, the window was lighted "night after night," but at last the time came when the priest died and the blinds were drawn. The only light inside is from candles burning at the dead man's head; this light is not seen from the street, where the window is lit only by "tawny gold" light reflected from the clouds. Inside, the narrator "groped" his way to a chair, and then learns of the episode in the confession-box. Darkness takes over. Sometimes the images of light against the dark are not literal, as in the previous instances, but are figurative. In "The Dead," for instance, we get this figurative description of Gabriel: "The dull fires of his lust began to glow angrily in his veins." Here again life or vitality is associated with light ("fire"). As in the other stories, the light does not last, for

Gabriel's lust soon disappears and he falls asleep in the night. In another story, "Ivy Day in the Committee Room," the fire is literal; some minor politicians are discussing an election in a room with a dying fire, and it is clear that they are the corrupt or dying left-overs of what was once a genuinely patriotic movement. We are told that the weather is unpleasant and that "the short day had grown dark." Several times we are told that the room is dark, the fire being inadequate. We learn from the dialogue that there is bribery, suspicion, selfishness, a total lack of idealism. In short, the physical locale--a darkening room, fitfully illuminated by a dying fire--is a way of representing the people who live in it.

Because it would be tedious to go through each story, describing the special sorts of darkness that appear in almost all, this paper will study a single story, "Araby," in a bit more detail. The gist of the plot is that a young boy, in love with a girl, promises to bring her something from a fair called Araby, but when he gets to the fair, just before closingtime, he finds that his romantic visions of himself as a heroic lover, and of the fair as a sort of enchanted place, are demolished by the tawdriness of the fair. This short summary gives only one hint, in the reference to closingtime, of the role that darkness plays in creating the atmosphere that helps to shape the characters, but in fact the story is filled with references to darkness. The narrator played in "dark muddy lanes," "dark dripping gardens," and "dark odorous stables," and he admires the girl from inside of his room, where he has pulled the shade "down to within an inch of the sash so that I could not be seen." On the day he is to go to the fair to bring back his trophy, his uncle does not get home until nine o'clock, and therefore the boy does not get to the fair until ten to ten, when "the greater part of the hall was in darkness." This is the way the story ends:

> I heard a voice call from one end of the gallery that the light was out. The upper part of the hall was now completely dark.
> Gazing up into the darkness I saw myself as a creature driven and derided by vanity; and my eyes burned with anguish and anger.

The narrator's sense of disillusionment is perfectly represented by the statement of the voice that "the light was out." The voice is stating a simple fact about the light in the hall, but the reader understands its relation to the narrator's state of mind. In the last sentence of the story, the narrator looks into the dark and sees nothing; his rich illusions, or delusions, have vanished, and he is surrounded by nothing, for he now has nothing within him.

Dublin probably is often dark; certainly night comes to Dublin as it comes to every other city, and one might try to argue that Joyce is merely being accurate in his depiction of dark days, and of nights. But when one rereads the stories, and notices how few are set in the daylight, and how often the darkness is stressed, and how appropriate it is to the spiritually impoverished characters in the book,

one realizes that Joyce is doing more than giving realistic
pictures of Dublin at a certain time of day. His descriptions of dark streets, dark rooms, and of fitful bits of
illumination, are also descriptions of a state of mind that
dominates the Dubliners in Dubliners.

The Dublin in *Dubliners* and the England in *Jude* are the Dublin
and England that Joyce and Hardy thought existed, but it must be
remembered that although an author *writes* a story, someone else *tells*
it. The story is seen from a particular **point of view.** A wide variety of
terms has been established to name differing points of view, but the
following labels are among the commonest. We can begin with two
categories: third-person points of view (in which the narrator is, in
the crudest sense, not a character in the story) and first-person points
of view (in which the "I" who narrates the story plays a part in it).

The **third-person point of view** itself has several subdivisions. At
one extreme is the **omniscient narrator.** He knows everything that is
going on; he can tell us the inner thoughts of all the characters. He
may editorialize, passing judgments, reassuring his reader, etc., in
which case he may sound like the author. Here is Hardy's omniscient
narrator in *Tess of the D'Urbervilles,* telling the reader that Tess was
mistaken in imagining that the countryside proclaimed her guilt:
"But this encompassment of her own characterization, based upon
shreds of convention, peopled by phantoms and voices antipathetic
to her, was a sorry and mistaken creation of Tess's fancy — a cloud
of moral hobgoblins by which she was terrified without reason." Still,
even this narrator is not quite Hardy; he does not allude to his other
books, his private life, or his hope that the book will sell. If he is
Hardy, he is only one aspect of Hardy, quite possibly a fictional
Hardy, a disembodied voice with particular characteristics.

Another sort of third-person narrator (**selective omniscient**) takes
up what Henry James called a "center of consciousness," revealing
the thoughts of one of the characters but (for the most part) seeing
the rest of the characters from the outside only. Wayne Booth, in a
penetrating study of Jane Austen's *Emma,* explains the effectiveness
of selective omniscience in this novel. He points out that Emma is
intelligent, witty, beautiful, and rich. But she is flawed by pride, and,
until she discovers and corrects her fault, she almost destroys herself
and her friends. How can such a character be made sympathetic, so
that we will hope for the happy conclusion to the comedy? "The

solution to the problem of maintaining sympathy despite almost crippling faults," Booth says,

> was primarily to use the heroine herself as a kind of narrator, though in third person, reporting on her own experience. . . . By showing most of the story through Emma's eyes, the author insures that we shall travel with Emma rather than stand against her. It is not simply that Emma provides, in the unimpeachable evidence of her own conscience, proof that she has many redeeming qualities that do not appear on the surface; such evidence could be given with authorial commentary, though perhaps not with such force and conviction. Much more important, the sustained inside view leads the reader to hope for good fortune for the character with whom he travels, quite independently of the qualities revealed.
>
> The Rhetoric of Fiction (Chicago, 1961), pp. 245–46

Booth goes on to point out, in a long and subtle analysis, that "sympathy for Emma can be heightened by withholding inside views of others as well as by granting them of her."

In writing about point of view, one of course tries to suggest what the author's choice of a particular point of view contributes to the story. Wayne Booth, we have just seen, shows how Jane Austen's third-person point of view helps to keep sympathetic a character who otherwise might be less than sympathetic. Booth states the problem — how to draw an intelligent but proud woman so that the reader will wish for a happy ending — and he presents his answer convincingly, moving from "It is not simply . . ." to "Much more important. . . ." (To reverse the order would cause a drop in interest.) He then moves from a discussion of the inside treatment of Emma to the outside treatment of the other characters, thus substantiating and enlarging his argument. Possibly one could reverse this procedure, beginning with a discussion of the treatment of the characters other than Emma and then closing in on Emma, but such an essay may seem slow in getting under way. The early part may appear unfocused. The reader will for a while be left wondering why in an essay on point of view in *Emma* the essayist does not turn to the chief matter, the presentation of the central character.

To continue our discussion of kinds of points of view: the third-person narrator, then, although not in the ordinary sense a character in the story, is an important voice in the story, who helps to give shape to it. Another type of third-person narrator is the so-called **effaced narrator.** He does not seem to exist, for he does not comment in his own voice (unlike the editorially omniscient narrator), and he does not enter any minds (unlike the omniscient or selective omniscient narrator). The reader hears dialogue and sees only what a camera or a fly on the wall would see. The following example is from Hemingway's "The Killers":

> The door of Henry's lunchroom opened and two men came in. They sat down at the counter.
> "What's yours?" George asked them.
> "I don't know," one of the men said. "What do you want to eat, Al?"
> "I don't know," said Al. "I don't know what I want to eat."

But even an effaced narrator has, if we think a moment, a kind of personality. The story he records may seem "cold" or "scientific" or "reportorial" or "objective," and such a **tone** or voice (attitude of the narrator, as it is detected) may be an important part of the story. Rémy de Gourmont's remark, quoted in Ezra Pound's *Literary Essays*, is relevant: "To be impersonal is to be personal in a special kind of way. . . . The objective is one of the forms of the subjective."

To turn to **first-person,** or **participant, points of view:** the "I" who narrates the story (recall that at the end of "Araby" the narrator says, "I saw myself as a creature driven and derided by vanity") may be a major character in it (as he is in "Araby," in *The Catcher in the Rye,* and in Dickens's *Great Expectations*), or he may be a minor character, a mere witness (Nick Carroway narrates the story of Gatsby in *The Great Gatsby*). A first-person narrator may not fully understand his own report. This is the **innocent-eye** device, in which a good part of the effect consists in the discrepancy between the narrator's imperfect awareness and the reader's superior awareness. The classic example is the narrator of Ring Lardner's "Haircut," a barber, who, thinking he is describing an accident, actually (the reader understands) describes a murder. Although we sometimes feel that a first-person narrator (Conrad's Marlow in several novels is an example) is a very thinly veiled substitute for the author, the words of a first-person narrator require the same kind of scrutiny that we give to the words of the other characters in a story or play. The reader must deduce the personality from what is said. For instance, the narrator of "Araby" never tells us that he was a good student; but, from such a passage as the following, we can deduce that he was a bookish boy until he fell in love: "I watched my master's face pass from amiability to sternness; he hoped I was not beginning to idle." A first-person narrator is not likely to give us the help that an editorially omniscient narrator gives. We must deduce that the narrator's uncle drinks too much from this passage from "Araby": "At nine o'clock I heard my uncle's latchkey in the hall-door. I heard him talking to himself and heard the hall-stand rocking when it had received the weight of his overcoat. I could interpret these signs."

In a first-person narrative it is sometimes difficult for the reader to interpret the signs. In a sense the author has given the reader two stories: the story the narrator tells and the story of a narrator telling a story. Henry James's tale, *The Turn of the Screw*, is told in the first person, beginning thus:

> The story had held us, round the fire, sufficiently breathless, but except the obvious remark that it was gruesome, as, on Christmas eve in an old house, a strange tale should essentially be, I remember no comment uttered till somebody happened to say that it was the only case he had met in which such a visitation had fallen on a child.

The unnamed narrator — we can call him Henry James, but only if we remember that he exists here only as narrator, not as the American expatriate, the brother of William James, etc. — is one of a group which has heard a ghost story. He goes on to introduce another member of the group, someone named Douglas:

> It was this observation that drew from Douglas — not immediately, but later in the evening — a reply that had the interesting consequence to which I call attention.

The narrator proceeds to say that two nights later Douglas told a ghost story concerning a governess and her two charges, a boy and a girl, who had been harried by the ghosts of two former servants. Douglas did not exactly tell the story, rather he read it from a manuscript written long ago by the governess. There are, then, three narrators: the "I" who addresses the reader; Douglas, who narrates the ghost story; and the governess, whose words Douglas reads aloud to the group. The heart of *The Turn of the Screw* is, therefore, the governess's long first-person narrative, which is read to a group by Douglas and which is recounted to the reader by one of the group, "I." If an essayist is writing about point of view in James's story, he will want to comment on this narrator within a narrator within a narrator. He will want to ask himself at least two questions: What broad effects does this framework have on the reader, and how reliable are Douglas and the governess as narrators?

Because the first question is simpler and less important, it is probably best to treat it first and get on to the larger matter. An essay might, then, at the outset, touch on the suitability of having a ghost story told by someone who has heard it from someone who saw the ghosts. Ghost stories are like that; we usually get them not firsthand but second- or thirdhand, and we listen with wonder and at the same time with a sense of doubt. The stories, like ghosts, are not within our grasp; we wish we could question the eyewitness, but we cannot. Having said this much, the essayist might add that because ghost stories belong primarily to the world of oral literature, where stories are told to a group rather than read by an individual, it is appropriate for this story, too, to be told to a group. James's first line, "The story had held us, round the fire," in some measure takes us into the world of oral literature, a world less intellectual than the world of books. Even this outermost narrator is simply one of "us," a nameless part of the community, a member of Douglas's audience two nights later.

The writer of an essay on point of view in *The Turn of the Screw* will next alert his reader to the fact that he has finished his discussion of the broad effects created by the framework and will now turn to the second, and more important, point: the degree to which the narrators' personalities color the events. Douglas explains that he met the governess when he was a university student; she was ten years older than he, and she seemed "worthy" and "clever"; he "liked her extremely." He means to assure his audience of her reliability, but the reader senses that Douglas was infatuated with her; the reader learns, too, that Douglas did not meet her until ten years after her ordeal with the ghosts, when she was no longer an "anxious girl out of a Hampshire vicarage," "young, untried, nervous." The essayist may decide that her personality indeed colors the happenings. If he does, he will collect the details about her provincial background and her in-experience, which made awesome the responsibility of bringing up two children. He will probably devote a paragraph to what he under-stands her intellectual and emotional state to have been at the time she accepted the job. If he sees her as unprepared and unstable, he will want to explain that Douglas's positive remarks about her must be taken only provisionally and as only Douglas's view; the real gov-erness is not simply the "worthy" girl Douglas thinks he is describ-ing, but she is the governess whom the reader perceives through Douglas's words and through her own. The essayist will give the evi-dence that supports his own view that she was unstable: various bits that emphasize her naiveté and her nervousness provide the back-ground. Then he will go on to examine her less direct revelations. At one point, for example, she compares herself and the little boy in her charge to "some young couple on their wedding-journey." He might notice that she sometimes says "I felt" and later reports as a fact the things she had only "felt," and that she is given to learn-ing things in a "flash of knowledge" rather than in a more acceptable way. An essayist on this topic will notice, too, the lack of corrobora-tion. The governess insists that the little girl saw the ghost, and she explains that the girl would lie and deny it if asked; there is, then, in her opinion, no need to check with the girl. The essayist might well conclude that the story is not so much a ghost story as a story about a neurotic governess whose fantasies drive the children to destruction.

In this sketch of an essay on point of view in *The Turn of the Screw*, one important matter may have been omitted: Is there any evidence, other than Douglas's testimony of the governess's good character, that conflicts with the thesis that she is neurotic? If there is, it must, of course, be accounted for. *Where* it will be accounted for depends upon what it is. As we have seen, Douglas's testimony can effectively be given immediately after the discussion of Douglas as a narrator and before the essayist's detailed discussion of the governess. About the only advice one can give is to put it at the appropriate place, the place where the reader *ought* to be told. Usually, as with the comment on Douglas's comments, it should precede your detailed refutation; if it follows, your essay may seem to run downhill. But in initially setting forth a position that will be refuted, the reader should be given a clear hint of what is to come; there is no point in setting forth an argument that at first seems convincing only to inform the reader that he has accepted an insubstantial argument. A clue such as "It may seem," or "Although at first glance one may believe," will often be enough, though sometimes one may want to be even more forthright: "The argument that the governess is reliable is based on two pieces of evidence, but neither is substantial. The first. . . ." Usually the most satisfactory formula is to state your view at some length, take account of the objections at the points where they might reasonably be offered, and move steadily toward developing your thesis.

Because modern fiction makes subtle use of point of view, it can scarcely be neglected in a discussion of what a story is about. Perhaps unfairly, modern criticism is usually unhappy with suggestions of the author's voice in older fiction. We would rather see than be lectured at. We are less impressed by "It was the stillness of an implacable force brooding over an inscrutable intention" (from Conrad's *Heart of Darkness*) than by this passage from the same book:

> Black shapes crouched, lay, sat between the trees, leaning against the trunks, clinging to the earth, half coming out, half effaced within the dim light, in all the attitudes of pain, abandonment, and despair. Another mine on the cliff went off, followed by a slight shudder of the soil under my feet. The work was going on. The work! And this was the place where some of the helpers had withdrawn to die.

The second quotation, but not the first, gives us the sense of reality that we have come to expect from fiction. (Still, this is a critical assumption that can be questioned.) Hardy's novels in particular have been censured on this account; the modern sensibility is uneasy when it hears Hardy's own voice commenting on the cosmic significance of the happenings, as when in *Tess of the D'Urbervilles* the narrator says: "In the ill-judged execution of the well-judged plan of things, the call seldom produces the comer, the man to love rarely coincides with the hour for loving." The passage goes on in this vein at some length. Even in passages of dialogue we sometimes feel that we are getting not a vision of life but a discourse on it, as in this famous exchange between Tess and her brother:

> "Did you say the stars were worlds, Tess?"
> "Yes."
> "All like ours?"
> "I don't know; but I think so. They sometimes seem to be like the apples on our stubbard-tree. Most of them splendid and sound — a few blighted."
> "Which do we live on — a splendid one or a blighted one?"
> "A blighted one."

We prefer the picture of the field at Flintcomb Ash, the pigeons, the rabbits, Stonehenge. Partly, we feel, overt commentary (even when put into the mouths of the characters) leaves the world of fiction and invites us to judge it separately, as philosophy. Partly, of course, the difficulty is that twentieth-century novelists and readers have come to expect the novel to do something different from what Hardy and his contemporaries expected it to do. As Virginia Woolf puts it in "Mr. Bennett and Mrs. Brown," the novelists before World War I "made tools and established conventions which do their business. But those tools are not our tools, and that business is not our business. For us those conventions are ruin, those tools are death." Mrs. Van Ghent concisely gives the modern objection: when the philosophic vision

> can be loosened away from the novel to compete in the general field of abstract truth — as frequently in Hardy — it has the weakness of any abstraction that statistics and history and science may be allowed to criticize; whether true or false for one generation or another, or for one reader or another, or even for one personal mood or another, its status as truth is relative to conditions of evidence and belief existing outside the novel and existing there quite irrelevant to whatever body of particularized life the novel itself might contain.
>
> *The English Novel*, p. 197

Mrs. Van Ghent goes on to explain that the philosophic vision has its proper place in the novel when it is "local and inherent there through a maximum of organic dependencies." She illustrates her point by quoting this passage from *Tess*, which describes the coming

of morning after Tess's horse has been accidentally stabbed to death
by the shaft of a mail cart.

> The atmosphere turned pale, the birds shook themselves in the hedges,
> arose, and twittered; the lane showed all its white features, and
> Tess showed hers, still whiter. The huge pool of blood in front of her
> was already assuming the iridescence of coagulation; and when the
> sun rose, a million prismatic hues were reflected from it. Prince lay
> alongside still and stark, his eyes half open, the hole in his chest
> looking scarcely large enough to have let out all that had animated him.

Part of Mrs. Van Ghent's comment runs thus:

> With the arousal and twittering of the birds we are aware of the
> oblivious manifold of nature stretching infinite and detached beyond
> the isolated human figure; the iridescence of the coagulating blood
> is, in its incongruity with the dark human trouble, a note of the
> same indifferent cosmic chemistry that has brought about the accident;
> and the smallness of the hole in Prince's chest, that looked "scarcely
> large enough to have let out all that had animated him," is the minor
> remark of that irony by which Tess's great cruel trial appears as a van-
> ishing incidental in the blind waste of time and space and biological
> repetition. Nevertheless, there is nothing in this event that has not the
> natural "grain" of concrete fact; and what it signifies — of the com-
> plicity of doom with the most random occurrence, of the cross-
> purposing of purpose in a multiple world, of cosmic indifference and
> of moral desolation — is a local truth of a particular experience and
> irrefutable as the experience itself.
>
> The English Novel, pp. 198–99

In attempting to take account of the **theme** of a work of fiction
(What does it add up to? What is the motif that holds the happenings together? What is the point? *Not:* How does it turn out? *Not:*
What happens?),* the essayist must consider the role of concrete
facts. The details add up, or, to use Flannery O'Connor's words,
they are "controlled by some overall purpose." The narrative of James
Joyce's "The Dead" tells of Gabriel's arrival at a party, the events
at the party, his subsequent departure, and his realization that his
wife is taken up with the thought of a boy, unknown to Gabriel, who
had loved her. As David Daiches points out in his essay (in *The Novel
and the Modern World*), on the theme of this story, about three-

---

* A theme in a literary work is not a thesis, an arguable message such
as "Men ought not to struggle against fate"; rather, it is something like
"Man's Struggle against Fate" or "The Process of Growing Up" or "The
Quest for Knowledge." The formulation of a theme normally includes an
abstract noun or a phrase. For some further comments on theme, see
pp. 91–93.

fourths of the story is devoted to episodes at the party. Daiches suggests that these episodes modify each other and embody the theme. That theme, he says, is the liberation of Gabriel from his own egotism. Here is the skeleton of Daiches's essay:

> The theme of "The Dead" is the liberation of Gabriel from his own egotism; this theme determines the episodes:
>
> > The first attack on his egotism (the caretaker's daughter is not impressed by him)
> >
> > Gabriel's response (he is a little distressed)
> >
> > The second attack (Miss Ivors attacks his individualism and questions his patriotism)
> >
> > Gabriel's response (he is distressed, but he calms himself by denigrating her, and he regains his composure when he sits at the head of the table)
> >
> > The third attack (D'Arcy's favorable reference to Caruso reveals the provincialism of the rest of the group, whose members have hardly heard of him)
> >
> > Gabriel continues in his role as the center of attention
> >
> > The fourth attack (D'Arcy's singing and playing take the limelight from Gabriel)
> >
> > The fifth attack (confident and desirous of his wife, Gabriel learns that her thoughts are of a boy he does not even know)
> >
> > Gabriel's response (humbled, he dozes off and becomes a part of all the blank, snow-covered world around him)
> >
> > Gabriel's new attitude resembles Joyce's ideal aesthetic attitude.

Daiches's method, clearly, is to move through the story, episode by episode.

Another method of talking about the theme is to focus on a single speech. A work, especially if it is told from an editorially omniscient point of view, may include an explicit statement of the theme, but it need not; think twice before you detach any passage and say that it states the theme. Be especially wary of assuming that the words of any character state the theme, though of course this is not to say that no character in any work of fiction ever says anything that can serve as a statement of the theme. The difficulty is that a character has a personality, and what he says is usually colored by this personality and the momentary situation. The statement, apt in the immediate context, may not adequately cover the entire work. Take, for example, Phoebe's comment to her brother

Holden Caulfield in *The Catcher in the Rye:* "You don't like *any*-thing that's happening." Many readers believe that Phoebe has put her finger on the matter: Holden doesn't like anything. But with a little work one can find a number of things Holden likes. He likes the kettle drummer at Radio City, he likes *The Return of the Native,* he likes the music of carousels, he likes his brother Allie, and he likes talking to Phoebe. She mentions that Allie is dead and so he "really" doesn't count, but Holden replies:

> I know he's dead! Don't you think I know that? I can still like him, though, can't I?

And when Phoebe says that talking to her "isn't anything *really,*" he insists it is:

> It is so something *really!* Certainly it is! Why the hell isn't it? People never think anything is anything *really.* I'm getting goddam sick of it.

Phoebe may have touched on an important point. An essay suggest-ing that *The Catcher* is about a boy whose perception of corruption is so keen that it overwhelms him and in turn corrupts his vision will make use of Phoebe's statement, but it will also establish the limitations of that statement. One other statement has fairly often been thought of as a summary of the theme of *The Catcher.* It is Mr. Antolini's diagnosis:

> This fall I think you're riding for — it's a special kind of fall, a horrible kind. The man falling isn't permitted to feel or hear him-self hit bottom. He just keeps falling and falling. The whole arrange-ment's designed for men who, at some time or other in their lives, were looking for something their own environment couldn't supply them with. So they gave up looking. They gave it up before they ever really even got started. . . . I can very clearly see you dying nobly, one way or another, for some highly unworthy cause.

Is this what *The Catcher* is about? Perhaps, but Mr. Antolini's words must be tested carefully against one's own perception of Holden. If an essay on the theme of *The Catcher* argues that Mr. Antolini states the theme with precision, it must go on to give evidence supporting this idea. Probably it will in its early stages want to indicate why Antolini can be taken as a reliable spokesman. It will, for example, have to face the objection that Salinger apparently alienates us from Mr. Antolini by making him a homosexual whose adjustment to his environment has in part taken the form of marriage to a woman whose close presence he avoids. Even before Mr. Antolini touches Holden, Holden has noticed that the Antolinis "were never in the same room at the same time. It was sort of funny." If the essayist believes that Mr. Antolini is a judicious spokesman, his reply may be threefold: Mr. Antolini must have some sort of distinguishing trait if he is to be believable; the fact that he is a homosexual does not in itself mean that he cannot state the theme of the book; and possibly his own alienation from the normal world may even help to give him awareness of Holden's alienation. The thesis of the overall argument, then, is not simply "The theme of *The Catcher in the Rye*" but something with more shape, "Mr. Antolini's diagnosis is apt." Some such angle as this is necessary when trying to write about the theme of a novel; such a work is much too long to proceed through, episode by episode, as Daiches does (p. 74) with Joyce's story, "The Dead." The essayist must, of course, be thoroughly familiar with the entire novel, but because he does not have at his disposal the space to take his reader through some fifty or sixty episodes, he must take hold of the theme another way. Here is the skeleton of an essay arguing that Mr. Antolini's speech brings us to the theme of the book:

(Topic idea of introductory paragraph) At the end of the novel, Holden has had a collapse and is undergoing psychoanalytic treatment. Mr. Antolini had predicted a fall.

(Topic idea of next paragraph) Although Mr. Antolini himself is an embodiment of the corrupt sexuality and phoniness that obsess Holden, his own alienation from the normal world may even help to give him an awareness of Holden's alienation.

(Topic idea of next paragraph) Holden fits Mr. Antolini's diagnosis in the following details. . . . (Whether or not the presentation of this evidence will take more than one paragraph depends upon the nature of the evidence. One paragraph might be devoted to evidence that Holden is looking for something that his environment cannot provide; another paragraph might be devoted to evidence that Holden is likely to settle "for some highly unworthy cause.")

(Topic idea of concluding paragraph) Although Mr. Antolini's words do not seem to make any impression on Holden; they impress the reader by their accuracy.

With detailed evidence fleshing these bare bones, we might get an essay that convinces and illuminates.

Concluding Remarks on Writing About Fiction

Here are some starting points for essays on fiction:

Plot: Does the plot grow out of the characters, or does it depend on chance or coincidence? Are there irrelevant episodes, or do episodes that at first seem irrelevant have a function? Does surprise play an important role, or does foreshadowing? Is the title a good one?

Character: Are there characters who by their similarities and differences define each other? How else is a particular character defined? (His words, actions, dress, setting, narrative point of view?) To what extent does a character change, and what causes the change?

Point of view: How does the point of view help to shape the theme? After all, the basic story of "Little Red Riding Hood" remains unchanged whether told from the wolf's point of view or from the girl's, but (to simplify grossly) if we hear the story from the wolf's point of view we may feel that the story is about terrifying yet pathetic compulsive neurotic behavior; if from the girl's point of view, about terrified innocence.

Setting: What is the relation of the setting to the plot and the characters? What would be lost if the setting were changed?

Style: What role is played by the author's style? Is the style simple, understated, figurative, or what, and why?

The least fruitful way to study a novel is to seek to extract whatever overt philosophizing it seems to contain and to discuss it as philosophy; the most fruitful way is to pay close attention to all the words. In writing an essay on a very short piece of fiction, a short short story, one can perhaps study in some detail all aspects of it — or all that one sees. But most fiction is too big for such analysis. Normally one decides either to examine a particular passage (sometimes called the **textural approach**) or to examine some significant thread (sometimes called the **structural approach**). In this book, David Lodge's essay (p. 79) on the first chapter of Dickens's *Hard Times* is an example of the former approach; John Daremo's essay (p. 83) on point of view in Faulkner's "A Rose for Emily" is an example of the latter. Notice, by the way, that Lodge wisely chooses the *first* chapter of *Hard Times*. Because the meaning of a later chapter is in part determined by what has preceded it, discussion of a later chapter is more cumbersome. (On the other hand, one must realize that an early passage derives part of its meaning from what happens later; the description of the blind street and the stuffy house in "Araby" achieves its fullest meaning at the end of the story, when the boy's imaginative world is dispersed and he finds himself in darkness.) A second difficulty with the textural approach is that the chosen passage may not be typical of the work as a whole. To choose the right passage one must have a good understanding of all the passages. The structural approach comes closer to dealing with the whole, but it too has a danger: in following a thread, say, the point of view in a novel, the role of landscape in a story, or a particular theme, it inevitably neglects other threads that, if followed, might lead to a rather different reading of the work. This means that even though the topic must be narrowed, one must have a grasp of the whole work and must follow a thread that is significant.

Sample Essays

The two essays printed below reveal different approaches. David Lodge, using the textural approach, examines a page from Dickens's *Hard Times*, giving it the sort of close reading that is commonly reserved for poetry. He shows how Dickens makes every word contribute to his portrait of Gradgrind and how the portrait contributes to the novel's central concern. John Daremo, using a structural approach, stands a little further back from his subject, surveying Faulkner's "A Rose for Emily" by an examination of the narrative point of view which controls our understanding of all that happens in the story. Where Lodge looks hard at words, Daremo looks hard at the narrator's interpretation of action in the light of character. (Lodge of course has ideas about the actions and the characters of the novel as a whole, and Daremo has ideas about the individual words, but on the whole the treatments are different.)

Because Lodge's essay is part of a chapter in a book, it does not have the neat opening and closing paragraphs that a good independent essay usually has. But it is carefully organized. The first paragraph is chiefly devoted to quoting the passage he will study. The next paragraph explains that in the quoted passage Dickens introduces "a judgment of a concept of education," and the following paragraph tells us that "fact" is a key word in this concept. Lodge supports his assertion by telling us exactly how often the word occurs, and by quoting an illustrative sentence. Next he says that the "concept of education" can be broken down into three categories, which he lists and goes on to discuss in the listed order. When he has finished with the third category he links it to the first. There is no need in this headnote to discuss further the organization; a reader of the essay will find that he moves easily from paragraph to paragraph — the sign of a well-organized essay.

Daremo's essay too is well-organized. The title accurately conveys its contents, the opening paragraph moves from the large matter of Faulkner's alleged sensationalism to a study of it in one story whose plot is briefly summarized, thereby letting the reader get his bearings. The body of the essay studies the problem, first by rejecting the idea that the narrator is an Innocent Eye and then by offering proof of the narrator's perceptive sympathy in recounting what superficially is a sensational tale. There are a fair number of supporting quotations, but most of them are brief and are therefore welcome. The final paragraph nicely turns back to the very beginning of the story, commenting on the relevance of the title to the story as Daremo interprets it.

David Lodge

The Rhetoric of a Page of *Hard Times**

The very first chapter of *Hard Times* affords an excellent illustration of Dickens's rhetoric, and it is short enough to be quoted and analysed in its entirety.

HARD TIMES
BOOK THE FIRST. SOWING

CHAPTER 1
The One Thing Needful

"Now, what I want is, Facts. Teach these boys and girls nothing but Facts. Facts alone are wanted in life. Plant nothing else, and root out everything else. You can only form the minds of reasoning animals upon Facts: nothing else will ever be of any service to them. This is the principle on which I bring up my own children, and this is the principle on which I bring up these children. Stick to Facts, Sir!"

The scene was a plain, bare, monotonous vault of a schoolroom, and the speaker's square forefinger emphasised his observations by underscoring every sentence with a line on the schoolmaster's sleeve. The emphasis was helped by the speaker's square wall of a forehead, which had his eyebrows for its base, while his eyes found commodious cellarage in two dark caves, overshadowed by the wall. The emphasis was helped by the speaker's mouth, which was wide, thin, and hard set. The emphasis was helped by the speaker's voice, which was inflexible, dry, and dictatorial. The emphasis was helped by the speaker's hair, which bristled on the skirts of his bald head, a plantation of firs to keep the wind from its shining surface, all covered with knobs, like the crust of a plum pie, as if the head had scarcely warehouseroom for the hard facts stored inside. The speaker's obstinate carriage, square coat, square legs, square shoulders — nay, his very neckcloth, trained to take him by the throat with an unaccommodating grasp, like a stubborn fact, as it was — all helped the emphasis.

"In this life, we want nothing but Facts, Sir; nothing but Facts!"

The speaker, and the schoolmaster, and the third grown person present, all backed a little, and swept with their eyes the inclined

* The title of this essay is the editor's.

plane of little vessels then and there arranged in order, ready to have imperial gallons of facts poured into them until they were full to the brim.

This chapter communicates, in a remarkably compact way, both a description and a judgment of a concept of education. This concept is defined in a speech, and then evaluated — not in its own terms, but in terms of the speaker's appearance and the setting. Dickens, of course, always relies heavily on the popular, perhaps primitive, assumption that there is a correspondence between a person's appearance and his character; and as Gradgrind is a governor of the school, its design may legitimately function as a metaphor for his character. Dickens also had a fondness for fancifully appropriate names, but — perhaps in order to stress the representativeness of Gradgrind's views — he does not reveal the name in this first chapter.[1]

Because of the brevity of the chapter, we are all the more susceptible to the effect of its highly rhetorical patterning, particularly the manipulation of certain repeated words, notably *fact*, *square*, and *emphasis*. The kind of education depicted here is chiefly characterized by an obsession with facts. The word occurs five times in the opening speech of the first paragraph, and it is twice repeated towards the end of the second, descriptive paragraph to prepare for the reintroduction of Gradgrind speaking — " 'we want nothing but Facts, Sir; nothing but Facts' "; and it occurs for the tenth and last time towards the end of the last paragraph. In Gradgrind's speeches the word is capitalized, to signify his almost religious devotion to Facts.

Gradgrind's concept of education is further characterized in ways we can group into three categories, though of course they are closely connected:

1. It is authoritarian, fanatical and bullying in its application.
2. It is rigid, abstract and barren in quality.
3. It is materialistic and commercial in its orientation.

The first category is conveyed by the structure of the second paragraph, which is dominated by "emphasis." This paragraph comprises six sentences. In the first sentence we are told how the "speaker's square forefinger emphasised his observations." The next four, central sentences are each introduced, with cumulative force, by the clause "The emphasis was helped," and this formula, translated from the passive to the active voice, makes a fittingly "emphatic" conclusion to

---

[1] Mary McCarthy has suggested that an anonymous "he" at the beginning of a novel usually moves the reader to sympathetic identification. That the effect is quite the reverse in this example shows that the effect of any narrative strategy is determined finally by the narrator's language.

the paragraph in the sixth sentence: "all helped the emphasis." This rhetorical pattern has a dual function. In one way it reflects or imitates Gradgrind's own bullying, overemphatic rhetoric, of which we have an example in the first paragraph; but in another way it helps to *condemn* Gradgrind, since it "emphasises" the narrator's own pejorative catalogue of details of the speaker's person and immediate environment. The narrator's rhetoric is, as it must be, far more skilful and persuasive than Gradgrind's.

The qualities in category 2 are conveyed in a number of geometrical or quasi-geometrical terms, *wide, line, thin, base, surface, inclined plane* and, particularly, *square* which recurs five times; and in words suggestive of barren regularity, *plain, bare, monotonous, arranged in order, inflexible.* Such words are particularly forceful when applied to human beings — whether Gradgrind or the children. The metamorphosis of the human into the non-human is, as we shall find confirmed later, one of Dickens's main devices for conveying his alarm at the way Victorian society was moving.

Category 3, the orientation towards the world of commerce, is perhaps less obvious than the other categories, but it is unmistakably present in some of the boldest tropes of the chapter: *commodious cellarage, warehouseroom, plantation, vessels, imperial gallons.*

The authoritarian ring of *"imperial"* leads us back from category 3 to category 1, just as *"under-scoring* every sentence with a *line"* leads us from 1 to 2. There is a web of connecting strands between the qualities I have tried to categorize: it is part of the rhetorical strategy of the chapter that all the qualities it evokes are equally applicable to Gradgrind's character, person, ideas, his school and the children (in so far as he has shaped them in his own image).

Metaphors of growth and cultivation are of course commonplace in discussion of education, and we should not overlook the ironic invocation of such metaphors, with a deliberately religious, prophetic implication (reinforced by the Biblical echo of the chapter heading, "The One Thing Needful"[2]) in the title of the Book, "SOWING," later to be followed by Book the Second, "REAPING," and Book the Third, "GARNERING." These metaphors are given a further twist in Gradgrind's recommendation to "Plant nothing else and root out everything else" (except facts).

If there is a flaw in this chapter it is the simile of the plum pie, which has pleasant, genial associations alien to the character of Gradgrind, to whose head it is, quite superfluously, applied. Taken as a whole, however, this is a remarkably effective and densely woven beginning of the novel.

[2] Chapter 2 of Book I is called "Murdering the Innocents."

The technique of the first chapter of *Hard Times* could not be described as "subtle." But subtle effects are often lost in a first chapter, where the reader is coping with the problem of "learning the author's language." Perhaps with some awareness of this fact, sharpened by his sense of addressing a vast, popular audience, Dickens begins many of his novels by nailing the reader's attention with a display of sheer rhetorical power, relying particularly on elaborate repetition. One thinks, for instance, of the fog at the beginning of *Bleak House* or the sun and shadow in the first chapter of *Little Dorrit*. In these novels the rhetoric works to establish a symbolic atmosphere; in *Hard Times*, to establish a thematic Idea — the despotism of Fact. But this abstraction — Fact — is invested with a remarkable solidity through the figurative dimension of the language.

The gross effect of the chapter is simply stated, but analysis reveals that it is achieved by means of a complex verbal activity that is far from simple. Whether it represents fairly any actual educational theory or practice in mid-nineteenth-century England is really beside the point. It aims to convince us of the *possibility* of children being taught in such a way, and to make us recoil from the imagined possibility. The chapter succeeds or fails as rhetoric; and I think it succeeds.

Dickens begins as he means to continue. Later in the novel we find Gradgrind's house, which, like the school-room, is a function of himself, described in precisely the same terms of fact and rigid measurement, partly geometrical and partly commercial.

> A very regular feature on the face of the country, Stone Lodge was. Not the least disguise toned down or shaded off that uncompromising fact in the landscape. A great square house, with a heavy portico darkening the principal windows, as its master's heavy brows over-shadowed his eyes. A calculated, cast up, balanced and proved house. Six windows on this side of the door, six on that side; a total of twelve in this wing, a total of twelve in the other wing; four and twenty carried over to the back wings. A lawn and garden and an infant avenue, all ruled straight like a botanical account-book. (I, iii)

It has been observed that Dickens individualizes his characters by making them use peculiar locutions and constructions in their speech, a technique which was particularly appropriate to serial publication in which the reader's memory required to be frequently jogged. This technique extends beyond the idiosyncratic speech of characters, to the language in which they are described. A key-word, or group of key-words, is insistently used when the character is first introduced, not only to identify him but also to evaluate him, and is invoked at various strategic points in the subsequent action. Dickens's remarkable metaphorical inventiveness ensures that continuity and rhetorical emphasis are not obtained at the expense of monotony. The application of the key-words of the first chapter to Mr. Gradgrind's house gives the same delight as the development of a metaphysical conceit. The observation that Mrs. Gradgrind, "whenever she showed a symptom of coming to life, was invariably stunned by some weighty piece of fact tumbling on her" (I, iv), affords a kind of verbal equivalent of knock-about comedy, based on a combination of expectancy (we know the word will recur) and surprise (we are not prepared for the particular formulation).

JOHN DAREMO

Insight into Horror: The Narrator in Faulkner's "A Rose for Emily"*

Having admitted, in the preface to the Modern Library edition of *Sanctuary* (1932), that after some failures he set out to make money by writing about the horrible and the obscene, Faulkner was regularly accused of turning out meaningless narratives which had only their sensationalism to recommend them. (In fact, however, the infamous preface to *Sanctuary* made the point that although he began the book with the crudest of motives, he rewrote it at the cost of time and money to make it into something worthy.) His most popular short story, "A Rose for Emily," written at about the same time as *Sanctuary*, on the surface at least shares a concern with the horrible and the obscene: Miss Emily Grierson, it turns out, has poisoned a lover who was about to desert her, has kept the rotting corpse in an upstairs bedroom, and on at least one occasion has lain next to it. Murder and a hint of necrophilia are pretty strong stuff, and yet, when one first reads this rather drily narrated story of a southern lady who retreated into a world of her own, one scarcely is aware of any sensationalism at all until the very end, when the corpse is discovered in bed, and a strand of Miss Emily's hair is found upon the adjacent pillow. This is shocking, no doubt. But on re-reading the story one sees that one's first reading was right: the story is not simply a horror story, designed to thrill, but a story in which horror plays a meaningful part. Despite the decaying mansion, the silent servant, and the corpse, all the usual properties in rather old-fashioned thrillers, "A Rose for Emily" — whether on the first reading or on the tenth — seems closely related to experience. Not that we know anyone who in fact has behaved precisely in this mad way; but, as Miss Emily's behavior is narrated, it seems plausible, fully in accord not merely with

* Faulkner's story is reprinted in the Appendix to this book, pp. 179–187.

some arbitrary fictional world but with our understanding of human behavior.

In large measure this sense of plausibility is conveyed to us by the unnamed narrator, who unobtrusively gives us a sense of the world in which Miss Emily lives, and whose responses — sometimes commonplace and sometimes deeply sympathetic — help to assure us that the story we hear is one that speaks to mankind. This narrator is never very precisely identified, and there are moments when he almost seems to be an Innocent Eye, a simple-minded recorder of a story whose implications escape him but reach us. Sometimes he seems to be a good deal less than deeply sensitive: he speaks of Miss Emily's aunt as "old Lady Wyatt, the crazy woman"; he talks easily of "niggers"; he confesses that because he and the other townspeople felt that Miss Emily's family "held themselves a little too high for what they really were," when at thirty Miss Emily was still unmarried "we were not pleased exactly, but vindicated." When her father died and Miss Emily was left in poverty, the narrator, like the other townspeople, could take some pleasure in seeing her reduced to the common level: "Now she too would know the old thrill and the old despair of a penny more or less."

But of course, as even this last brief quotation suggests, the narrator is no simpleton. If his feelings are those of common humanity, he not only shares our feelings, but, more important, he *knows* what these feelings are, he can describe them and thus he helps us to understand the character and also ourselves. We recognize this ability, and we therefore have confidence in his narrative: we heed the story not only because it is curious but because, guided by the narrator, we feel that it deserves our respectful attention. These are both motifs introduced in the first sentence: "When Miss Emily Grierson died, our whole town went to her funeral: the men through a sort of respectful affection for a fallen monument, the women mostly out of curiosity to see the inside of her house, which no one save an old manservant — a combined gardener and cook — had seen in at least ten years." The narrator shares the women's curiosity and the men's respect, and by reading the story we too become implicated. There is, of course, a certain snoopiness involved in telling a story about someone ·else, or in reading one, but there can also be respect for the subject, and this the narrator of "A Rose for Emily" unobtrusively but abundantly conveys.

For example, the narrator sees old Miss Emily's ugliness ("She looked bloated. . . . Her eyes, lost in the fatty ridges of her face, looked like two small pieces of coal pressed into a lump of dough"), but he also remembers her when, many years earlier, her father drove with a horsewhip a suitor from the door, and Miss Emily was "a slender figure in white in the background." After the death of her tyrannical father, and before she became bloated, she bore "a vague resemblance to those angels in colored church windows — sort of tragic and serene." On the whole, the narrator is compassionate. He helps us to understand why Miss Emily for three days after the death of her father insisted that he was not dead: "We did not say she was crazy then. We believed she had to do that. We remembered all the young men her father had driven away, and we knew that with nothing left, she would have to cling to that which had robbed her, as people will."

The insight is presented simply, almost as an afterthought: Miss Emily acted "as people will," and it is easy for us to give no thought to the narrator even while we accept his explanation that a woman whose father has robbed her of a husband will cling to the only man who had played an important role in her life, even when he is dead. (And of course later she will cling to her lover, Homer Barron, by murdering him and keeping his corpse in the bedroom. The narrator does not go on to put it this way, but, given his comments on Miss Emily's relationship to her father, we easily make the connection. We do so not because we are superior to a simple-minded Innocent Eye narrator, but because the narrator has astutely shown us the way, and then in a gentlemanly fashion has not gone on to labor the point.)

I have been saying that if we regard Miss Emily with some respect — as well as with some curiosity and with some horror — it is largely because the narrator treats her, on the whole, with respect. We can, of course, say that Miss Emily earns respect by her aloofness and her strength of purpose when, for example, she scorns the town's opinions and drives in the buggy with Homer Barron, a Yankee laborer, or when she cows the druggist into selling arsenic, or when she cows the aldermen who come to collect taxes. But we learn all such things through the narrator, and if we speak of her aloofness or strength of purpose rather than of, say, her arrogance or madness, it is because he has helped us to think this way of her, to see her not as a monster but as a human being with feelings like our own. The narrator's imaginative sympathy is evident throughout, even in its wry tolerance of "a member of the rising generation" who is unable to tolerate the stench on Miss Emily's property, but the sympathy is perhaps most evident in the wonderful description of the memories of the very old men who come to Miss Emily's funeral. For old men, the narrator tells us, "the past is not a diminishing road, but, instead, a huge meadow which no winter ever quite touches, divided from them now by the narrow bottleneck of the most recent decade of years." The two metaphors, meadow and bottleneck, give us a sense of what the minds of old people may be like, conveying both rich expansiveness and narrowness. And just as the narrator had not been so presumptuous as to tell us that Miss Emily's mad (but understandable) insistence that her father was not dead is related to her later murder of Homer Barron in her mad effort to preserve their relation as lovers, so now he does not presume to tell us that Miss Emily, like these old men at her funeral, had shut off "the most recent decade" and had been living, with Homer's corpse, in a meadow of memory.

But of course the horror is not revealed until the last two paragraphs, when we learn that Miss Emily had murdered Homer and had kept the rotting corpse in bed. The horror is not minimized. In the penultimate paragraph we are told of the "fleshless grin" and the "rotted" body. But here too we sense a compassionate voice. The talk of "niggers" and of "the crazy woman," which earlier had at most been sporadic, now is totally banished and the language and the vision evoke the Bible:

> The body had apparently once lain in the attitude of an embrace, but now the long sleep that outlasts love, that conquers even the grimace of love, had cuckolded him. What was left of him, rotted beneath what was left of the nightshirt, had become inextricable from the bed in which he lay; and upon him and upon the pillow beside him lay that even coating of the patient and biding dust.

The final paragraph, commenting on the strand of hair on the pillow beside Homer, makes it clear that Emily had lain next to the corpse, and the effect is shocking but the revelation is not inconsistent with what has come before.

Nor is the final paragraph, I think, the last word in the story. I suppose that at the end almost every reader calls back to mind the title of the story, and briefly wonders why it is "A Rose for Emily." Almost immediately, I suppose, the question answers itself, even in the mind of the reader who has not thought much about the unobtrusive narrator of the story. The telling of this tale about a woman who, deprived of a husband, murdered her lover before he could desert her, is itself the rose, the community's tribute (for the narrator insistently speaks of himself as "we") to the intelligible humanity in a woman whose unhappy life might seem monstrous to less sympathetic observers.

4

DRAMA

WRITING ABOUT DRAMA

Most of the world's great plays may be put into one of two classes: tragedy and comedy. Roughly speaking, tragedy dramatizes the conflict between the vitality of the single life and the laws or limits of life (the tragic hero reaches his heights, going beyond the experiences of other men, at the cost of his life), and comedy dramatizes the vitality of the laws of social life (the good life is seen to reside in the shedding of individualism in favor of a union with a genial and enlightened society). These points must be amplified a bit before we go on to the further point that, of course, any important play does much more than can be put into such crude formulas.

In **tragedy,** usually, the tragic hero goes beyond the standards to which reasonable men adhere; he does some fearful deed which ultimately destroys him but at the same time shows him (paradoxically) to be in some way more fully a living being — a man who has experienced life more fully, whether by heroic action or by capacity for enduring suffering — than the men around him. Othello kills Desdemona, Lear gives away his crown and banishes his one loving daughter, Antony loses his share of the Roman Empire; but all of these men seem to live more fully — for one thing, they experience a kind of anguish unknown to those who surround them and who outlive them. (If the hero does not die, he usually is left in some death-like state, as is the blind Oedipus in *King Oedipus.*) We see humanity pushed to an extreme; in his agony and grief the hero enters a world unknown to the rest and reveals magnificence. After his departure from the stage, we are left in a world of littler men. The closing lines of almost any of Shakespeare's tragedies can be used to illustrate the point. *King Lear,* for example, ends thus:

> The oldest hath borne most: we that are young
> Shall never see so much, nor live so long.

87

Tragedy commonly involves **irony** of two sorts: unconsciously ironic deeds and unconsciously ironic speeches. **Ironic deeds** have some consequence more or less the reverse of what the doer intends. Macbeth thinks that by killing Duncan he will gain happiness, but he finds that his deed brings him sleepless nights. Brutus thinks that by killing Caesar he will bring liberty to Rome, but he brings tyranny. In an unconsciously **ironic speech,** the speaker's words mean one thing to him but something more significant to the audience, as when King Duncan, baffled by Cawdor's treason, says:

> There's no art
> To find the mind's construction in the face:
> He was a gentleman on whom I built
> An absolute trust.

At this moment Macbeth, whom we have already heard meditating the murder of Duncan, enters. Duncan's words are true, but he does not apply them to Macbeth, as the audience does. A few moments later Duncan praises Macbeth as "a peerless kinsman." Soon Macbeth will indeed become peerless, when he kills Duncan and ascends to the throne.* Sophocles's use of ironic deeds and speeches is so pervasive, especially in *King Oedipus*, that **Sophoclean irony** has become a critical term. Here is a critic summarizing the ironies of *King Oedipus*:

> As the images unfold, the enquirer turns into the object of enquiry, the hunter into the prey, the doctor into the patient, the investigator into the criminal, the revealer into the thing revealed, the finder into the thing found, the savior into the thing saved ("I was saved, for some dreadful destiny"), the liberator into the thing released ("I released your feet from the bonds which pierced your ankles" says the Corinthian messenger), the accuser becomes the defendant, the ruler the subject, the teacher not only the pupil but also the object lesson, the example.
>
> Bernard Knox, "Sophocles' Oedipus," in *Tragic Themes in Western Literature*, ed. Cleanth Brooks (New Haven, 1955), pp. 10–11

---

* Ironic deeds, or happenings, and unconsciously ironic speeches must be distinguished from **verbal irony,** which is produced when the speaker is conscious that his words mean something different from what they say. In *Macbeth* Lennox says: "The gracious Duncan / Was pitied of Macbeth. Marry, he was dead! / And the right valiant Banquo walked too late. / . . . / Men must not walk too late." He *says* nothing about Macbeth having killed Duncan and Banquo, but he *means* that Macbeth has killed them.

Notice, by the way, the neatness of this sentence; it is unusually long, but it does not ramble, it does not baffle, and it does not suggest a stuffy writer. The verb "turns" governs the first two-thirds; and after the second long parenthesis, when there is danger that the messenger's speech will cause the reader to forget the verb, the writer provides another verb, "becomes."

When the deed backfires, or has a reverse effect such as Macbeth's effort to gain happiness has, we have what Aristotle called a **peripeteia,** or a **reversal.** When a character comes to perceive what has happened (Macbeth's "I have lived long enough: my way of life / Is fall'n into the sere, the yellow leaf"), he experiences (in Aristotle's language) an **anagnorisis** or **recognition.** In his analysis of drama Aristotle says that the tragic hero comes to grief through his **hamartia,** a term sometimes translated as **tragic flaw** but perhaps better translated as **tragic error.** Thus, it is a great error for Othello to trust Iago and to strangle Desdemona, for Lear to give away his kingdom, and for Macbeth to decide to help fulfill the prophecies. If we hold to the translation "flaw," we begin to hunt for a fault in their characters; and we say, for instance, that Othello is gullible, Lear self-indulgent, Macbeth ambitious, or some such thing. In doing this, we may overlook their grandeur. To take a single example: Iago boasts he can dupe Othello because

> The Moor is of a free and open nature
> That thinks men honest that but seem to be so.

We ought to hesitate before we say that a man who trusts men because they seem to be honest has a flaw.

When writing about tragedy, probably the commonest essay topic is on the tragic hero. Too often the hero is judged mechanically: he must be noble, he must have a flaw, he must do a fearful deed, he must recognize his flaw, he must die. The previous paragraph suggests that Shakespeare's practice makes doubtful one of these matters, the flaw. A student might be similarly cautious about accepting the rest of the package unexamined. On the other hand, if "tragedy" is to have any meaning — any use as a term — it must have some agreed-upon attributes. An essay that seeks to determine whether or not a character is a tragic character ought at its outset to make clear its conception of tragedy and the degree of rigidity, or flexibility, with which it will interpret some or all of its categories. For example, it may indicate that although nobility is a *sine qua non*, nobility is not equivalent to high rank. A middle-class figure with certain mental or spiritual characteristics may, in such a view, be an acceptable tragic hero.

An essay closely related to the sort we have been talking about measures a character by some well-known theory of tragedy. For example, one can measure Willy Loman, in *Death of a Salesman*, against Miller's essays on tragedy or against Aristotle's remarks on tragedy. The organization of such an essay is usually not a problem: isolate the relevant aspects of the theoretical statement, and then examine the character to see if, point by point, he illustrates them. But remember that even if Willy Loman fulfills Arthur Miller's idea of a tragic figure, you need not accept him as tragic; conversely, if he does not fulfill Aristotle's idea, you need not deny him tragic status. Aristotle may be wrong.

In **comedy**, the fullest life is seen to reside within social norms: at the beginning of a comedy we find banished dukes, unhappy lovers, crabby parents, jealous husbands, and harsh laws; but at the end we usually have a unified and genial society, often symbolized by a marriage feast to which everyone, or almost everyone, is invited. Early in *A Midsummer Night's Dream*, for instance, we meet quarreling young lovers and a father who demands that his daughter either marry a man she does not love or enter a convent. Such is the Athenian law. At the end of the play the lovers are properly matched, to everyone's satisfaction.

Speaking broadly, most comedies fall into one of two classes: **satiric comedy** and **romantic comedy**. In the former, the emphasis is on the obstructionists — the irate fathers, hardheaded business men, and other members of the Establishment who at the beginning of the play seem to hold all of the cards, preventing joy from reigning. They are held up to ridicule because they are monomaniacs enslaved to themselves, acting mechanistically (always irate, always hardheaded) instead of responding genially to the ups and downs of life. The outwitting of these obstructionists often provides the resolution to the plot. Jonson, Molière, and Shaw are in this tradition; their comedy, according to an ancient Roman formula, "chastens morals with ridicule." In romantic comedy (one thinks of Shakespeare's *A Midsummer Night's Dream*, *As You Like It*, and *Twelfth Night*) the emphasis is put on a pair or pairs of delightful people who engage our sympathies as they run their obstacle race to the altar. There are obstructionists here too, but the emphasis is elsewhere.

Essays on comedy often examine the nature of the humor. Why is an irate father, in this context, funny? Or why is a young lover, again in this context, funny? Commonly one will find that at least some of the humor is in the disproportionate nature of their activities (they get terribly excited) and in their inflexibility. In both of these qualities they are rather like the cat in animated cartoons, who repeatedly chases the mouse to his hole and who repeatedly bangs his head against the wall. The following is a skeleton of a possible essay on why Jacques in *As You Like It* is amusing:

> Jaques is insistently melancholy. In the Eden-like Forest of Arden, he sees only the dark side of things.
>
> His monomania, however, is harmless to himself and to others; because it causes us no pain, it may entertain us.
>
> Indeed, we begin to look forward to his melancholy speeches. We delight in hearing him fulfill our expectations by wittily finding gloom where others find mirth.
>
> We are delighted, too, to learn that this chastizer of others has in fact been guilty of the sort of behavior he chastizes.
>
> At the end of the play, when four couples are wed, the inflexible Jaques insists on standing apart from the general rejoicing.

Such might be the gist of an essay. It needs to be supported with details, and it can be enriched, for example, by a comparison between his sort of jesting and Touchstone's; but it is at least a promising draft of an outline.

Every play, of course, is different from every other play; each is a unique and detailed statement, and the previous paragraphs give only the broadest outlines — comedies and tragedies seen at a distance, as it were. The analyst's job is to try to study the differences as well as the similarities, in an effort (in Henry James's words) "to appreciate, to appropriate, to take intellectual possession, to establish in fine a relation with the criticized thing and make it one's own."

The best way to make a work of art one's own is (again in Henry James's words) "to be one of the people on whom nothing is lost." If we have perceived the work properly, we ought to be able to formulate its **theme,** its underlying idea. Some critics, it is true, have argued that the concept of theme is meaningless. They hold that *Macbeth,* for example, gives us only an extremely detailed history of one imaginary man. In this view, *Macbeth* says nothing to you or me; it only says what happened to some imaginary man. Even *Julius Caesar* says nothing about the historical Julius Caesar or about the nature of Roman politics. Here we can agree; no one would offer Shakespeare's play as evidence of what the historical Caesar said or did. But surely the view that the concept of theme is meaningless, and that a work tells us only about imaginary creatures, is a desperate one. We *can* say that we see in *Julius Caesar* the fall of power, or (if we are thinking of Brutus) the vulnerability of idealism, or some such things. To the reply that these are mere truisms, we can counter: Yes, but the truisms are presented in such a way that they take on life and become a part of us rather than remain things of which we say "I've heard it said, and I guess it's so." And surely we are in no danger of equating the play with the theme that we sense underlies it. We never believe that our statement of the theme is the equivalent of the play itself. We recognize that the play presents the theme with such detail that our statement is only a wedge to help us enter into the play so that we may more fully appropriate it. Joseph Wood Krutch discusses at some length the themes of *Death of a Salesman* and *A Streetcar Named Desire* on pages 111–15, but a briefer illustration may be helpful here. A critic examining Ibsen's achievements begins by trying to see what some of the plays are in fact about.

> We must not waste more than a paragraph on such fiddle-faddle as the notion that *Ghosts* is a play about venereal disease or that *A Doll's House* is a play about women's rights. On these terms, *King Lear* is a play about housing for the elderly and *Hamlet* is a stage-debate over the reality of spooks. Venereal disease and its consequences are represented onstage in *Ghosts;* so, to all intents and purposes, is incest; but the theme of the play is inherited guilt, and the sexual pathology of the Alving family is an engine in the hands of that theme. *A Doll's House* represents a woman imbued with the idea of becoming a person, but it proposes nothing categorical about women becoming people; in fact, its real theme has nothing to do with the sexes. It is the irrepressible conflict of two different personalities which have founded themselves on two radically different estimates of reality.
>
> Robert M. Adams, "Ibsen on the Contrary," in *Modern Drama*, ed. Anthony Caputi (New York, 1966), p. 345

Such a formulation can be most useful; a grasp of the theme helps us to see what the plot is really all about, what the plot suggests in its universal meaning or applicability.

A few words about the preceding quotation may be useful here. Notice that Adams's paragraph moves from a vigorous colloquial opening through some familiar examples, including a brief comparison with plays by another dramatist, to a fairly formal close. The disparity in tone between opening and closing is not distressing because even in the opening we sense the writer's mastery of his material, and we sympathize with his impatience. Adams's next paragraph, not given here, extends his suggestion that the plays are not about nineteenth-century problems: he argues that under the bourgeois décor, under the frock coat and the bustle, we detect two kinds of people — little people and great people. His third paragraph elaborates this point by suggesting that, allowing for variations, the dichotomy consists of satyrs and saints, and he provides the details necessary to make this dichotomy convincing. Among Ibsen's little people, or satyrs, are Parson Manders, Peter Stockmann, Hjalmar Ekdal, and Torvald Helmer; among the great people, or saints, are Mrs. Alving, Thomas Stockmann, Gregers Werle, and Nora Helmer. In short, Adams's argument about Ibsen's themes advances steadily, and is convincingly illustrated with concrete references.

Although **action** commonly denotes physical movement, some critics (influenced by Aristotle's statement that a drama is an imitation of an action) use it in a sense equivalent to theme. In this sense, the action is the underlying happening — the inner happening — for example, "the enlightenment of a man" or "the coming of unhappiness to a man" or "the finding of the self by self-surrender." Francis Fergusson suggests that an expression in *Macbeth* to the effect that Macbeth "outran the pauser, reason" describes the action of the play. A paragraph from his chapter on *Macbeth* may clarify this conception:

> To "outrun" reason suggests an impossible stunt, like lifting oneself by one's own bootstraps. It also suggests a competition or race, like those of nightmare, which cannot be won. As for the word "reason," Shakespeare associates it with nature and nature's order, in the individual soul, in society, and in the cosmos. To outrun reason is thus to violate nature itself, to lose the bearings of common sense and of custom, and to move into a spiritual realm bounded by the irrational darkness of Hell one way, and the superrational grace of faith the other way. As the play develops before us, all the modes of this absurd, or evil, or supernatural, action are attempted, the last being Malcolm's and Macduff's acts of faith.
>
> *The Human Image in Dramatic Literature*
> (New York, 1957), p. 118

In this view, the dramatist conceives of an action and then imitates it or sets it forth by means of, first of all, a plot and characters, then by means of language, gesture, and perhaps spectacle and music. When the Greek comic dramatist Menander told a friend he had finished his play and now had only to write it, he must have meant that he had the action or the theme firmly in mind, and had worked out the plot and the requisite characters. All that remained was to set down the words.

Plot is variously defined, sometimes as equivalent to "story" (in this sense a synopsis of *Julius Caesar* has the same plot as *Julius Caesar*), but more often, and more usefully, as the dramatist's particular *arrangement of the story*. Thus, because Shakespeare's *Julius Caesar* begins with a scene dramatizing an encounter between plebeians and tribunes, its plot is different from that of a play on Julius Caesar in which such a scene (not necessary to the story) is omitted. Richard G. Moulton, discussing the early part of Shakespeare's plot in *Julius Caesar*, examines the relationship between the first two scenes.

> . . . The opening scene strikes appropriately the key-note of the whole action. In it we see the tribunes of the people — officers whose whole

raison d'être is to be the mouthpiece of the commonalty — restraining their own clients from the noisy honors they are disposed to pay Caesar. To the justification in our eyes of a conspiracy against Caesar, there could not be a better starting-point than this hint that the popular worship of Caesar, which has made him what he is, is itself reaching its reaction-point. Such a suggestion moreover makes the whole play one complete *wave* of popular fickleness from crest to crest.

The second is the scene upon which the dramatist mainly relies for the *crescendo* in the justification of the conspirators. It is a long scene, elaborately contrived so as to keep the conspirators and their cause before us at their very best, and the victim at his very worst. . . .

Shakespeare as a Dramatic Artist (Oxford, 1893), pp. 188–89

Moulton's discussion of the plot continues at length. One can argue that he presents too favorable a view of the conspirators (when he says we see the conspirators at their best he seems to overlook their fawning), but that is not our concern here; here we have been talking about the process of examining juxtaposed scenes, a process Moulton's words illustrate well. Handbooks on the drama often suggest that a plot (arrangement of happenings) should have a **rising action**, a **climax**, and a **falling action**. This sort of plot can be diagramed as a pyramid: the tension rises through complications or **crises** to a climax, at which point the climax is the apex, and the tension allegedly slackens as we witness the **dénouement** (unknotting). Shakespeare sometimes used a pyramidal structure, placing his climax neatly in the middle of what seems to us to be the third of five acts. Roughly the first half of *Romeo and Juliet*, for example, shows Romeo winning Juliet; but when in III.i he kills her cousin Tybalt, Romeo sets in motion (it is often said) the second half of the play, the losing of Juliet and of his own life. Similarly, in *Julius Caesar*, Brutus rises in the first half of the play, reaching his height in III.i, with the death of Caesar; but later in this scene he gives Marc Antony permission to speak at Caesar's funeral, and thus he sets in motion his own fall, which occupies the second half of the play. In *Macbeth*, the protagonist attains his height in III.i ("Thou hast it now: King"), but he soon perceives that he is going downhill:

> I am in blood
> Stepped in so far, that, should I wade no more,
> Returning were as tedious as go o'er.

In *Hamlet*, the protagonist proves to his own satisfaction Claudius's guilt in III.ii (by the play within the play), but almost immediately he begins to worsen his position, by failing to kill Claudius when he is an easy target (III.iii) and by contaminating himself with the murder of Polonius (III.iv).

Of course, no law demands such a structure, and a hunt for the pyramid usually causes the hunter to overlook all the crises but the middle one. William Butler Yeats once suggestively diagrammed a good plot not as a pyramid but as a line moving diagonally upward, punctuated by several crises. Perhaps it is sufficient to say that a good plot has its moments of tension, but that the location of these will vary with the play. They are the product of **conflict,** but it should be noted that not all conflict produces tension; there is conflict but little tension in a ball game when the home team is ahead 10–0 and the visiting pitcher comes to bat in the ninth inning with two out and none on base.

Regardless of how a plot is diagramed, the **exposition** is that part which tells the audience what it has to know about the past, the **antecedent action.** Two gossiping servants who tell each other that after a year away in Paris the young master is coming home tomorrow with a new wife are giving the audience the exposition. The exposition in Shakespeare's *The Tempest* is almost ruthlessly direct: Prospero tells his naive daughter, "I should inform thee farther," and for about one hundred and fifty lines he proceeds to tell her why she is on an almost uninhabited island. Prospero's harangue is punctuated by his daughter's professions of attention; but the Elizabethans (and the Greeks) sometimes tossed out all pretense at dialogue, and began with a **prologue,** like the one spoken by the Chorus at the outset of *Romeo and Juliet:*

> Two households, both alike in dignity
> In fair Verona, where we lay our scene,
> From ancient grudge break to new mutiny,
> Where civil blood makes civil hands unclean.
> From forth the fatal loins of these two foes
> A pair of star-crossed lovers take their life. . . .

But the exposition may also extend far into the play, being given in small, explosive revelations.

Exposition has been discussed as though it consists simply of informing the audience about events; but exposition can do much more. It can give us an understanding of the characters who themselves are talking about other characters, it can evoke a mood, and it can generate tension. When we summarize the opening act, and treat it as "mere exposition," we are probably losing what is in fact dramatic in it. Moulton, in his analysis of the first two scenes in *Julius Caesar,* does not make the mistake of thinking that the first scenes exist merely to tell the audience certain facts.

An analysis of plot, then, will consider the arrangement of the episodes, the effect of juxtapositions, as well as the overall story. A useful essay can be written on the function of one scene. Such an essay may point out, for example, that the curious scene (IV.iii) in which Malcolm, Macduff, and Ross converse near the palace of the King of England serves to indicate that even good men must tell lies during Macbeth's reign, that Macbeth has the vile qualities that Malcolm pretends to have, and that Macbeth has failed — as the King of England has not — to be a source of health to the realm. Sometimes an analysis of plot will examine the relationships between the several stories in a play: A *Midsummer Night's Dream* has supernatural lovers, mature royal lovers, young Athenian lovers, a bumpkin who briefly becomes the lover of the fairy queen, and a play (put on by the bumpkins) about legendary lovers. How these are held together and how they help to define each other and the total play are matters that concern anyone looking at the plot of A *Midsummer Night's Dream*. Richard Moulton suggests that Shakespeare's subplots "have the effect of assisting the main stories, smoothing away their difficulties and making their prominent points yet more prominent." He demonstrates his thesis at some length, but a very brief extract from his discussion of the Jessica-Lorenzo story in *The Merchant of Venice* may be enough to suggest the method. The main story concerns Shylock and his rivals, Antonio, Bassanio, and Portia. Shylock's daughter Jessica is not needed for the narrative purpose of the main story. Why then did Shakespeare include her? Part of Moulton's answer runs thus:

> A Shylock painted without a tender side at all would be repulsive . . . and yet it appears how this tenderness has grown hard and rotten with the general debasement of his soul by avarice, until, in his ravings over his loss, his ducats and his daughter are ranked as equally dear.

> > I would my daughter were dead at my foot, and the jewels in her ear! Would she were hearsed at my foot, and the ducats in her coffin!

> For all this we feel that he is hardly used in losing her. Paternal feeling may take a gross form, but it is paternal feeling none the less, and cannot be denied our sympathy; bereavement is a common ground upon which not only high and low, but even the pure and the outcast, are drawn together. Thus Jessica at home makes us hate Shylock; with Jessica lost we cannot help pitying him.
> > > *Shakespeare as a Dramatic Artist*, p. 79

Below is a student's essay on the structure of Tennessee Williams's *The Glass Menagerie*. It proceeds a bit mechanically, moving (after the first two paragraphs) scene by scene through the play, but the writer notices some interesting things about the shape of the plot and he makes his points clearly.

The Solid Structure of The Glass Menagerie

In the "Production Notes" Tennessee Williams calls The
Glass Menagerie a "memory play," a term that the narrator in
the play also uses. Memories often consist of fragments of
episodes which are so loosely connected that they seem
chaotic, and therefore we might think that The Glass Menagerie will consist of very loosely related episodes. However, the play covers only one episode and though it gives
the illusion of random talk, it really has a firm structure
and moves steadily toward a foregone conclusion.

Tennessee Williams divides the play into seven scenes.
The first scene begins with a sort of prologue and the last
scene concludes with a sort of epilogue that is related to
the prologue. In the prologue Tom addresses the audience
and comments on the 1930's as a time when America was
"blind" and was a place of "shouting and confusion." Tom
also mentions that our lives consist of expectations, and
though he does not say that our expectations are unful-
filled, near the end of the prologue he quotes a postcard
that his father wrote to the family he deserted: "Hello--
Goodbye." In the epilogue Tom tells us that he followed his
"father's footsteps," deserting the family. And just before
the epilogue, near the end of Scene VII, we see what can be
considered another desertion: Jim explains to Tom's sister
Laura that he is engaged and therefore cannot visit Laura
again. Thus the end is closely related to the beginning,

and the play is the steady development of the initial implications.

The first three scenes show things going from bad to
worse. Amanda is a nagging mother who finds her only relief
in talking about the past to her crippled daughter Laura and
her frustrated son Tom. When she was young she was beautiful and was eagerly courted by rich young men, but now the
family is poor and this harping on the past can only bore or
infuriate Tom and embarrass or depress Laura, who have no
happy past to look back to, who see no happy future, and who
can only be upset by Amanda's insistence that they should
behave as she behaved long ago. The second scene deepens
the despair: Amanda learns that the timorous Laura has not
been attending a business school but has retreated in terror
from this confrontation with the contemporary world.
Laura's helplessness is made clear to the audience, and so
is Amanda's lack of understanding. Near the end of the
second scene, however, Jim's name is introduced; he is a boy
Laura had a crush on in high school, and so the audience
gets a glimpse of a happier Laura and a sense that possibly
Laura's world is wider than the stifling tenement in which
she and her mother and brother live. But in the third
scene things get worse, when Tom and Amanda have so violent
an argument that they are no longer on speaking terms. Tom
is so angry with his mother that he almost by accident
destroys his sister's treasured collection of glass animals,
the fragile lifeless world which is her refuge. The apart-

ment is literally full of the "shouting and confusion" that Tom spoke of in his prologue.

The first three scenes have revealed a progressive worsening of relations; the next three scenes reveal a progressive improvement in relations. In Scene IV Tom and his mother are reconciled, and Tom reluctantly--apparently in an effort to make up with his mother--agrees to try to get a friend to come to dinner so that Laura will have "a gentleman caller." In Scene V Tom tells his mother that Jim will come to dinner on the next night, and Amanda brightens, because she sees a possibility of security for Laura at last. In Scene VI Jim arrives, and despite Laura's initial terror, there seems, at least in Amanda's eyes, to be the possibility that things will go well.

The seventh scene, by far the longest, at first seems to be fulfilling Amanda's hopes. Despite the ominous fact that the lights go out because Tom has not paid the electric bill, Jim is at ease. He is an insensitive oaf, but that doesn't seem to bother Amanda, and almost miraculously he manages to draw Laura somewhat out of her sheltered world. Even when Jim in his clumsiness breaks the horn off Laura's treasured glass unicorn, she is not upset. In fact, she is almost relieved because the loss of the horn makes the animal less "freakish" and he "will feel more at home with the other horses." In a way, of course, the unicorn symbolizes the crippled Laura, who at least for the moment feels less freakish and isolated now that she is somewhat reunited with society through Jim. But this is a play about life in a blind and confused world, and though in a previous age the father escaped, there can be no escape now. Jim reveals that he is engaged, Laura relapses into "desolation," Amanda relapses into rage and bitterness, and Tom relapses into dreams of escape. In a limited sense Tom does escape. He leaves the family and joins the merchant marine, but his last speech or epilogue tells us that he cannot escape the memory of his sister: "Oh, Laura, Laura, I tried to leave you behind me, but I am more faithful than I intended to be!" And so the end of the last scene brings us back again to the beginning of the first scene: we are still in a world of "the blind" and of "confusion." But now at the end the darkness is deeper, the characters are lost forever in their unhappiness as Laura "blows the candles out," the darkness being literal but also symbolic of their extinguished hopes.

Numerous devices, such as repeated references to the absent father, to Amanda's youth, to Laura's victrola and of course to Laura's glass menagerie help to tie the scenes together into a unified play. But beneath these threads of imagery, and recurring motifs, is a fundamental pattern which involves the movement from nagging (Scenes I and II) to open hostilities (Scene III) to temporary reconciliation (Scene IV) to false hopes (Scenes V and VI) to an impossible heightening of false hopes and then, in a swift descent, to an inevitable collapse (Scene VII). Tennessee Williams has

constructed his play carefully. Like Ibsen, if Williams
were introduced to an architect he might say, "Architecture
is my business too."

The danger in writing about structure, especially if one proceeds by
beginning at the beginning and moving steadily to the end, is that
one will simply tell the plot. This essay on *The Glass Menagerie* manages to say things about the organization of the plot even as it tells
the plot. It has a point, hinted at in the title, developed in the body
of the essay, and wrapped up in the last line.

Before we proceed to talk about gestures, setting, and characterization, it may be useful to touch on dramatic **conventions.** An artist
and his audience have some tacit — even unconscious — agreements.
When we watch a motion picture and see an image dissolve and then
reappear, we understand that some time has passed. Such an un-
realistic, but widely accepted, device is a convention. In the theater,
we sometimes see on the stage a room, realistic in all details except
that it lacks a fourth wall; were that wall in place, we would see it
and not the interior of the room. We do not regret the missing wall,
and indeed we are scarcely aware that we have entered into an agree-
ment to pretend that this strange room is an ordinary room with the
usual number of walls. Sometimes the characters in a play speak verse,
although outside of the theater no human beings speak verse for more
than a few moments. Again we accept the device because it allows the
author to make a play, and we want a play. In *Hamlet* the characters
are understood to be speaking Danish, in *Julius Caesar* Latin, in *A
Midsummer Night's Dream* Greek, yet they all speak English for our
benefit. Two other conventions are especially common in older drama:
the **soliloquy** and the **aside.** In the former, although a solitary character speaks his thoughts aloud, we do not judge him to be a lunatic;
in the latter, a character speaks in the presence of others but is understood not to be heard by them, or to be heard only by those to whom
he directs his words. The soliloquy and the aside strike us as artificial
— and they are. But they so strike us only because they are no longer
customary. Because we are accustomed to it, we are not bothered by
the artificiality of music accompanying dialogue in a motion picture.
The conventions of the modern theater are equally artificial but are
so customary that we do not notice them. The Elizabethans, who
saw a play acted without a break, would probably find strange our
assumption that, when we return to the auditorium after a ten-minute
intermission, the ensuing action may be supposed to follow immediately the action before the intermission.

The language of a play, broadly conceived, includes the **gestures** that the characters make and the settings in which they make them. As Ezra Pound somewhere says, "The medium of drama is not words, but persons moving about on a stage using words." When Shaw's Major Barbara, in a Salvation Army shelter, gives up the Army's insignia, pinning it on the collar of her millionaire father, who has, she says, bought the Army, the gesture is at least as important as the words that accompany it. Gesture can be interpreted even more broadly: the mere fact that a character enters, leaves, or does not enter may be highly significant. John Russell Brown comments on the actions and the absence of certain words that in *Hamlet* convey the growing separation between Gertrude and Claudius.

> Their first appearance together with a public celebration of marriage is a large and simple visual effect, and Gertrude's close concern for her son suggests a simple, and perhaps unremarkable modification. . . . But Claudius enters without Gertrude for his "Prayer Scene" (III.iii) and, for the first time, Gertrude enters without him for the Closet Scene (III.iv) and is left alone, again for the first time, when Polonius hides behind the arras. Thereafter earlier accord is revalued by an increasing separation, often poignantly silent, and unexpected. When Claudius calls Gertrude to leave with him after Hamlet has dragged off Polonius' body, she makes no reply; twice more he urges her and she is still silent. But he does not remonstrate or question; rather he speaks of his own immediate concerns and, far from supporting her with assurances, becomes more aware of his own fears:
>
> > O, come away!
> > My soul is full of discord and dismay.
> > (IV.i.44–45)
>
> Emotion has been so heightened that it is remarkable that they leave together without further words. The audience has been aware of a new distance between Gertrude and Claudius, of her immobility and silence, and of his self-concern, haste and insistence.
>
> *Shakespeare's Plays in Performance* (New York, 1967), p. 139

Sometimes the dramatist helps us to interpret the gestures; Shaw and O'Neill give notably full stage directions, but detailed stage directions before the middle of the nineteenth century are rare.

Drama of the nineteenth and early twentieth centuries is often thought to be "realistic," but of course even a realistic playwright or stage designer selects his materials. A realistic **setting** (indication of the locale), then, can say a great deal, can serve as a symbol. Here is Ibsen on nonverbal devices:

> I can do quite a lot by manipulating the prosaic details of my plays so that they become theatrical metaphors and come to mean more than what they are; I have used costume in this way, lighting, scenery, landscape, weather; I have used trivial everyday things like

inky fingers and candles; and I have used living figures as symbols of spiritual forces that act upon the hero. Perhaps these things could be brought into the context of a modern realistic play to help me to portray the modern hero and the tragic conflict which I now understand so well.

> Quoted by John Northam, "Ibsen's Search for the Hero," in *Ibsen*, ed. Rolf Fjelde (Englewood Cliffs, N.J., 1965), p. 99

Ibsen uses two suggestive details in the setting of *Hedda Gabler*: early in the play Hedda is distressed by the sunlight that shines through the opened French doors, a detail that we later see helps to reveal her fear of the processes of nature. More evident and more pervasive is her tendency, when she cannot cope with her present situation, to move to the inner room, at the rear of the stage, in which hangs a picture of her late father.

Contemporary dramatists are often explicit about the symbolic qualities of the setting. Below is an example from O'Neill's *Desire under the Elms*. Only a part of the initial stage direction is given.

> The house is in good condition but in need of paint. Its walls are a sickly grayish, the green of the shutters faded. Two enormous elms are on each side of the house. They bend their trailing branches down over the roof. They appear to protect and at the same time subdue. There is a sinister maternity in their aspect, a crushing, jealous absorption. . . . They are like exhausted women resting their sagging breasts and hands and hair on its roof. . . .

A second example is part of Miller's description of the set in *Death of a Salesman*:

> Before us is the Salesman's house. We are aware of towering, angular shapes behind it, surrounding it on all sides. Only the blue light of the sky falls upon the house and forestage; the surrounding area shows an angry glow of orange. As more light appears, we see a solid vault of apartment houses around the small, fragile-seeming home.

These directions and the settings they describe are symbols that help to give the plays their meaning. Not surprisingly, O'Neill's play has Freudian overtones, Miller's (in a broad sense) Marxist overtones. O'Neill is concerned about passion, Miller (note the "solid vault of apartment houses" that menaces the salesman's house) about social forces that warp the individual. An essay might examine in detail the degree to which the setting contributes to the theme of the play. Take, for example, O'Neill's setting. The maternal elms are the most important aspect, but an essayist might first point out that the "good condition" of the house suggests it was well built, presumably some years ago. The need of paint, however, suggests both present neglect and indifference to decoration, and indeed the play is partly concerned with a strong, miserly father who regards his sons as decadent. The house, "a sickly grayish," helps to embody the suggestion of old strength but present decadence. One might continue through the stage direction, explaining the relevance of the details. Contrasts between successive settings can be especially important.

Because Shakespeare's plays were performed in broad daylight on a stage that (compared with Ibsen's, O'Neill's, and Miller's) made little use of scenery, he had to use language to manufacture his settings. But the attentive ear, or the mind's eye, responds to these settings too. Early in *King Lear*, when Lear reigns, we hear that we are in a country "With plenteous rivers, and wide-skirted meads"; later, when Lear is stripped of his power, we are in a place where "For many miles about / There's scarce a bush." (Incidentally, the vogue for the relatively bare stage which has been with us for a couple of decades is not merely an attempt to clear the stage of unnecessary furniture; in many plays it functions as a symbol of man's barren existence or of his existential plight. That is, the very sparseness of the decor or the black backdrop says something about the people who move on the stage.)

Characterization, or personality, is defined, as in fiction (see p. 54), by what the characters do (a stage direction tells us that "Hedda paces up and down, clenching her fists"), by what they say (she asks her husband to draw the curtains), by what others say about them, and by the setting in which they move. The characters are also defined in part by other characters whom they in some degree resemble. Hamlet, Laertes, and Fortinbras have each lost their fathers, but Hamlet spares the praying King Claudius, whereas Laertes, seeking vengeance on Hamlet for murdering Laertes's father, says he would cut Hamlet's throat in church; Hamlet meditates about the nature of action, but Fortinbras leads the Norwegians in a military campaign and ultimately acquires Denmark. Here is Kenneth Muir commenting briefly on the way in which Laertes helps us to see Hamlet more precisely. (Notice how Muir first offers a generalization, then supports it with details, and finally offers an even more important generalization that effectively closes his paragraph.)

> In spite of Hamlet's description of him as "a very noble youth," there is a coarseness of fibre in Laertes which is revealed throughout the play. He has the stock responses of a man of his time and position. He gives his sister copy-book advice; he goes to Paris (we are bound to suspect) to tread the primrose path; and after his father's death and again at his sister's grave he shows by the ostentation and "bravery of his grief" that he pretends more than he really feels. He has no difficulty in raising a successful rebellion against Claudius, which suggests that the more popular prince could have done the same.

Laertes, indeed, acts more or less in the way that many critics profess to think Hamlet ought to act; and his function in the play is to show precisely the opposite. Although Hamlet himself may envy Laertes' capacity for ruthless action we ought surely to prefer Hamlet's craven scruples.

Shakespeare: The Great Tragedies (London, 1961), pp. 12–13

Muir returned to the subject two years later, treating it more fully in an essay which is reprinted below, pp. 109–111. A comparison of the two versions reveals that the longer one is by no means simply a wordier version. The additional words convey additional perceptions.

Other plays, of course, provide examples of such **foils**, or characters who set one another off. Macbeth and Banquo both hear prophecies, but they act and react differently; Brutus is one kind of assassin, Cassius another, and Casca still another. Any analysis of a character, then, will probably have to take into account, in some degree, the other characters that help to show what he is, that help to set forth his **motivation** (grounds for action, inner drives, goals). In Ibsen's *A Doll's House*, Dr. Rank plays a part in helping to define Nora:

This is not Rank's play, it is Nora's. Rank is a minor character — but he plays a vital dramatic role. His function is to act as the physical embodiment, visible on the stage, of Nora's moral situation as she sees it. Nora is almost hysterical with terror at the thought of her situation — almost, but it is part of her character that with great heroism she keeps her fears secret to herself; and it is because of her reticence that Rank is dramatically necessary, to symbolize the horror she will not talk about. Nora feels, and we feel, the full awfulness of Rank's illness, and she transfers to herself the same feeling about the moral corruption which she imagines herself to carry. Nora sees herself, and we see her seeing herself (with our judgment), as suffering from a moral disease as mortal, as irremediable as Rank's disease, a disease that creeps on to a fatal climax. This is the foe that Nora is fighting so courageously.

John Northam, "Ibsen's Search for the Hero," p. 103

Finally, a warning about character: in most drama, every character is a more or less unreliable spokesman. What he says is conditioned by his personality and by the people to whom he is speaking. (An exception: One can assume that when a character soliloquizes he is telling the truth as he sees it; at such a moment there is no one on whom he is trying to make an impression.) Here, for example, is Claudius's speech telling Hamlet that Hamlet's grief for his father is excessive.

'Tis sweet and commendable in your nature, Hamlet,
To give these mourning duties to your father,

But you must know your father lost a father,
That father lost, lost his, and the survivor bound
In filial obligation for some term
To do obsequious sorrow. But to persever
In obstinate condolement is a course
Of impious stubbornness. 'Tis unmanly grief.
It shows a will most incorrect to heaven,
A heart unfortified, a mind impatient,
An understanding simple and unschooled.
For what we know must be and is as common
As any the most vulgar thing to sense,
Why should we in our peevish opposition
Take it to heart? Fie, 'tis a fault to heaven,
A fault against the dead, a fault to nature,
To reason most absurd, whose common theme
Is death of fathers, and who still hath cried,
From the first corse till he that died today,
"This must be so." We pray you throw to earth
This unprevailing woe, and think of us
As of a father, for let the world take note
You are the most immediate to our throne,
And with no less nobility of love
Than that which dearest father bears his son
Do I impart toward you. For your intent
In going back to school in Wittenberg,
It is most retrograde to our desire,
And we beseech you, bend you to remain
Here in the cheer and comfort of our eye,
Our chiefest courtier, cousin, and our son.   (I.ii.87–117)

What can one write about this speech? Out of context, it is reasonable enough; and certainly the point that everyone's father dies is
unexceptionable. But the speech exists within a context. We have
earlier seen the ghost of the late king, and Horatio has suggested that
ghosts walked "a little ere the mightiest Julius fell," thus implanting
in our minds the possibility that the ghost in *Hamlet* too is somehow
related to an assassination. (The relation is twofold: King Hamlet
was assassinated, and Claudius, his successor, will be assassinated at
the end of the play.) Moreover, Hamlet's wry comments (in the
speech preceding the quotation) about "the fruitful river in the eye"
and other highly visible manifestations of sorrow serve to diminish
Claudius's easy oratory. Most important, we notice, on rereading the
scene after we have read the entire play and learned that Claudius
murdered his brother, that Claudius, in the quoted speech, accuses
Hamlet of impiety. In fact, it is Claudius, and not Hamlet, who has
committed "a fault to heaven, / A fault against the dead, a fault to
nature," and the odiousness of this fault is emphasized by Claudius's

own pat reference to "the first corse" (corpse), for this first corpse was that of Abel, killed by his brother, as King Hamlet was killed by his brother. One might notice, too, Claudius's insistence that Hamlet remain in Denmark, where Claudius can keep an eye on him, though a few moments earlier Claudius granted Laertes leave to return to Paris. In short, a speech that seems plausible and even pious is the utterance of a murderer who daringly (or guiltily?) glances at his own crime in the reference to Abel, who cunningly suggests that his opponent is sinful, and who virtually imprisons his opponent under the guise of offering fatherly comfort. Charles Lamb has a comment relevant to this point that one must consider the context: "Everything, in heaven and earth, in man and in story, in books and in fancy, acts by confederacy, by juxtaposition, by circumstance and place."

Concluding Remarks on Writing About Drama

Among the questions one may ask as one sits down to write about a play are: What sort of **character** is So-and-so? How is he defined? If he is tragic, does the tragedy proceed from a flaw in his character, from an intellectual error, from the malice of others, from sheer chance? If he is comic, do we laugh with him or at him? Does the **plot** depend on chance? If there is a subplot, is it related? Are there irrelevant scenes? What is the function of a particular scene? Is the **setting** functional?

In writing about drama, most of us are likely to pay most of our attention to the words on the page, an understandable procedure if we regard drama as literature. Probably the great majority of essays are about the characterization of So-and-so. These essays usually look at a character's words, actions, and the setting in which he moves, as well as at what others say about him and do to him. With a play of great complexity, for example, one of Shakespeare's major plays, a short essay may do well to take an even smaller topic, such as Iago's use of prose (Why does he sometimes speak in prose, sometimes in verse, and what does it tell us about him?) or Hamlet's bawdy talk (Why does this prince sometimes make off-color remarks?). Even here we will not be able merely to hunt through the play looking at Iago's prose or Hamlet's bawdry; we will have to pay some attention to other uses of prose in *Othello*, or to other jesting in *Hamlet*, if we are to see the exact nature of the problem we have chosen to isolate.

But words are not, it has been argued above, the only language of drama, and a student will sometimes want to explore matters of staging. What is especially difficult, for most of us confronted with only a printed page, is to catch the full dramatic quality of a play — to read the words and also to have a sense of how they will sound in the context of gestures and a setting. We tend to read drama as literature rather than as dramatic literature, or theater. When the author is Shakespeare or Shaw, we can sometimes justly examine his works as literature, although even here we may find that things that seem flat on the page come alive in the theater. (Those unfunny clowns in Shakespeare are usually performed today by minor actors on the assumption that the parts are of no value; when cast well — in Shakespeare's day some of the best-known actors were those who played the clowns — these parts of the play take on meaning.) Of the two essays on drama included in this book, Kenneth Muir's is the more theatrical. Muir tries to give us a sense of contrasting characters. Joseph Wood Krutch discusses the themes of *Death of a Salesman* and of *A Streetcar Named Desire*, with a glance at the tradition of tragic literature. Both methods can be fruitful.

Sample Essays

Kenneth Muir's essay on "Hamlet's Foil" is about Laertes, but like any good essay on a relatively minor aspect of a play it illuminates a larger matter. Muir's title itself hints at the point: Laertes is seen in relation to Hamlet. Muir proceeds chronologically, giving us a sense of Laertes's doings from beginning to end, but he does not merely tell the plot. Rather, while he seems to be telling the plot he is commenting on Laertes's personality and on Hamlet's too, usually pointing out Hamlet's superiority. (He misses a chance in the first sentence of the second paragraph, when he says that Hamlet and Laertes have both returned to Denmark for Claudius's coronation; surely Hamlet returned for his father's funeral.) This summary of the action — really much more than a summary because it is accompanied by thoughtful commentary — is framed by an opening paragraph that makes the basic point that Laertes is Hamlet's foil, and by a closing paragraph that draws some broad conclusions.

Muir's topic is relatively narrow, a comparison between two characters in one play. Joseph Wood Krutch, however, ranges over Arthur Miller's *Death of a Salesman* and Tennessee Williams's *A Streetcar Named Desire*, seeking to get at the broad underlying ideas and to place them in a tradition of tragic drama. Krutch's first paragraph introduces both Arthur Miller and Tennessee Williams, and the next two paragraphs talk about both playwrights, but once the frame has been established Krutch sets out to discuss Miller first, and then Williams. The procedure is sensible, in accord with the usually sound advice, "One thing at a time." *Death of a Salesman* is not, of course, forgotten in the latter part of the essay, where it is contrasted thus in a discussion of A *Streetcar Named Desire:* "Even more conspicuously than in the case of Arthur Miller's play, an alternate reading of the situation [in A *Streetcar*] is possible." But Miller does eventually disappear from the discussion, as he almost surely would not disappear if these pages (extracted from a book on modern drama) had originally been intended to stand by themselves.

KENNETH MUIR

Hamlet's Foil

Laertes, like Fortinbras and Horatio, is Hamlet's foil; and his situation in the second half of the play is very like Hamlet's own. Hamlet has a father killed and a mother stained, and he has the task of vengeance imposed upon him by the ghost of his father; Laertes has a father killed, he is afraid that his sister will be stained, and she is driven mad — and the culprit in both cases is the avenger of the main plot.

Laertes, like Hamlet, has come to Elsinore for Claudius's coronation; he wishes to return to France, as Hamlet wishes to return to Wittenberg. The two men are on the stage at the same time, but they do not speak to each other. In the next scene Laertes warns Ophelia against Hamlet, apparently believing that he will try to seduce her. Ophelia, aware of the double standard for men and women, mildly retorts that she hopes he will practise what he preaches. Laertes, in his turn, has to listen to a sermon from his father. In the very revealing scene between Polonius and Reynaldo, it is clear that they both expect Laertes to be a bit of a rake. Polonius's method of extracting information about his son reveals a lack of trust and a coarseness of fibre in the father, and it suggests that, compared with Hamlet, Laertes is less idealistic and more easy-going in his morals.

Laertes returns from Paris on receiving the news of his father's death. Although it is obvious that he is not so devoted to his father as Hamlet was to his, he immediately takes steps to avenge Polonius's death, raises a rebellion, storms the palace, and has Claudius at his mercy. We are meant to understand that the more popular Prince could have done the same.

One has the feeling that Laertes knows exactly how he should react to every situation, according to the conventional views of the time, and that he behaves accordingly. It was the natural result of being brought up in a house where "what is done" was always more important than what ought to be done. When, for example, the Queen urges him to be calm, he bursts out:

> That drop of blood that's calm proclaims me bastard;
> Cries cuckold to my father. . . .

The rhetorical over-emphasis, apparent also in the graveyard scene, shows how even his initial sincerity becomes vulgarised.

The King has no difficulty in persuading Laertes that he is not to blame for Polonius's death, and he is about to tell him of the news he is expecting from England, when letters arrive from Hamlet himself, and he knows that his plot has failed. Immediately, he begins another plot, casting Laertes as the chief actor. He approaches the subject very gingerly, but when Laertes declares that he would cut Hamlet's throat in the church, the King realises that he need not have been so careful; and we are reminded of the way Hamlet would not kill the King while he was praying. The plot requires that Hamlet shall not peruse the foils, and Claudius admits that his intended victim is "Most generous, and free from all contriving." This plot has the advantage that the Queen might suppose that the unbated foil was an accident; but Laertes nullifies this advantage, even though it makes Hamlet's death more certain, by proposing to anoint his sword with poison. To buy poison in case of need exhibits a deeper depravity in Laertes than he has yet revealed; and it is this refinement which is the cause of his own death. The King, who has used poison before, decides to provide a poisoned chalice in case Hamlet escapes the "venom'd stuck"; but, as Macbeth reminds us, "even-handed justice Commends the ingredience of our poison'd chalice To our own lips." The murderous pact is sealed by the news of Ophelia's death.

The next time we see Laertes, at the grave of his sister, Hamlet calls him with unconscious irony "a very noble youth." But he regains some sympathy by his exchange with the churlish priest, and does not entirely lose it when he leaps into the grave and asks to be buried alive. But, here again, Laertes is going beyond what he really feels, as Hamlet is quick to recognise. This is the first time that Shakespeare brings the two men face to face. Hamlet has only just learnt that Ophelia is dead, that the Queen hoped they would marry, that his killing of her father had led to her madness, and to her death; and, though he rants to outface Laertes, he convinces us that he loved her more than one brother, if not more than forty thousand. The encounter by the grave of the woman they both loved confirms Laertes in his resolution to murder Hamlet. Yet, when it comes to the point, he is ashamed of what he is doing. In answer to Hamlet's apology that he had "shot his arrow o'er the house" and hurt his brother (as Laertes would have been if Hamlet had married Ophelia), Laertes says that although he will not be officially reconciled until his case has been considered by a tribunal, he will nevertheless receive Hamlet's "offer'd love like love, And will not wrong it."

When Laertes asks for a foil, Hamlet quibbles on the word:

I'll be your foil, Laertes; in mine ignorance
Your skill shall, like a star i' th' darkest night,
Stick fiery off indeed.

But Laertes, as we have seen, is a foil to Hamlet in another sense.

We may suppose that Laertes's guilty conscience prevents him from displaying the skill of which Lamord had spoken, for Hamlet scores the first two hits. At last, almost against his conscience, Laertes attacks Hamlet before he is ready and scores the necessary hit. Hamlet, although not realising the full extent of the treachery, disarms Laertes and secures the unbated rapier. Laertes is wounded before the King can intervene, and admits that he has met his deserts. In his dying moments he reveals the King's villainy and exchanges forgiveness with Hamlet.

Laertes is the ruthless avenger that Hamlet, with half his mind, wishes to be; and he throws into relief the hesitations and craven scruples of the hero. He is almost what some of Hamlet's critics blame him for not being, and he might almost have been put into the play to show them how wrong they were. "By the image of my cause," Hamlet told Horatio earlier, "I see the portraiture of his." It is one measure of the gulf between the two avengers that Laertes could never have used these words about Hamlet.

Joseph Wood Krutch

Moral Vision in Arthur Miller and Tennessee Williams*

Neither Miller's *Death of a Salesman* nor Tennessee Williams' *A Streetcar Named Desire* is a cheerful play. Both end with what looks less like a tragic affirmation than like a simple confession of defeat. Neither Willy Loman nor Blanche Dubois is likely to strike the spectator as a very dignified or very noble character, and both are completely destroyed — as, say, Hamlet and Othello are not completely destroyed — when the story ends. Loman is a suicide and Blanche is being led away to a madhouse.

Obviously neither Miller nor Williams plainly commits himself as do Maxwell Anderson and O'Neill to either the form or the ethical content of classic tragedy. Moreover, neither exhibits, as plainly

* The title of this essay is the editor's.

as it seems to me O'Neill exhibits, a determination to seek persistently for something in the universe outside man to which he can appeal and "belong." It is possible to interpret *Death of a Salesman* as brutal naturalism and *A Streetcar Named Desire* as a sort of semisurrealist version of the Strindbergian submission to destructive obsessions.

If such is a proper summation, then Miller and Williams, the two most widely discussed American playwrights of the moment, follow O'Neill and Anderson only as Sean O'Casey followed Synge. They represent, that is to say, the collapse of a reaction and illustrate, as did O'Casey, an irresistible pull in the direction of nihilism and despair.

Perhaps, indeed, that is the proper interpretation to be put upon their work and their current popularity. I am unwilling, however, to leave the subject without suggesting the possibility that there may be something to be said on the other side, and at the risk of being accused of overinterpretation, I should like to say it.

So far as *Death of a Salesman* is concerned, it seems reasonable to suppose that it is intended as something a little more than merely detached "scientific" naturalism. Most spectators, I think, assume that it embodies some "social criticism," and most, I imagine, assume that the social criticism is of a sort by now very traditional. In this view, Willy Loman is the victim of an unjust competitive society. He was first corrupted by its false ideals and then exploited by those shrewder and more ruthless than himself. Society made him what he was, and in a better society his fate would have been a happier one. In all this there is, of course, nothing incompatible with what I have been loosely calling "modernism." The doctrine and methods of the naturalists lend themselves very readily to such "social significance."

What makes it impossible to dismiss *Death of a Salesman* as merely left-wing naturalism is the curious fact that Miller himself seems to be some sort of pluralist and that his play could be interpreted, not as a demonstration of the workings of social determinism, but as a study of the effects of moral weakness and irresponsibility. Willy Loman is a victim of society, but he is also a victim of himself. He accepted an essentially vulgar and debased as well as a false system of values. He himself says, and the audience seems to be expected to believe him, that he might have led a happy life if he had followed his own bent and become, for example, a carpenter, instead of submitting to the prejudice which makes a salesman more respectable than a man who works with his hands. His tragic guilt — and it is his, not society's — was, in this view, a very old-fashioned one. He was not true to himself. Thus the moral of the play becomes a classical moral and must necessarily presume both the existence of the classical ego and the power to make a choice.

Seen in this light, Miller becomes a moralist, at least in the sense and in much the same fashion that Ibsen was still a moralist. He has found his way back along the road which leads to determinism and the disappearance of the ego at least to the point where the dramatic disciples of Ibsen first entered upon it, and *Death of a Salesman* thus becomes a qualified reaffirmation of the individual's privilege of being, within certain limits, what he chooses to be.

The case of Tennessee Williams is different but equally dubious. As I have already suggested, the most obvious interpretations put him plainly among the despairing explorers of pathological states of mind just as the obvious interpretations put Arthur Miller among the sociological naturalists. In all his most striking plays, *The Glass Menagerie, Summer and Smoke,* and *A Streetcar Named Desire,* the chief character is obsessed, and in the last two the obsession takes a sexual form. Madness seems to interest the author more than anything else, and at least in the third and most successful of the plays a quasi-expressionist technique is used for the purpose of persuading the audience to see certain of the events from the standpoint of the heroine's abnormality rather than from its own presumably objective point of view.

In each of the three plays there is another recurrent theme. Each of the heroines numbers among her obsessions the fact that she is or was "a lady." In each the ideal of respectability, the sense that her parents and her remoter ancestors lived in accordance with some code to which she herself would like to be loyal but which no one with whom she comes in contact acknowledges, is so strong as to appear crucial. In *The Glass Menagerie* the mother sees her family disintegrating because it no longer finds her dream of respectability anything but annoying. In both *Summer and Smoke* and *A Streetcar Named Desire* the heroine seems to succumb to crude sexuality because she has so fanatically refused to accept a normal life among people who appear to her as hopelessly unrefined.

Tennessee Williams grew up in the South. Like so many other Southern writers, the existence of a decayed aristocracy was one of the inescapable facts of the society with which he was most familiar. That representatives of such a decayed aristocracy should appear in his plays may mean no more than that they were part of his experience. Nevertheless it seems to me obvious that his persistent concern with them does have a greater significance. These helpless survivors from the past, feeble and pathetic clingers to a dead tradition, take on the importance of symbols. They are not accidental facts; they mean something.

JOSEPH WOOD KRUTCH 113

Upon the answer to the question "What do they mean? Of what are they symbols?" depends the whole meaning of the plays so far as our own special theme is concerned. Let us consider it in connection with A *Streetcar Named Desire*.

Blanche DuBois, a decayed aristocrat and a fanatical lady, has already lost her position as a schoolteacher because she is also a nymphomaniac. As the curtain rises we see her arriving alone and seeking refuge in the squalid home of her sister Stella, who has married a crude and brutal young man of foreign extraction. This sister has made what the psychologists would call "a satisfactory adjustment." She has rejected and forgotten the traditions of her past. She has accepted the frank squalor of her surroundings and the ignorant brutality of her husband, chiefly because she is reveling delightedly in his abundant and animalistic sexuality. Blanche, the nymphomaniac, is horrified by what some would call her sister's "normality." She makes a feeble and ridiculous attempt to instruct both the sister and her husband in the genteel tradition, and she is violently repelled by their contented animality. But because she can neither lead their life nor the genteel life of which she dreams, her last defenses crumble and she is led away to an asylum, certifiably insane.

Everything depends upon, as the phrase goes, which side the author is on. It appears that to many members of the audience this question presents no difficulty. They are, and they assume that the author is, on the side of the sister. She is "healthy," "adjusted," "normal." She lives in the present; she accepts things as they are; and she will never be confined to a madhouse. Her husband is crude, even somewhat brutal, but he is also virile; he is the natural man and one of literature's many kinsmen of Lady Chatterley's lover. Virility, even orgiastic virility, is the proper answer to decadence. Stella, the representative of a decayed aristocracy, is rejuvenated by a union with a representative of "the people."

Even more conspicuously than in the case of Arthur Miller's play, an alternate reading of the situation is possible. In Miller one suspects a sort of pluralism. In Williams the question presents itself instead under the form of an ambiguity.

By this I mean that while one section of the audience takes the side of Stella almost as a matter of course another section understands and shares Blanche's revulsion. Her instincts are right. She is on the side of civilization and refinement. But the age has placed her in a tragic dilemma. She looks about for a tradition according to which she may live and a civilization to which she can be loyal. She finds none. Ours is a society which has lost its shape.

Behind her lies a past which, at least in retrospect, seems to have been civilized. The culture of the Old South is dead, and she has good reason to know that it is. It is, however, the only culture about which she knows anything. The world of Stella and of her husband is a barbarism, — perhaps, as its admirers would say, a vigorous barbarism — but a barbarism nonetheless. Blanche chooses the dead past and becomes the victim of that impossible choice. But she does choose it rather than the "adjustment" of her sister. At least she has not succumbed to barbarism.

As I have said, one's choice of sides will depend largely upon one's attitude toward Stella's "virile" husband. The real question is whether he is villain or hero. If we knew which he is to his creator, we should know whether Williams should be classified among that group of "moderns" who see in a return to the primitive the possible rejuvenation of mankind or whether he belongs rather with traditionalists, such as the esoteric T. S. Eliot on the one hand or the popular Maxwell Anderson on the other, who maintain that from the past itself we shall still have to learn if we are ever to learn at all what civilization means.

I cannot tell you what Williams thinks or says. I can, after due warning, report a very significant thing which he is said to have said. At third hand I have it that when queried in conversation about the meaning of A *Streetcar Named Desire*, or rather about the significance of its chief male character, he replied: "It means that if you do not watch out the apes will take over."

If this report is accurate, and I repeat that I have it only at third hand, the question is answered. Williams, despite all the violence of his plays, despite what sometimes looks very much like nihilism, is really on the side of what modernists would call the Past rather than the Future — which means, of course, on the side of those who believe that the future, if there is to be any civilized future, will be less new than most modern dramatists from Ibsen on have professed to believe.

5

POETRY

Aristotle suggested that the arts arise out of two impulses: the impulse for harmony and the impulse to imitate. Let us take these one at a time.

We are all familiar with the desire to make a pattern. We straighten pictures on the walls (we like parallel lines), and we arrange the silverware on the table in a way that pleases. (Even chimpanzees are said to show what is called an instinct for closure. If they are given paint and a brush and a paper on which two-thirds of a circle has been painted, they will sometimes complete the circle.) We make patterns too out of sounds; if we forget a line of a song, we do not leave an unpleasant blank, but we feel compelled to fill it out by humming or by uttering nonsense syllables such as *da da da da da*. Sometimes the sounds make a sort of sense, but the sense scarcely seems important. The following lines have pleased for generations, presumably because of their catchiness rather than because of any message.

> Pease-porridge hot,
> Pease-porridge cold,
> Pease-porridge in the pot
> Nine days old.

Something about meter, rhythm, and rhyme will be said below, but for the moment we can say that one source of pleasure in poetry is afforded by its harmonious pattern of sounds.

The meaning affords a second source of pleasure. Poetry is sound and sense, and in this connection we may briefly consider Aristotle's statement that the second psychological impulse behind the arts is the impulse to imitate. Children mimicking their parents or playing

116

cops and robbers provide examples of the impulse to imitate. And it is easy to see that a landscape painting is a sort of imitation (in pigment) of a landscape; a piece of sculpture is an imitation (in wood or stone) of, say, Moses; a historical novel is an imitation (in words) of some aspect of a period of time; a play is an imitation (in words and gestures) of the doings of men. Because in ordinary language, however, "imitation" has a pejorative overtone, the idea may become more acceptable if we substitute "representation" or "re-creation." Now, this representation is not an exact duplicate; as the previous chapter mentioned, no one believes that *Julius Caesar* is a mirror image of what happened in Rome two thousand years ago. Shakespeare took some hints from history (a leader assassinated), but he invented speeches and even some characters. And his *Julius Caesar* offers itself as a coherent and meaningful work; Caesar may never have said this or done that, but Shakespeare's words combine to give us an imitation that helps us to see the invisible relationships in our own world, somewhat as a mimic of X suddenly — by heightening certain features of X's gestures and intonations — makes us see and hear things we had not before noticed in X. Through the imitation, we perceive, let us say, the insecurity that underlies X's words and gestures. But this is to speak of drama and impersonation, not specifically of poetry. In what sense is nondramatic poetry an imitation? And let us make the problem more difficult by eliminating such narratives as *The Odyssey* and *Paradise Lost*, for clearly they imitate — that is, they present in words — actions that allegedly happened long ago. Let us talk at first about what is commonly called lyric poetry.

The **lyric** commonly presents a speaker expressing an emotion. The name suggests that it was once a song to be accompanied by a lyre, and although the genre now includes much that cannot possibly be sung, let us begin with the singable.

ROBERT BURNS
Auld Lang Syne°   *long ago*

Should auld acquaintance be forgot,
    And never brought to mind?
Should auld acquaintance be forgot,
    And auld lang syne!   4

    For auld lang syne, my jo,
      For auld lang syne,
    We'll tak a cup o' kindness yet
      For auld lang syne.   8

And surely ye'll be your pint-stowp!°   *pay for your pint-cup*
    And surely I'll be mine!

And we'll tak a cup o' kindness yet
  For auld lang syne.   12

We twa hae run about the braes,°   *slopes*
  And pu'd the gowans° fine;   *daisies*
But we've wander'd mony a weary fitt
  Sin auld lang syne.   16

We twa hae paidl'd i' the burn,°   *brook*
  From morning sun till dine;°   *dinner, noon*
But seas between us braid hae roar'd,
  Sin auld lang syne.   20

And there's a hand, my trusty fiere!°   *friend*
  And gie's a hand o' thine!
And we'll tak a right guid-willie-waught,°   *hearty swig*
  For auld lang syne.   24

It is not stretching a point to say that Burns's song imitates, or re-
creates, a state that we all know in some degree. There are moments
of conviviality that are suffused with a sense of the irrevocable past.
This last sentence is an inept summary of the poem, but it affords a
prologue to a simple question that may clarify the point: Do we
not — and do not innumerable people who sing "Auld Lang Syne"
on New Year's Eve — feel that Burns has perfectly caught, or imi-
tated, a state of mind? Is not "Auld Lang Syne" an embodiment or
imitation of a human experience? We value its sound (we may not
even know the meanings of some of the words), and we also value its
sense, the representation of a moment of human behavior. We hear
a voice that is not at all literally like any voice we have ever heard
(no one talks in rhymes) but that nevertheless makes us say, "Yes,
I understand that experience. I see what that state of mind is."

  Here is another voice, very far from a singing one:

ALEXANDER POPE
from *An Essay on Man*

Awake, my St. John!° leave all meaner things   *Henry St. John,*
To low ambition, and the pride of kings.   *pronounced "Sinjun"*
Let us (since life can little more supply
Than just to look about us and to die)
Expatiate free o'er all this scene of Man;   5
A mighty maze! but not without a plan;
A wild, where weeds and flowers promiscuous shoot,
Or garden, tempting with forbidden fruit.
Together let us beat this ample field,
Try what the open, what the covert yield;   10

The latent tracts, the giddy heights, explore
Of all who blindly creep, or sightless soar;
Eye nature's walks, shoot folly as it flies,
And catch the manners living as they rise;
Laugh where we must, be candid where we can,   15
But vindicate the ways of God to man.

This poem proceeds for hundreds of lines, and we may not feel that
Pope vindicates the ways of God to man, but again we catch a human voice. It begins authoritatively ("Awake") and yet jocosely (low
things, it says, are the concern of kings). Then, in the third and
fourth lines, a touch — but a highly controlled touch — of pathos
is introduced in the parenthetic reference to the brevity of man's
life. Next, the speaker suggests that the world is a sort of large estate
harboring all sorts of creatures. He almost seems supercilious in his
reference to shooting down folly (i.e., some people are compared to
stupid game birds), but his good-natured "Laugh where we must,
be candid [i.e., generous] where we can" reminds us of the traditional and reasonable view that wrongdoing appears funny (because
it is self-defeating) to the good man. We continue to listen with interest to this speaker who, in the last line of this verse paragraph,
reaffirms his high purpose with an echo from Milton's *Paradise Lost*.
What we have is a man talking easily and intimately about something important. We read Pope's *Essay on Man*, looking out both
for the "ideas" he sets forth, which may or may not prove convincing, and for the voice or mind or personality, that is, for an imitation
of a man thinking.

The **voice,** or **persona** (Latin for mask), or **mask,** that speaks the
poem is not identical with the poet who writes it. The author counter-
feits the speech of a person in a particular situation. Robert Browning
invented a Renaissance duke who speaks "My Last Duchess"; Robert
Frost in "Stopping by Woods on a Snowy Evening" invented the
speech of a man who, sitting in a horse-drawn sleigh, is surveying
woods that are "lovely, dark and deep."

The speaker's voice, of course, often has the ring of the author's
own voice, and to make a distinction between speaker and author
may at times seem perverse. Robert Burns sometimes lets us know
that the poem is spoken by "Rob"; he may address his wife by name;
beneath the title "To a Mouse" he writes, "On Turning Up Her
Nest with the Plow, November, 1785," and beneath the title "To a
Mountain Daisy" he writes, "On Turning One Down with the Plow
in April, 1786." Still, even in these allegedly autobiographical poems,
it may be convenient to distinguish between author and speaker;
the speaker is Burns the lover, or Burns the meditative man, or Burns
the compassionate man, not simply Robert Burns the poet.

The voice is established not only by broad strokes but by such details as **alliteration** (the repetition of initial consonants), **assonance** (the repetition of vowel-sounds), and rhyme. (More will be said about rhyme later.) F. W. Bateson, in *English Poetry*, aptly notes the role that alliteration plays in reinforcing the contemptuous tone we hear in "Die and endow a college or a cat," a line from Pope's "Epistle to Bathurst." Bateson points out that "the *d*'s hint that there is a subtle identity in the dying and the endowing (the only interest that the world takes in this particular death is in the testamentary endowments), and the *c*'s point the contrast between founding colleges and financing cats' homes."

From the whole of language, one consciously or unconsciously selects certain words and grammatical constructions; this selection constitutes one's **diction**. It is partly by the diction that we come to know the speaker of a poem. "Auld" and "twa" tell us that the speaker of "Auld Lang Syne" is a Scot. In the passage from Pope's *Essay on Man*, "expatiate," "promiscuous," and "vindicate" tell us that the speaker is an educated man. Of course, some words are used in both poems: "my," "to," "and." The fact remains, however, that although a large part of language is shared by all speakers, some parts of language are used only by certain speakers.

Like some words, some grammatical constructions are used only by certain kinds of speakers. Consider these two passages:

In Adam's fall
We sinnèd all.   (from *The New England Primer*)

Of Man's first disobedience, and the fruit
Of that forbidden tree whose mortal taste
Brought death into the World, and all our woe,
With loss of Eden, till one greater Man
Restore us, and regain the blissful seat,
Sing, Heavenly Muse, that, on the secret top
Of Oreb, or of Sinai, didst inspire
That shepherd who first taught the chosen seed
In the beginning how the heavens and earth
Rose out of Chaos. . . .

(Milton, from *Paradise Lost*)

There is an enormous difference in the diction of these two passages. Milton, speaking as an inspired poet who regards his theme as "a great argument," appropriately uses words and grammatical constructions somewhat removed from common life. Hence, while the anonymous author of the primer speaks directly of "Adam's fall," Milton speaks allusively of the fall, calling it "Man's first disobedience."

Milton's sentence is nothing that any Englishman ever said in conversation; its genitive beginning, its length (the sentence continues for six lines beyond the quoted passage), and its postponement of the main verb until the sixth line mark it as the utterance of a poet working in the tradition of Latin poetry. The primer's statement, by its choice of words as well as by its brevity, suggests a far less sophisticated speaker.

A speaker (or voice, to use the previous terminology) has attitudes toward himself, his subject, and his audience, and (consciously or unconsciously) he chooses his words, pitch, and modulation accordingly; all these add up to his **tone.** In written literature, tone must be detected without the aid of the ear; the reader must understand by the selection and sequence of words the way (i.e., playfully, angrily, confidentially, ironically, etc.) in which they are meant to be heard. The reader must catch what Frost calls "the speaking tone of voice somehow entangled in the words and fastened to the page for the ear of the imagination." *

Our interest in the shifting tones in the voice that speaks the words should not, of course, cause us to neglect the words themselves, the gist of the idea expressed. If we **paraphrase** (reword) the first two lines of Pope's *Essay on Man*, we get something like this: "Wake up, my friend St. John [the man addressed was Henry St. John], leave low things to such lowly people as are ambitious and (equally low) to arrogant monarchs." A paraphrase at least has the virtue of making us look hard at all of the words. In paraphrasing Pope, for example, we come to see that "my" in the first line reveals the intimacy which Pope feels toward St. John. If you paraphrase the next six lines of Pope's *Essay*, and then closely compare your paraphrase with Pope's words, you are doing some of the homework preliminary to writing an explication (see pp. 7–10) of the lines. To take the most obvious example: You will probably be able to see the implication that is in Pope's "garden, tempting with forbidden fruit." You may need a dictionary to see the multiple meanings in "Expatiate" and "promiscuous." But the point of a paraphrase is not to enlarge your vocabulary; it is an exercise designed to help you understand at least the surface meaning, and it will usually help you to understand at least some of the implicit meaning. Furthermore, a paraphrase makes you see that the poet's words — if the poem is a good one — are ex-

---

* This discussion concentrates on the speaker's tone. But sometimes one can also talk of the author's tone, that is, of the author's attitude toward his invented speaker. The speaker's tone might, for example, be angry, but the author's tone (as detected by the reader) might be humorous.

actly right, better than the words you might substitute. It becomes clear that the thing said in the poem — not only the "idea" expressed but the precise tone with which it is expressed — is a sharply defined experience.

The following is an anonymous quatrain, written in England about 1500.

> Western wind, when wilt thou blow,
>   The small rain down can rain?
> Christ, if my love were in my arms,
>   And I in my bed again.

This poem defies paraphrase, not because it is obscure or nonsensical, but because the surface statement is so lucid. The most one can do in paraphrasing the first line is to say something like "O west wind [the opening is vocative, the wind is being addressed], when will you come?" About the only distortion from ordinary language in the poem is "small rain," where we would normally speak of the "light rain" or "gentle rain." But an explication will point out that much more is going on in the poem than a word-for-word substitution can indicate. The first two lines indicate that the speaker longs for the spring — the time of light rain and the time when the west wind (warmed by the Gulf Stream) blows in England. In the next two lines he expresses his unhappiness that he is not with his beloved. What is the connection between the first two and the last two lines? Among the answers are these: spring is commonly associated with lovers; spring is a time of warmth and revitalization, and love is associated with warmth and with new birth. The first two lines implicitly tell us it is winter, and the lover in effect compares the world's wintry state with his own wintriness (sense of coldness, barrenness) caused by the absence of his beloved. "Christ" in the third line may be both an agonized expletive and an invocation: he calls on Christ, who Himself was reborn in the spring (the Resurrection), and who is the giver of new life to men who sense the emptiness of their present lives. The previous sentences are tiresomely wordy (about a hundred words in place of the poem's twenty-six), but perhaps they help to illuminate the highly complex experience that we overhear in these four lines. Again, we are overhearing or witnessing an experience, not receiving an edifying message. The poem does not offer any answers to the questions: How shall I live? How can I regain the lover I have lost? It does, however, in memorable words, so perfectly catch a human experience that we feel the experience is available for us to look at, in contrast to our own daily experiences which are so much a welter that we can scarcely know them. In the preface to his *Collected*

Poems, Robert Frost, somewhat cryptically and punningly, talks about these matters of sound and sense and the knowledge of life that they afford:

> The sound is the gold in the ore. Then we will have the sound out alone and dispense with the inessential. We do till we make the discovery that the object in writing poetry is to make all poems sound as different as possible from each other, and the resources for that of vowels, consonants, punctuation, syntax, words, sentences, meter are not enough. We need the help of context — meaning — subject matter. . . . The possibilities for tune from the dramatic tones of meaning struck across the rigidity of a limited meter are endless, and we are back in poetry as merely one more art of having something to say, sound or unsound. Probably better if sound, because deeper and from wider experience. . . . [A poem] begins in delight and ends in wisdom . . . [and] a clarification of life — not necessarily a great clarification, such as sects and cults are founded on, but in a momentary stay against confusion. . . . For me the initial delight is in the surprise of remembering something I didn't know I knew. I am in a place, a situation, as if I had materialized from cloud or risen out of the ground.

Robert Frost has said, "Poetry provides the one permissible way of saying one thing and meaning another." This, of course, is an exaggeration, but it shrewdly suggests the importance of **figurative language** — saying one thing in terms of something else. Words have their literal meaning, but they can also be used so that something other than the literal meaning is implied. "My love is a rose" is, literally, nonsense, for she is not a five-petaled, many-stamened plant with a spiny stem. But the suggestions of "rose" include "delicate beauty," "soft," "perfumed," and thus the word "rose" can be meaningfully applied — figuratively rather than literally — to "my love." The girl is fragrant; her skin is perhaps like a rose in texture and (in some measure) color; she will not keep her beauty long. The poet, that is, has communicated a perception very precisely. His discovery is not world-shaking; it is less important than the discovery of America or the discovery that the meek are blessed, but it *is* a discovery and it offers that "clarification" and "momentary stay against confusion" that Frost spoke of.

People who write about poetry have found it convenient to name the various kinds of figurative language. Just as the student of geology employs special terms, such as kames and eskers, the student of literature employs special terms to name things as accurately as possible. The next few pages give the most common terms.

In a **simile** items from different classes are explicitly compared by a connective such as "like," "as," or "than," or by a verb such as "appears" or "seems." (If the objects compared are from the same class, e.g., "New York is like London," no simile is present.)

> Float like a butterfly, sting like a bee.   (Muhammad Ali)

> It is a beauteous evening, calm and free.
> The holy time is quiet as a Nun,
> Breathless with adoration.   (Wordsworth)

> How sharper than a serpent's tooth it is
> To have a thankless child.   (Shakespeare)

> Seems he a dove? His feathers are but borrowed.   (Shakespeare)

A **metaphor** asserts the identity, without a connective such as "like" or a verb such as "appears," of terms that are literally incompatible.

> She is the rose, the glory of the day.   (Spenser)

> Yes! it's true all my visions
> have come home to roost at last.   (Brautigan)

Notice how in the last example only one of the terms ("visions") is stated; the other ("chickens") is implied in "have come home to roost." In the following poem, Keats's excitement on reading Chapman's translation of Homer is communicated first through a metaphor and then through a simile.

JOHN KEATS
On First Looking into Chapman's Homer

> Much have I traveled in the realms of gold,
> And many goodly states and kingdoms seen;
> Round many western islands have I been
> Which bards in fealty to Apollo hold.
> Oft of one wide expanse have I been told   5
> That deep-browed Homer ruled as his demesne;
> Yet did I never breathe its pure serene
> Till I heard Chapman speak out loud and bold:
>
> Then felt I like some watcher of the skies
> When a new planet swims into his ken;   10
> Or like stout Cortez when with eagle eyes
> He stared at the Pacific — and all his men
> Looked at each other with a wild surmise —
> Silent, upon a peak in Darien.

We might pause for a moment to take a closer look at Keats's poem. If you write an essay on the figurative language in this sonnet,

you will probably discuss the figure involved in asserting that reading is a sort of traveling (it brings us to unfamiliar worlds), and especially that reading brings us to realms of gold. Presumably the
experience of reading is valuable. "Realms of gold" not only continues
and modifies the idea of reading as travel, but in its evocation of El
Dorado (an imaginary country in South America, thought to be rich
in gold and therefore the object of search by Spanish explorers of
the Renaissance) it introduces a suggestion of the Renaissance appropriate to a poem about a Renaissance translation of Homer. The
figure of traveling is amplified in the next few lines, which assert that
the "goodly states and kingdoms" and "western islands" are ruled by
poets who owe allegiance to a higher authority, Apollo. The beginning
of the second sentence (line 5) enlarges this already spacious area
with its reference to "one wide expanse," and the ruler of this area
(unlike the other rulers) is given the dignity of being named. He is
Homer, "deep-browed," "deep" suggesting not only his high, or perhaps furrowed, forehead but the profundity of the thoughts behind
the forehead. The speaker continues the idea of books as remote
places, but now he also seems to think of this place as more than a
rich area; instead of merely saying that until he read Chapman's translation he had not "seen" it (as in line 2) or "been" there (line 3),
he says he never breathed its air. That is, the preciousness is not
material but ethereal, not gold but something far more exhilarating
and essential. This reference to air leads easily to the next dominant
image, that of the explorer of the illimitable skies (so vast is Homer's
world) rather than of the land and sea. But the explorer of the skies
is conceived as watching an *oceanic* sky. In hindsight we can see that
the link was perhaps forged earlier in line 7, with "serene" (a vast
expanse of air *or* water); in any case, there is an unforgettable rightness in the description of the suddenly discovered planet as something
that seems to "swim" into one's ken. After this climactic discovery
we return to the Renaissance Spanish explorers (though, in fact,
Balboa, and not Cortez, was the discoverer of the Pacific) by means
of a simile that compares the speaker's rapture with Cortez's as he
gazed at the expanse before him. The writer of an essay on the figurative language in a poem should, in short, try to call attention to the
aptness (or ineptness) of the figures and to the connecting threads
that make a meaningful pattern.

Two types of metaphor deserve special mention. In **synecdoche**
the whole is replaced by the part, or the part by the whole. For example, "bread," in "Give us this day our daily bread," replaces all
sorts of food. In **metonymy** something is named that replaces something closely related to it. For example, James Shirley names certain

objects, using them to replace social classes to which they are related:

> Scepter and crown must tumble down
> And in the dust be equal made
> With the poor crooked scythe and spade

The attribution of human feelings or characteristics to abstractions or to inanimate objects is called **personification.**

> The fixed bells rang, their voices
> came like boats over the oil-slicks.   (Olson)

Olson attributes voices to bells. Of all figures, personification most surely gives to airy nothings a local habitation and a name:

> There's Wrath who has learnt every trick of guerilla warfare,
> The shamming dead, the night-raid, the feinted retreat.   (Auden)

> Hope, thou bold taster of delight.   (Crashaw)

Crashaw's personification, "Hope, thou bold taster of delight," is also an example of the figure called **apostrophe,** an address to a person or thing not literally listening. Wordsworth begins a sonnet by apostrophizing Milton:

> Milton, thou shouldst be living at this hour,

and Ginsberg apostrophizes "gusts of wet air":

> Fall on the ground, O great Wetness.

What conclusions can we draw about figurative language? First, figurative language, with its literally incompatible terms, forces the reader to attend to the connotations (suggestions, associations) rather than to the denotations (dictionary definitions) of one of the terms. Second, although figurative language is said to differ from ordinary discourse, it is found in ordinary discourse as well as in literature. "It rained cats and dogs," "War is hell," "Don't be a pig," "Mr. Know-all," and other tired figures are part of our daily utterances. But through repeated use, these, and most of the figures we use, have lost whatever impact they once had and are only a shade removed from expressions which, though once figurative, have become literal: the *eye* of a needle, a *branch* office, the *face* of a clock. Third, good figurative language is usually concrete, condensed, and interesting. The concreteness lends precision and vividness; when Keats writes that he felt "like some watcher of the skies / When a new planet swims into his ken," he more sharply characterizes his feelings than if he had said, "I felt excited." His simile isolates for us a precise kind of excitement, and the metaphoric "swims" vividly brings up the oceanic aspect of the sky. The effect of the second of these three qualities, condensation, can be seen by attempting to paraphrase some of the figures. A paraphrase will commonly use more words than the original, and it will have less impact — as the gradual coming of night usually has less impact on us than a sudden darkening of the sky, or as a prolonged push has less impact than a sudden blow. The third quality, interest, is largely dependent on the previous two: the successful figure often makes us open our eyes wider and take notice. Keats's "deep-browed Homer" arouses our interest in Homer as "thoughtful Homer" or "meditative Homer" does not. Similarly, when W. B. Yeats says:

> An aged man is but a paltry thing,
> A tattered coat upon a stick, unless
> Soul clap its hands and sing, and louder sing
> For every tatter in its mortal dress,

the metaphoric identification of an old man with a scarecrow jolts us out of all our usual unthinking attitudes about old men as kind, happy folk who are content to have passed from youth into age.

When we read "rose," we may more or less call to mind a picture of a rose, or perhaps we are reminded of the odor or texture of a rose. Whatever in a poem appeals to any of our senses (including sensations of heat and pressure as well as of sight, smell, taste, touch, sound) is an **image.** In short, images are the sensory content of a work, whether literal or figurative. When a poet says "My rose," and he is speaking about a rose, we have no figure of speech — though we still have an image. If, however, "My rose" is a shortened form of "My love is a rose," some would say that he is using a metaphor, but others would say that because the first term is omitted ("My love is"), the rose is a **symbol.** A poem about the transience of a rose might compel the reader to feel that the transience of female beauty is the larger theme even though it is never explicitly stated. This is John Ciardi's point when he speaks (p. 150) of "the poet's essential duplicity." "The poet," Ciardi explains, "pretends to be talking about one thing, and all the while he is talking about many others." The horse in "Stopping by Woods on a Snowy Evening" is a horse and is also, Ciardi suggests, "that order of life that does not understand why a man stops in the wintry middle of nowhere to watch the snow come down."

Some symbols are **conventional symbols** — people have agreed to accept them as standing for something other than their literal meanings: a poem about the cross would probably be about Christianity; similarly, the rose has long been a symbol for love. In Virginia Woolf's novel *Mrs. Dalloway*, the husband communicates his love by proffering this conventional symbol: "He was holding out flowers — roses, red and white roses. (But he could not bring himself to say he loved her; not in so many words.)" Objects that are not conventional symbols, however, may also give rise to rich, multiple, indefinable associations. The following poem uses the traditional symbol of the rose, but uses it in a nontraditional way.

WILLIAM BLAKE
The Sick Rose

O rose, thou art sick!
The invisible worm
That flies in the night,
In the howling storm,

Has found out thy bed
Of crimson joy,
And his dark secret love
Does thy life destroy.

One might perhaps argue that the worm is "invisible" (line 2) merely because it is hidden within the rose, but an "invisible worm / That flies in the night" is more than a long, slender, soft-bodied, creeping animal; and a rose that has, or is, a "bed / Of crimson joy" is more than a gardener's rose. Blake's worm and rose suggest things beyond themselves — a stranger, more vibrant world than the world we are usually aware of. One finds oneself half-thinking, for example, that the worm is male, the rose female, and the poem is about the violation of virginity. Or that the poem is about the destruction of beauty: woman's beauty, rooted in joy, is destroyed by a power that feeds on her. But these interpretations are not fully satisfying: the poem presents a worm and a rose, and yet it is not merely about a worm and a rose. These objects resonate, stimulating our thoughts toward something else, but the something else is elusive, whereas it is not elusive in Burns's "My love is like a red, red rose."

A symbol, then, is an image so loaded with significance that it is not simply literal, and it does not simply stand for something else; it is both itself *and* something else that it richly suggests, a kind of manifestation of something too complex or too elusive to be otherwise revealed. Blake's poem is about a blighted rose and at the same time about much more. In a symbol, as Thomas Carlyle wrote, "the Infinite is made to blend with the Finite, to stand visible, and as it were, attainable there."

Here is a student's essay on Blake's "The Sick Rose," relating the symbolism to the speaker and audience.

Speaker and Audience in "The Sick Rose"

Blake's "The Sick Rose" seems, on first reading, to be addressed to a rose, but despite "O rose" of the first line, further reading reveals two other audiences: the speaker, if he is not a madman, is addressing a special kind of rose, a rose that can listen, and, second, he is addressing himself. Another way of putting these points is to say that the rose is in some measure a woman, and second, it is in some measure any person, male or female, here including the speaker.

The first point, that the rose is no ordinary rose, is evident from the fact that it is attacked by an "invisible worm/ That flies in the night" and that feels a "dark secret love" for the rose. Of course the worm might be invisible merely because it is concealed within the rose, and the "bed" of line 5 might simply be a flower bed, but other words, such as "joy" (line 6) and "love" (line 7) serve to bring the rose and the worm close to the human world. The flower bed thus suggests a bed of love, or rather (since the love is specifically said to be "dark" and "secret" and destructive) a bed of lust. The worm suggests the destructive male, partly because it is phallic, partly perhaps because the biblical tradition holds that the serpent in the garden is male, and mostly because the worm may reasonably be conceived of as different in sex from the flower, the rose being conventionally female.

Thus far the poem would seem, then, to be addressed to

a woman, or at least to a rose that partakes of human female characteristics. But repeated rereading suggests that the poet is not so much addressing something or someone in front of him, but is thinking aloud. Despite "O rose," he is in good measure addressing himself, meditating upon a fact of life. Beauty and love are destroyed in the "night" and "howling storm" by furtive lust ("dark secret love"). The first step beyond seeing the rose and worm as merely a rose and a worm is to see them as also a woman and a man; the next step is to see them as the beauty that anyone, regardless of gender, may have, and the destructiveness that is similarly beyond gender. Because the speaker is clearly so sympathetic to the object he addresses that he is virtually soliloquizing, it is reasonable to say that the speaker and his audience and his subject are one. He may reasonably be thought of as thinking about a process that is going on inside of himself, as well as about some external destruction of feminine beauty by male lust.

The previous sentences, with their abstractions, may seem far from the poem, and indeed their language and the language of the poem are utterly different. But the language of the poem sets up vibrations or emanations that may be legitimately pursued; to say that the poem starts with a rose and a worm and leads us back to the speaker and even to ourselves is scarcely an exaggeration.

This essay on symbolism is temperate, but essays on symbolism often have a way of seeming far-fetched to instructors, just as, perhaps, instructors' classroom references to symbolism may at first seem far-fetched to students. As a rough rule of thumb, beware of saying X equals, or symbolizes, Y, unless there are rather evident and insistent connections between X and Y. One reference to the darkness of night does not justify your talking about the night as symbolic of evil; one reference to water does not justify your talking about water as symbolic of life-giving forces. But a pattern of contrasting references to day and night, or to water versus an arid landscape, calls for such interpretations. As John Ciardi points out (p. 154), Frost's *repetition* of "miles to go before I sleep" forces us to give the words more than their usual significance, transforms "miles" and "sleep" into symbols. Remember, too, that although some things by their nature are likely to be symbolic of certain qualities (e.g., railroad trains of unfeeling industrialism, stars of spiritual or intellectual illumination, water of life), we should not respond automatically to these things as we do to red and green traffic lights. The poet shapes our responses, and an automatic response may preclude a more appropriate response. In Matthew Arnold's "To Marguerite — Continued," the sea plays an important role. The poem begins "Yes! in the sea of life enisled," and it ends with a reference to "The unplumbed, salt, estranging sea." In this poem Arnold conceives of men as islands, creatures tragically *separated* by water. The student who writes about the life-giving symbol of water in this poem ignores the fact that Arnold specifies that it estranges and is salty, that is, undrinkable. Such a reading will distort the poem more than a reading that sees the water only as water rather than emblematic of the gulfs (figurative language keeps slipping in, even in analysis) that separate men. Mary McCarthy's comments on symbolism in fiction (p. 60) are relevant here. Keep in mind the fact that in literature things *are*; they may also *represent*, but don't lose sight of what they are.

The arrangement of the parts, the manner of organization of the entire poem is its **structure**. Every poem has its own structure, but if we stand back from a given poem we may see that the structure is one of three common sorts: repetitive structure, narrative structure, or logical structure. **Repetitive structure** is especially common in lyrics that are sung, where a single state of mind is repeated from stanza to stanza so that the stanzas are pretty much interchangeable. As we read through "Auld Lang Syne," for instance, we get reaffirmation rather than progression. Here is a passage from Whitman's *By Blue Ontario's Shore* that similarly has a repetitive structure:

> I will confront these shows of the day and night,
> I will know if I am to be less than they,

I will see if I am not as majestic as they,
I will see if I am not as subtle and real as they,
I will see if I am to be less generous than they.

In a poem with a **narrative structure** (we are not talking about "narrative poems," poems that tell a story, such as *The Odyssey* or *The Rime of the Ancient Mariner*, but about a kind of lyric poem) there is a sense of advance. Blake's "The Sick Rose" (p. 128) is an example. What comes later in the poem could not come earlier. The poem seems to get somewhere, to settle down to an end. A lyric in which the speaker at first grieves and then derives some comfort from the thought that at least he was once in love similarly has a narrative structure. Here is a short but detailed examination by F. W. Bateson of a poem with narrative structure, Wordsworth's "A slumber did my spirit seal." Although "She" in line three is unnamed, it is customary to call her Lucy because that name is given in some other poems associated with this one in Wordsworth's *Lyrical Ballads*. The poem consists of two quatrains:

A slumber did my spirit seal;
    I had no human fears:
She seemed a thing that could not feel
    The touch of earthly years.

No motion has she now, no force;
    She neither hears nor sees;
Rolled round in earth's diurnal course,
    With rocks, and stones, and trees.

Bateson writes:

The structural basis of the poem is clearly the contrast between the two verses. Verse one deals with the past (there are no less than four verbs in a past tense — *did, had, seemed, could*). Lucy had been such a vital person that the possibility of her growing old or dying had not crossed Wordsworth's mind. Verse two concerns the present (in addition to the *now* in the first line there are three main verbs in the present tense — *has, hears, sees*). Lucy is dead. The invulnerable Ariel-like creature is now as lifeless and immobile as stocks and stones. And the contrast is emphasized by the repetition of *earth*: Lucy, who had seemed immune from the passage of *earthly years*, must now submit to *earth's diurnal course*. So far from escaping the *touch* of years she is now undergoing a daily contact with the earth. The use of the solemn Latinism *diurnal*, the only three-syllable word in this mainly monosyllabic poem, completes the contrast. But the final impression the poem leaves is not of two contrasting moods, but of a single mood mounting to a climax in the pantheistic magnificence of the last two lines. How then is the surface conflict reconciled? The metre certainly makes its contribution. The identity of the metrical pattern in the two verses — which is paralleled by the virtual identity of the word-order l. 5 repeats l. 1, abstract noun + verb + pronoun + abstract noun, l. 6 repeats l. 2, and l. 8 and l. 4 both have nouns but no verb) — suggests an underlying identity of mood. The gap between the two verses is also bridged by the negatives. There are no less than six negatives in the first six lines. Indeed, as the first line really means "I was not mentally awake," all the sentences are essentially negative propositions, until we reach the tremendous positive of the last two lines. Finally, the description of the living Lucy as a mere *thing* has prepared the transition to the dead Lucy who is passively *rolled*. The rhymes have no special significance, as far as I can see, but the alliterations should not be overlooked. The initial *s*'s in l. 1 do not seem to me of much interest (it is much the weakest line in the poem), though they may be intentional, but the *r*'s in ll. 7–8 are masterly. There are no less than three initial *r*'s and four internal *r*'s in the last twelve words,[1] and they provide a kind of cohesive cement to the lines. The implication is that the pantheistic universe is solidly *one*. The parallel lines in verse one are without alliteration, and its absence confirms the suggestion of fragility in the living Lucy (a *thing* who can only be described in negative terms).

[1] The *r*'s in *earth's diurnal course* are not sounded in modern English. Wordsworth, however, certainly sounded them. Hazlitt had found "a strong tincture of the northern *burr*" in his voice when they first met in 1798 (the year before "A slumber did my spirit seal" was written). See Hazlitt's "My First Acquaintance with Poets."

English Poetry (London, 1950), pp. 33–34

This essay comes from a chapter in which Mr. Bateson has been arguing for "the all-importance of meaning in poetry and the comparative insignificance of sound," hence perhaps his somewhat driving, or no-nonsense, manner.

The third kind of structure commonly found is **logical structure.** The speaker argues a case, and he comes to some sort of conclusion. Probably the most famous example of a poem that moves to a resolution through an argument is Andrew Marvell's "To His Coy Mistress." The speaker begins, "Had we but world enough, and time" (i.e., "if"), and for twenty lines he sets forth what he might do. At the twenty-first line he says, "But," and he indicates that the preceding twenty lines, in the subjunctive, are not a description of a real condition. The real condition (as he sees it) is that Time oppresses us, and he sets this idea forth in lines 21–32. In line 34 he begins his conclusion, "Now therefore," clinching it in line 45 with "Thus."

Here is another example of a poem with a logical structure.

John Donne
The Flea

Mark but this flea, and mark in this
How little that which thou deniest me is;
It sucked me first, and now sucks thee,
And in this flea our two bloods mingled be.
Thou knowest that this cannot be said   5
A sin, nor shame, nor loss of maidenhead;
    Yet this enjoys before it woo,
    And pampered swells with one blood made of two,
    And this, alas, is more than we would do.

O stay! Three lives in one flea spare,   10
Where we almost, yea, more than married are;
This flea is you and I, and this
Our marriage bed and marriage temple is.
Though parents grudge, and you, we're met
And cloistered in these living walls of jet.   15
    Though use make you apt to kill me,
    Let not to that, self-murder added be,
    And sacrilege, three sins in killing three.

Cruel and sudden! Hast thou since
Purpled thy nail in blood of innocence?   20
Wherein could this flea guilty be,
Except in that drop which it sucked from thee?
Yet thou triumph'st and saist that thou
Find'st not thyself, nor me, the weaker now.
    'Tis true. Then learn how false, fears be;   25
    Just so much honor, when thou yield'st to me,
    Will waste, as this flea's death took life from thee.

The speaker is a lover who begins by assuring his mistress that sexual intercourse is of no more serious consequence than a flea bite. Between the first and second stanzas the woman has apparently threatened to kill the flea, moving the lover to exclaim in line 10, "O stay! Three lives in one flea spare." In this second stanza he reverses his argument, now insisting on the importance of the flea, arguing that since it has bitten both man and woman it holds some of their lives as well as its own. Unpersuaded of its importance, the woman kills the flea between the second and third stanzas; and the speaker uses her action to reinforce his initial position, when he says, beginning in line 25, that the death of the flea has no serious consequences and her yielding to him will have no worse consequences.

Among the commonest devices in poems with logical structure (although this device is employed elsewhere too) is **verbal irony.** The speaker's words mean more or less the opposite of what they seem to say. Sometimes it takes the form of **understatement** (as when Andrew Marvell's speaker remarks with cautious wryness, "The grave's a fine and private place, / But none, I think, do there embrace"), sometimes the form of **overstatement,** or **hyperbole** (as when Donne's speaker says that in the flea he and the lady are "more than married"). Another common device in poems with a logical structure is **paradox:** the assertion of an apparent contradiction, as in "This flea is you and I." But again it must be emphasized that irony and paradox are not limited to poems with a logical structure. In "Auld Lang Syne," for instance, there is the paradox that the remembrance of joy evokes a kind of sadness, and there is understatement in "we've wandered mony a weary fitt," which stands (roughly) for something much bigger, such as "we have had many painful experiences." The student who wishes to see irony and paradox examined as structural principles should consult Cleanth Brooks's *The Well-Wrought Urn.*

CONCLUDING REMARKS ON WRITING ABOUT POETRY

A good essay is based on a genuine response to the poem; a response may in part be stimulated by considering the following questions. Exactly what sort of person is the speaker? (Is he fully aware of himself? Is he sentimental? Ironic? Does he joke in earnest?) Does the poem proceed in a straightforward way, or at some points does the poet reverse his course, altering his tone or perception? Do certain words have rich and relevant associations that relate to other words to help to define the theme? What is the role of the figurative language, if any? (Does it help to define the speaker or the theme? What is to be taken symbolically, and what literally?) What is the role of sound effects, including repetitions of sound and of entire words, and shifts in versification?

Writing about poetry may seem to be easier than writing about fiction or drama because most poems that the student encounters are fairly short. He can usually keep the entire work before his eyes, and he need not be endowed with an exceptional memory. But the brevity may be deceptive. Because most of us are not used to reading poetry, we overlook a good deal of its complexity. Prose (the point will be mentioned again) runs straight on, but poetry is always turning back on itself, complicating its pattern of sound and of meaning. Of course the prose of fiction is not the prose of a newspaper or of a history book; it too is not used merely as a vehicle to give information about something outside of itself; rather, as David Lodge indicates in his essay on *Hard Times,* word by word it builds its own world. (Another way of putting it: The words of newspapers and textbooks aim, or should aim, at being inconspicuous. They are a sort of window, or telescope, through which we see things, but generally we do not value them for themselves. We look beyond them. They are road signs, telling us where Boston is, or how to get to the expressway. But the words of a piece of literature, especially of a poem, are among the things we are looking at and looking for.) Still, fiction tells a story, and the story is a major part of its interest. We are not expected to dwell on each word in a story; the narrative line carries us forward. But in poetry we are supposed to delight in the words themselves or, better, in their combinations, as well as in the experience they point to. The poet assumes his readers will enjoy his virtuoso performance with words. Alexander Pope may not have been fully conscious of exactly what he was doing when he wrote "Die and endow a college or a cat," but he probably would have been delighted with F. W. Bateson's perceptive analysis (p. 120) of the line. (Quite likely Pope *was* fully conscious; the man who wrote the lines about Ajax and Camilla — see below, pp. 138–39 — cared about the minutest problems of poetry. In any case, as Robert Frost has said, the poet deserves credit for anything good that is found in the poem.) A poet exploits more fully than does the writer of fiction such devices as alliteration and rhythm; a substantial part of the meaning of his work resides in them. Frost touched on this matter when he defined poetry as "what gets lost in translation." Auden touched on it when he said that his ideal reader notices misprints.

This is not to say that poetry is all sound and no sense but only that the sound plays a larger part in making the sense than it does in expository prose and even in fiction. The so-called musical qualities of poetry are among the hardest to discuss, for two reasons: first, we are not much aware of these resources because few of us write poetry, and we therefore sometimes do not notice them; second, when we do notice them, we are likely to talk wildly about them. Once we have learned that there is such a thing as onomatopoeia (see p. 143), we may too quickly find the sound echoing the sense, even when it does not. About the only advice one can give is this: Read the poem over and over, aloud at least a couple of times, and try to hear as well as see what is going on. But once you have noticed things, don't believe them until further rereading convinces you that they are really there. Be especially cautious about large claims for the effect of the sound of a single word. But keep a shrewd eye (and ear) open for the effects of combinations of sounds, such as those pointed out in Pope. Here is the first stanza of Walter Savage Landor's "Past Ruined Ilion" followed by some perceptive comments by Monroe Beardsley on the combinations of sounds.

> Past ruined Ilion Helen lives,
>> Alcestis rises from the shades;

Verse calls them forth; 'tis verse that gives
    Immortal youth to mortal maids.

Beardsley says:

> The "n" sound in "ruined Ilion Helen" ties them together in a single catastrophe. The "v" of "verse" and the "f" of "forth" bring them together, suggesting that the statement "Verse calls them forth" is naturally true. "Maids" is given irony because its meaning contrasts with the meaning of the two words that are connected with it, "shades" by rhyme and "mortal" by alliteration. The sound-parallelism of "Immortal" and "mortal" reinforces the slight paradox of the claim that the youth of the maid will outlive the maid.
>
> *Aesthetics* (New York, 1958), pp. 236–37

For example, notice that Beardsley says that "the 'n' sound in 'ruined Ilion Helen' ties them together in a single catastrophe." He does *not* say that the "n" sound is catastrophic or that it is mournful. He notes combinations, relationships between words, and he also relies on the meanings of the words. He can speak of "a single catastrophe" because "ruined" *means* ruined. Ilion (Troy) is a vanished city, and Helen is long dead. He does not make extravagant claims for the inherent meaning of the "n" sound. But he has seen some connections, and he talks plausibly about them.

An explication or an analysis of a single poem will normally require some comment on the sound patterns, but not every essay on poetry need concern itself with such patterns. Good papers can be written on the development of an image or of a motif in a group of poems, for example, Frost's use of woods or stars, or Yeats's use of the legend of Helen of Troy. A paper that traces a recurrent image or motif may reveal a meaning, generated by a group of poems, that is barely perceptible in a single poem. The essayist who takes on such a job is the sort of reader Yeats had in mind when he wrote in one of his prefaces, "I must leave my myths and images to explain themselves as the years go by and one poem lights up another." But whatever the topic and the approach, the essayist's goal is to illuminate.

RHYTHM AND VERSIFICATION: A GLOSSARY

Rhythm (most simply, in English poetry, stresses at regular intervals) has a power of its own. A highly pronounced rhythm is common in such forms of poetry as charms, college yells, and lullabies; all of them are aimed at inducing a special effect magically. It is not surprising that *carmen*, the Latin word for verse or song, is also the Latin word for charm and the word from which "charm" is derived.

In much poetry rhythm is only half-heard, but its omnipresence is suggested by the fact that when poetry is printed it is customary to begin each line with a capital letter. Prose (from Latin *prorsus*, "forward," "straight on") keeps running across the paper until the right-hand margin is reached, and then, merely because the paper has given out, the writer or printer starts again at the left, with a small letter. But verse (Latin *versus*, "a turning") often ends well short of the right-hand margin, and the next line begins at the left— usually with a capital — not because paper has run out but because the rhythmic pattern begins again. Lines of poetry are continually reminding us that they have a pattern.

A word of caution: A mechanical, unvarying rhythm may be good to put the baby to sleep, but it can be deadly to readers who wish to keep awake. A poet varies his rhythm according to his purpose; he ought not to be so regular that he is (in W. H. Auden's words) an "accentual pest." In competent hands, rhythm contributes to meaning; it says something. Ezra Pound has a relevant comment: "Rhythm *must* have meaning. It can't be merely a careless dash off, with no grip and no real hold to the words and sense, a tumty tum tumty tum tum ta." Consider this description of Hell from *Paradise Lost* (stressed syllables are marked by /; unstressed syllables by ⌣):

> Rócks, cáves, lákes, féns, bógs, déns, aňd shádes ǒf deáth.

Milton immediately follows one heavy stress with another (in contrast to the iambic feet — alternating unstressed and stressed syllables — that are the norm in the poem), helping to communicate the "meaning" — the oppressive monotony of Hell. As a second example, consider the function of the rhythm in two lines by Alexander Pope:

> Wȟen Ájax stríves sǒme róck's vást weíght tǒ thrów,
>
> Tȟe líne tóo lábǒrs, aňd tȟe wórds móve slów.

The stressed syllables do not merely alternate with the unstressed ones; rather, the great weight of the rock is suggested by three consecutive stressed words, "rock's vast weight," and the great effort involved in moving it is suggested by another three consecutive stresses, "line too labors," and by yet another three, "words move slow." Note, also, the abundant pauses within the lines. In the first line, for example, unless one's speech is slovenly, one must pause at least slightly after "Ajax," "strives," "rock's," "vast," "weight," and "throw." The grating sounds in "Ajax" and "rock's" do their work, too, and so do the explosive *t*'s. When Pope wishes to suggest lightness, he reverses his procedure, and he groups *un*stressed syllables:

Not so, when swift Camilla scours the plain,

Flíes o'er th' unbénding córn, and skíms alóng the máin.

This last line has twelve syllables, and is thus longer than the line about Ajax, but the addition of "along" helps to communicate lightness and swiftness because in this line (it can be argued) neither syllable of "along" is strongly stressed. If "along" is omitted, the line still makes grammatical sense and becomes more "regular," but it also becomes less imitative of lightness.

The very regularity of a line may be meaningful too. Shakespeare begins a sonnet thus:

When Í do cóunt the clóck that télls the tíme.

This line about a mechanism runs with appropriate regularity. (It is worth noting, too, that "count the clock" and "tells the time" emphasize the regularity by the repetition of sounds and syntax.) But notice what Shakespeare does in the middle of the next line:

And sée the bráve dáy súnk in hídeous níght.

The technical vocabulary of **prosody** (the study of the principles of verse structure, including meter, rhyme, and other sound effects, and stanzaic patterns) is large. An understanding of these terms will not turn anyone into a poet, but it will enable one to discuss some aspects of poetry more efficiently. The following are the chief terms of prosody.

Most English poetry has a pattern of **stressed (accented)** sounds, and this pattern is the **meter** (from the Greek word for "measure"). Although in Old English poetry (poetry written in England before the Norman-French Conquest in 1066) a line may have any number of unstressed syllables in addition to four stressed syllables, most poetry written in England since the Conquest not only has a fixed number of stresses in a line but also a fixed number of unstressed syllables before or after each stressed one. (One really ought not to talk of "unstressed" or "unaccented" syllables, since to utter a syllable — however lightly — is to give it some stress. But the fact is that "unstressed" or "unaccented" are parts of the established terminology of versification.)

In a line of poetry the **foot** is the basic unit of measurement. It is on rare occasions a single stressed syllable; but generally a foot consists of two or three syllables, one of which is stressed. The repetition of feet, then, produces a pattern of stresses throughout the poem.

Two cautions:

1. A poem will seldom contain only one kind of foot throughout; significant variations usually occur, but one kind of foot is dominant.

2. In reading a poem, one pays attention to the sense as well as to the metrical pattern. By paying attention to the sense, one often finds that the stress falls on a word that according to the metrical pattern would be unstressed. Or a word that according to the pattern would be stressed may be seen to be unstressed. Furthermore, by reading for sense one finds that not all stresses are equally heavy; some are almost as light as unstressed syllables, and sometimes there is a **hovering stress,** that is, the stress is equally distributed over two adjacent syllables. To repeat: One reads for sense, allowing the syntax to help indicate the stresses.

The most common feet in English poetry are:

iamb (adjective: **iambic**): one unstressed syllable followed by one stressed syllable. The iamb, said to be the most common pattern in English speech, is surely the most common in English poetry. It is called a **rising meter,** the foot rising toward the stress. The following example has five iambic feet:

˘ ΄ I saw | ˘ ΄ the sky | ˘ ΄ descend | ˘ ΄ ing black | ˘ ΄ and white.   (Robert Lowell)

trochee (trochaic): one stressed syllable followed by one unstressed; a **falling meter,** the foot falling away from the stress.

΄ ˘ Let her | ΄ ˘ live to | ΄ ˘ earn her | ΄ ˘ dinners.   (J. M. Synge)

anapest (anapestic): two unstressed syllables followed by one stressed; a rising meter.

˘ ˘ ΄ There are man | ˘ ˘ ΄ y who say | ˘ ˘ ΄ that a dog | ˘ ˘ ΄ has his day.
(Dylan Thomas)

dactyl (dactylic): one stressed syllable followed by two unstressed; a falling meter. This trisyllabic foot is common in light verse or verse suggesting joy, but its use is not limited to such material, as Longfellow's *Evangeline* shows. Thomas Hood's sentimental "The Bridge of Sighs" begins:

΄ ˘ ˘ Take her up | ΄ ˘ ˘ tenderly.

spondee (spondaic): two stressed syllables; most often used as a substitute for an iamb or trochee; it neither rises nor falls.

Smárt lád, | to slíp | betimes | awáy.   (A. E. Housman)

Because the **pyrrhic** foot (two unstressed syllables) lacks a stress, it is often not considered a legitimate foot in English.

A metrical line consists of one or more feet and is named for the number of feet in it. The following names are used:

monometer:	one foot	**pentameter:**	five feet
dimeter:	two feet	**hexameter:**	six feet
trimeter:	three feet	**heptameter:**	seven feet
tetrameter:	four feet	**octameter:**	eight feet

A line is scanned for the kind and number of feet in it, and the **scansion** tells you if it is, say, anapestic trimeter (three anapests):

As I came | to the edge | of the woods.   (Frost)

Another example, this time iambic pentameter:

Since brass, nor stone, nor earth, nor boundless sea.

(Shakespeare)

A line ending with a stress has a **masculine ending**; a line ending with an extra unstressed syllable has a **feminine ending.** The lines above by Synge and Hood have feminine endings; those by Lowell, Thomas, Housman, Frost, and Shakespeare have masculine endings. The **caesura** (usually indicated by the symbol //) is a slight pause within the line. It need not be indicated by punctuation, and it does not affect the metrical count:

Awake, my St. John! // leave all meaner things
To low ambition, // and the pride of kings.
Let us // (since Life can little more supply
Than just to look about us // and to die)
Expatiate free // o'er all this scene of Man;
A mighty maze! // but not without a plan;
A wild, // where weeds and flowers promiscuous shoot;
Or garden, // tempting with forbidden fruit.   (Pope)

The varying position of the caesura helps to give Pope's lines an informality that plays against the formality of the pairs of rhyming lines.

An **end-stopped line** concludes with a distinct syntactical pause, but a **run-on line** has its sense carried over into the next line without syntactical pause. (The running-on of a line is called **enjambment**.) In the following passage, only the first is a run-on line:

> Yet if we look more closely we shall find
> Most have the seeds of judgment in their mind:
> Nature affords at least a glimmering light;
> The lines, though touched but faintly, are drawn right.   (Pope)

Meter produces **rhythm,** recurrences at equal intervals, but rhythm (from a Greek word meaning "flow") is usually applied to larger units than feet. Often it depends most obviously on pauses. Thus, a poem with run-on lines will have a different rhythm from a poem with end-stopped lines, even though both are in the same meter. And prose, though it is unmetrical, can thus have rhythm, too. In addition to being affected by syntactical pause, rhythm is affected by pauses due to consonant clusters and the length of words. Polysyllabic words establish a different rhythm from monosyllabic words, even in metrically identical lines. One can say, then, that rhythm is altered by shifts in meter, syntax, and the length and ease of pronunciation. But even with no such shift, even if a line is repeated verbatim, a reader may sense a change in rhythm. The rhythm of the final line of a poem, for example, may well differ from that of the line before, even though in all other respects the lines are identical, as in Frost's "Stopping by Woods on a Snowy Evening," which concludes by repeating "And miles to go before I sleep." One may simply sense that this final line ought to be spoken, say, more slowly and with more stress on "miles."

Though rhythm is basic to poetry, **rhyme** is not. Rhyme is the repetition of the identical or similar stressed sound or sounds. It is, presumably, pleasant in itself; it suggests order; and it also may be related to meaning, for it brings two words sharply together, often implying a relationship, as Pope's "throne" and "alone." **Perfect** or **exact rhymes** occur when differing consonant-sounds are followed by identical stressed vowel-sounds, and the following sounds, if any, are identical (foe : toe; meet : fleet; buffer : rougher). Note that perfect rhyme involves identity of sound, not of spelling. "Fix" and "sticks," like "buffer" and "rougher," are perfect rhymes.

In **half-rhyme** (or **slant-rhyme, approximate-rhyme, near-rhyme, off-rhyme**), only the final consonant-sounds of the rhyming words are identical; the stressed vowel-sounds as well as the initial consonant-sounds, if any, differ (soul : oil; mirth : forth; trolley : bully). **Eye-rhyme** is not really rhyme; it merely looks like rhyme (cough : bough : rough). In **masculine rhyme** the final syllables are stressed and, after their differing initial consonant-sounds, are identical in sound (stark :

mark; support : retort). In **feminine rhyme** (or **double-rhyme**) stressed rhyming syllables are followed by identical unstressed syllables (revival : arrival; flatter : batter). **Triple-rhyme** is a kind of feminine rhyme in which identical stressed vowel-sounds are followed by two identical unstressed syllables (machinery : scenery; tenderly : slenderly). **End-rhyme** (or **terminal-rhyme**) has the rhyming word at the end of the line. **Internal rhyme** has at least one of the rhyming words within the line (Wilde's "Each narrow *cell* in which we *dwell*").

Alliteration is sometimes defined as the repetition of initial sounds ("All the *aw*ful *au*guaries" or "*B*ring me my *b*ow of *b*urning gold"), sometimes as the prominent repetition of a consonant ("a*f*ter li*f*e's *f*itful *f*ever"). **Assonance** is the repetition, in words in proximity, of identical vowel-sounds preceded and followed by differing consonant-sounds. Whereas "tide" and "hide" are rhymes, "tide" and "mine" are assonantal. **Consonance** is the repetition of identical consonant-sounds and differing vowel-sounds in words in proximity (fail : feel; rough : roof; pitter : patter). Sometimes consonance is more loosely defined merely as the repetition of a consonant (fai*l* : pee*l*). **Onomatopoeia** is said to occur when the sound of a word echoes or suggests the meaning of a word. "Hiss" and "buzz" are onomatopoetic. There is a mistaken tendency to see onomatopoeia everywhere, for example, in "thunder" and "horror." Many words sometimes thought to be onomatopoetic are not clearly imitative of the thing they denote; they merely contain some sounds which — when we know what the word means — seem to have some resemblance to the thing they denote. Tennyson's lines from "Come down, O maid" are usually cited as an example of onomatopoeia:

> The moan of doves in immemorial elms
> And murmuring of innumerable bees.

Lines of poetry are commonly arranged in a rhythmical unit called a **stanza** (from an Italian word meaning a "room" or "stopping-place"). Usually all the stanzas in a poem have the same rhyme pattern. A stanza is sometimes called a **verse**, though "verse" may also mean a single line of poetry. (In discussing stanzas, rhymes are indicated by identical letters. Thus, *abab* indicates that the first and third lines rhyme with each other, while the second and fourth lines are linked by a different rhyme. An unrhymed line is denoted by x.) Common stanzaic forms in English poetry are the following:

couplet: stanza of two lines, usually, but not necessarily, with end-rhymes. "Couplet" is also used for a pair of rhyming lines. The **octosyllabic couplet** is iambic or trochaic tetrameter:

> Had we but world enough, and time,
> This coyness, lady, were no crime.   (Marvell)

heroic couplet: a rhyming couplet of iambic pentameter, often "closed," that is, containing a complete thought, with a fairly heavy pause at the end of the first line and a still heavier one at the end of the second. Commonly, there is a parallel or an antithesis within a line, or between the two lines. It is called heroic because in England, especially in the eighteenth century, it was much used for heroic (epic) poems.

> Some foreign writers, some our own despise;
> The ancients only, or the moderns, prize.   (Pope)

triplet (or **tercet**): a three-line stanza, usually with one rhyme.

> Whenas in silks my Julia goes
> Then, then (methinks) how sweetly flows
> That liquefaction of her clothes.   (Herrick)

quatrain: a four-line stanza, rhymed or unrhymed. The **heroic** (or **elegiac**) **quatrain** is iambic pentameter, rhyming *abab*. The **ballad stanza** is a quatrain alternating iambic tetrameter with iambic trimeter lines, usually rhyming *xaxa*. Sometimes it is followed by a **refrain,** a line or lines repeated several times.

sonnet: a fourteen-line poem, predominantly in iambic pentameter. The rhyme is usually according to one of the two following schemes. The **Italian** (or **Petrarchan**) **sonnet** has two divisions: the first eight lines (rhyming *abba abba*) are the **octave,** the last six (rhyming *cd cd cd*, or a variant) are the **sestet.** Keats's "On First Looking into Chapman's Homer" (p. 124) is an Italian sonnet. The second kind of sonnet, the **English** (or **Shakespearean**) **sonnet,** is usually arranged into three quatrains and a couplet, rhyming *abab cdcd efef gg*. In many sonnets there is a marked correspondence between the rhyme scheme and the development of the thought. Thus an Italian sonnet may state a generalization in the octave and a specific example in the sestet. Or an English sonnet may give three examples — one in each quatrain — and draw a conclusion in the couplet.

A good deal of English poetry is unrhymed, much of it in **blank verse,** that is, unrhymed iambic pentameter. Introduced into English poetry by Surrey in the middle of the sixteenth century, late in the century it became the standard medium (especially in the hands of Marlowe and Shakespeare) of English drama. In the seventeenth century, Milton used it for *Paradise Lost,* and it has continued to be used in both dramatic and nondramatic literature. For an example see the passage from Milton on page 120. A passage of blank verse that has a rhetorical unity is sometimes called a **verse paragraph.**

The second kind of unrhymed poetry fairly common in English, especially in the twentieth century, is **free verse** (or ***vers libre***): rhythmical lines varying in length, adhering to no fixed metrical pattern and usually unrhymed. The pattern is often largely based on repetition and parallel grammatical structure. Though such a form may appear unrestrained, as T. S. Eliot (a practitioner) has said, "No *vers* is *libre* for the man who wants to do a good job." For a sample of free verse, see the passage from Whitman on page 132.

Sample Essays

Each of these two essays on poetry looks closely at a short poem. Mark Van Doren, after an awkward start ("is *not* . . . *not* . . . *un-*. . . . Perhaps no *p*oem is *p*erfect . . . *p*erhaps . . . a*pp*earance . . . *p*erfection . . . sus*p*icious a*pp*earance . . . *p*oem . . . *p*ut" — all this within two sentences), seeks to demonstrate that "the poem as a whole is fine, but . . . [it] goes steadily downhill." After an initial paragraph on the origin of the poem and a second paragraph on the motif of solitude, he moves forward stanza by stanza. Part of the excellence of this essay is in the judicious balancing of praise and blame. It is easy to write an attack but hard to keep the reader from wondering why you are bothering to write about something you dislike, and it is hard to avoid sounding supercilious. Van Doren, even while commenting adversely, keeps us aware of his respect for the work; he never allows us to think that he believes he is superior to the thing he is discussing. John Ciardi, with a vigor and a breeziness that come from having established himself as a poet and a critic, examines Robert Frost's "Stopping by Woods on a Snowy Evening." Ciardi's essay, as he points out at the start, is about poetry; and his remarks about Frost's poem are offered in the course of making the point that poetry is "duplicity." Reasonably, then, after he finishes his discussion of "Stopping by Woods," he returns, in his last paragraph, to some discussion of "every truly good poem."

Mark Van Doren
Wordsworth's "The Solitary Reaper"*

William Wordsworth

The Solitary Reaper

Behold her, single in the field,
    Yon solitary Highland lass!

* The title of this essay is the editor's.

Reaping and singing by herself;
    Stop here, or gently pass! 4
Alone she cuts and binds the grain,
And sings a melancholy strain;
O listen! for the vale profound
Is overflowing with the sound. 8

No nightingale did ever chaunt
    More welcome notes to weary bands
Of travelers in some shady haunt,
    Among Arabian sands: 12
A voice so thrilling ne'er was heard
In spring-time from the cuckoo-bird,
Breaking the silence of the seas
Among the farthest Hebrides. 16

Will no one tell me what she sings? —
    Perhaps the plaintive numbers flow
For old, unhappy, far-off things,
    And battles long ago: 20
Or is it some more humble lay,
Familiar matter of today?
Some natural sorrow, loss, or pain,
That has been, and may be again? 24

Whate'er the theme, the maiden sang
    As if her song could have no ending;
I saw her singing at her work,
    And o'er the sickle bending; — 28
I listened, motionless and still;
And, as I mounted up the hill,
The music in my heart I bore,
Long after it was heard no more. 32

The fact that this poem is not equally good in all of its parts does not mean that it is unadmirable. Perhaps no poem is perfect or could be; and perhaps an appearance of perfection is the most suspicious appearance a poem can put up. At any rate, here is a famous poem that deserves its fame, and yet each stanza is inferior to the one before it. The first, which is the best, has none before it, and in fact contains or expresses the whole of the impulse that was moving Wordsworth as he wrote. Not as he saw this Highland girl, for he never saw her. He read about her in a prose book of travels, Thomas Wilkinson's *Tour in Scotland*. Wilkinson saw the solitary lass, and wrote a sentence about her which made Wordsworth in effect see her too — made him, that is, see her as a poet. Many great poems have come thus out of books: most commonly, out of prose books. Prose discovers the matter and leaves it clear; after which the poet has only to write his poem as if the matter of it were his own, as indeed it comes to be.

Wordsworth is most deeply interested in the fact that this girl in his mind's eye inhabits a solitude. . . . There are many solitudes, and the present one is Wordsworth's own of which he always wrote so well. He puts the reaper into it and makes her belong there, a figure undefined except by the fact that she stands alone in a world which has no content other than her thought and feeling. Her mood at the moment is melancholy in the sweet way that Wordsworth understood so well. Good and healthy persons, in harmony with their surroundings, are both sad and happy there. They do not comprehend their universe as it weighs upon them, but they love it and can therefore bear its weight — gravely, because it is so huge and old, but joyfully too because they feel their strength as they do so.

The first eight lines say all that Wordsworth really has to say about this, and about the girl who is his symbol. "Behold her, single in the field." She is single; she is solitary; she is by herself; she is alone — we are told four times, in five lines, that this is true, as if nothing else matters, and nothing does for Wordsworth. Also, she is singing. She is a peasant girl, and she is singing as her kind is disposed to do, sadly, sweetly, and powerfully to herself. The folk knows, if civilized men do not, how the weight of the world is borne by those whose turn has come to be alive in it. Such is Wordsworth's deepest conviction as in his imagination he watches the girl. The eight lines put her clearly before us, bending gracefully as she sings some song of which he says only that it is melancholy, and that it is loud enough to fill a whole valley.

> O listen! for the vale profound
> Is overflowing with the sound.

If these are the best lines in the poem, the reason is their mysterious power to create the thing they mention. The deep valley fills with music as we listen; and overflows. This is partly a matter of onomatopoeia in the lines themselves, and partly a matter of their rhythmical relation to the six lines above. The eight-line stanza Wordsworth has decided to use — perhaps he is deciding only now — consists of a quatrain and two couplets. To point this out is not to explain the force we feel in the series as Wordsworth manages it. Few poems have begun more happily, or so rapidly achieved so much momentum. The initial quatrain, tetrameter except for its short fourth line which so sensibly halts us for a scrutiny of the thing, the person to be seen — the girl herself, bending down and rising up, reaping and soliloquizing — is followed, once we have checked our progress and stopped to gaze, by two melodious pairs of lines whose rhymes flow into one another as if by magic, producing in us a lively sense of the music which takes its rise in the maiden, fills the valley around her, keeps on filling it, and overflows. The two couplets are in a sense one sound, drawn out indefinitely and continuing in our ears, so that the remainder of the poem, no matter what it may say, will be assured of an accompaniment, a ground harmony, a remembered song that hums in the mind long after its occasion has ceased.

Having done this much — and it was a great thing to do — Wordsworth henceforth is reduced to conscious reflection upon his subject. The reflections are fine and the poem as a whole is fine, but nothing in it, not even the second stanza, quite matches that opening section in which the subject was created — all at once created, by no effort that could be observed, and by no means that we may be altogether sure of naming rightly.

The first reflection takes the form of a comparison. The song we heard was beautiful and strong; there is no doubt of that; but Wordsworth must suspect us of doubt, or he would not tell us how much better it was than something else. Than the voice of the Arabian nightingale; or the voice of the cuckoo in spring, among the farthest Hebrides. South or north, he insists, there is nothing to compare; and yet the comparison proceeds. The fact that it is a double comparison does not help to justify it. The girl's song is said to be more exciting than either of two distant sounds; and we believe this, yet are left thinking of those distant sounds, which replace hers. The second of them in particular is rendered with genius. The two compound words in line 14, "spring-time" and "cuckoo-bird," reinforce each other so freshly that one of them seems to spring out of the other as a rocket springs out of itself, bounding off with redoubled speed and joy. In two strokes of its wings the line mounts high and flies away, taking us with it to remote and moveless seas which nevertheless tremble when this sound arrives. "Breaking" is the word. It creates the very silence it shatters, softly and far away.

The stanza is noble, yet less so than the one that rendered it unnecessary. And the rest of the poem goes steadily downhill. The third stanza is of all things a rhetorical question, or worse yet, a pair of them. "Will no one tell me what she sings?" Certainly no one will, for Wordsworth is the authority. He does not understand these Highland words, or the girl is too far away for them to be heard, but that is no matter. The net meaning of the song is his to know if anybody is to know it, and he should not be asking for assistance. Lines 18–20 are agreeably suggestive of a romantic burden which the words may bear; and as such they are preferable to the couplets (21–24) he dutifully writes because he remembers his own theory that great poetry comes out of familiar and domestic things as well as out of battles long ago; it is not a useful theory at the moment, but he jogs on through it, finishing the stanza at last. He has long since lost contact with his subject in its purity. The quatrain of this stanza was intrinsically better than its couplets; but it was in the quatrain that he strayed away, farther even than he had gone in the magnificent stanza about the sands of Arabia and the Hebridean seas.

The last stanza recovers a fragment of the magic that is gone, but only a fragment. "Whate'er the theme" — it begins prosaically, still reflecting upon a very unimportant topic. It moves then into a series of lines whose function is to fix in us a sense of the song's immortality. We had that sense at the end of the first stanza, and noted it then. There is no object to our being reminded of it at the end of the poem — the poem, Wordsworth seems to be saying, will end but the song will not — and yet there is little chance that we shall be excited by learning something we already know. Wordsworth throws his discourse into the past tense — "I saw her," "I listened" — but this is a mere device of syntax. "I listened, motionless and still." That is better, for it suspends both him and us in a state of listening where it is possible to lose ourselves. This had been, however, our original state, which the second and third stanzas interrupted; and perhaps it is not available to us again. Indeed it is not, or to Wordsworth either, judging by the pious assurance he gives us in the last three lines that he will not forget an unforgettable experience. The experience, in fact, is dead; though we can always revive it by returning and rereading stanza one. That is the contribution of the poem, and it alone makes the entire work admirable.

JOHN CIARDI

Robert Frost: The Way to the Poem

ROBERT FROST

Stopping by Woods on a Snowy Evening

Whose woods these are I think I know.
His house is in the village though;
He will not see me stopping here
To watch his woods fill up with snow.   4

My little horse must think it queer
To stop without a farmhouse near
Between the wood and frozen lake
The darkest evening of the year.   8

He gives his harness bells a shake
To ask if there is some mistake.
The only other sound's the sweep
Of easy wind and downy flake.   12

The woods are lovely, dark and deep.
But I have promises to keep,
And miles to go before I sleep,
And miles to go before I sleep.   16

The School System has much to say these days of the virtue of reading widely, and not enough about the virtues of reading less but in
depth. There are any number of reading lists for poetry, but there is
not enough talk about individual poems. Poetry, finally, is one poem
at a time. To read any one poem carefully is the ideal preparation for
reading another. Only a poem can illustrate how poetry works.

Above, therefore, is a poem — one of the master lyrics of the
English language, and almost certainly the best-known poem by an
American poet. What happens in it? — which is to say, not *what* does
it mean, but *how* does it mean? How does it go about being a human
re-enactment of a human experience? The author — perhaps the thou-
sandth reader would need to be told — is Robert Frost.

Even the TV audience can see that this poem begins as a seemingly simple narration of a seemingly simple incident but ends by
suggesting meanings far beyond anything specifically referred to in
the narrative. And even readers with only the most casual interest in
poetry might be made to note the additional fact that, though the
poem suggests those larger meanings, it is very careful never to abandon
its pretense to being simply narration. There is duplicity at work. The
poet pretends to be talking about one thing, and all the while he is
talking about many others.

Many readers are forever unable to accept the poet's essential
duplicity. It is almost safe to say that a poem is never about what it
seems to be about. As much could be said of the proverb. The bird
in the hand, the rolling stone, the stitch in time never (except by
an artful double deception) intend any sort of statement about birds,
stones, or sewing. The incident of this poem, one must conclude, is
at root a metaphor.

Duplicity aside, this poem's movement from the specific to the
general illustrates one of the basic formulas of all poetry. Such a
grand poem as Arnold's "Dover Beach" and such lesser, though unfortunately better-known, poems is Longfellow's "Village Blacksmith"
and Holmes's "Chambered Nautilus" are built on the same progression. In these three poems, however, the generalization is markedly
set apart from the specific narration, and even seems additional to

the telling rather than intrinsic to it. It is this sense of division one has in mind in speaking of "a tacked-on moral."

There is nothing wrong-in-itself with a tacked-on moral. Frost, in fact, makes excellent use of the device at times. In this poem, however, Frost is careful to let the whatever-the-moral-is grow out of the poem itself. When the action ends the poem ends. There is no epilogue and no explanation. Everything pretends to be about the narrated incident. And that pretense sets the basic tone of the poem's performance of itself.

The dramatic force of that performance is best observable, I believe, as a progression in three scenes.

In scene one, which coincides with stanza one, a man — a New England man — is driving his sleigh somewhere at night. It is snowing, and as the man passes a dark patch of woods he stops to watch the snow descend into the darkness. We know, moreover, that the man is familiar with these parts (he knows who owns the woods and where the owner lives), and we know that no one has seen him stop. As scene one forms itself in the theatre of the mind's-eye, therefore, it serves to establish some as yet unspecified relation between the man and the woods.

It is necessary, however, to stop here for a long parenthesis: Even so simple an opening statement raises any number of questions. It is impossible to address all the questions that rise from the poem stanza by stanza, but two that arise from stanza one illustrate the sort of thing one might well ask of the poem detail by detail.

Why, for example, does the man not say what errand he is on? What is the force of leaving the errand generalized? He might just as well have told us that he was going to the general store, or returning from it with a jug of molasses he had promised to bring Aunt Harriet and two suits of long underwear he had promised to bring the hired man. Frost, moreover, can handle homely detail to great effect. He preferred to leave his motive generalized. Why?

And why, on the other hand, does he say so much about knowing the absent owner of the woods and where he lives? Is it simply that one set of details happened in whereas another did not? To speak of things "happening in" is to assault the integrity of a poem. Poetry cannot be discussed meaningfully unless one can assume that everything in the poem — every last comma and variant spelling — is in it by the poet's specific act of choice. Only bad poets allow into their poems what is haphazard or cheaply chosen.

The errand, I will venture a bit brashly for lack of space, is left generalized in order the more aptly to suggest *any* errand in life and, therefore, life itself. The owner is there because he is one of the forces of the poem. Let it do to say that the force he represents is the village of mankind (that village at the edge of winter) from which the poet finds himself separated (has separated himself?) in his moment by the woods (and to which, he recalls finally, he has promises to keep). The owner is he-who-lives-in-his-village-house, thereby locked away from the poet's awareness of the-time-the-snow-tells as it engulfs and obliterates the world the village man allows himself to believe he "owns." Thus, the owner is a representative of an order of reality from which the poet has divided himself for the moment, though to a certain extent he ends by reuniting with it. Scene one, therefore, establishes not only a relation between the man and the woods, but the fact that the man's relation begins with his separation (though momentarily) from mankind.

End parenthesis one, begin parenthesis two.

Still considering the first scene as a kind of dramatic performance of forces, one must note that the poet has meticulously matched the simplicity of his language to the pretended simplicity of the narrative. Clearly, the man stopped because the beauty of the scene moved him, but he neither tells us that the scene is beautiful nor that he is moved. A bad writer, always ready to overdo, might have written: "The vastness gripped me, filling my spirit with the slow steady sinking of the snow's crystalline perfection into the glimmerless profundities of the hushed primeval wood." Frost's avoidance of such a spate illustrates two principles of good writing. The first, he has stated himself in "The Mowing": "Anything *more* than the truth would have seemed too weak" (italics mine). Understatement is one of the basic sources of power in English poetry. The second principle is to let the action speak for itself. A good novelist does not tell us that a given character is good or bad (at least not since the passing of the Dickens tradition): he shows us the character in action, and then, watching him, we know. Poetry, too, has fictional obligations: even when the characters are ideas and metaphors rather than people, they must be *characterized in action*. A poem does not *talk about* ideas; it *enacts* them. The force of the poem's performance, in fact, is precisely to act out (and thereby to make us act out emphatically, that is, to *feel out*, that is, *to identify with*) the speaker and why he stopped. The man is the principal actor in this little "drama of why," and in scene one he is the only character, though, as noted, he is somehow related to the absent owner.

End second parenthesis.

In scene two (stanzas two and three) a *foil* is introduced. In fiction and drama, a foil is a character who "plays against" a more important character. By presenting a different point of view or an opposed set of motives, the foil moves the more important character to react in ways that might not have found expression without such opposition. The more important character is thus more fully revealed — to the reader and to himself. The foil here is the horse.

The horse forces the question. Why did the man stop? Until it occurs to him that his "little horse must think it queer" he had not asked himself for reasons. He had simply stopped. But the man finds himself faced with the question he imagines the horse to be asking: what *is* there to stop for out there in the cold, away from bin and stall (house and village and mankind?) and all that any self-respecting beast could value on such a night? In sensing that other view, the man is forced to examine his own more deeply.

In stanza two the question arises only as a feeling within the man. In stanza three, however (still scene two), the horse acts. He gives his harness bells a shake. "What's wrong?" he seems to say. "What are we waiting for?"

By now, obviously, the horse — without losing its identity as horse — has also become a symbol. A symbol is something that stands for something else. Whatever that something else may be, it certainly begins as that order of life that does not understand why a man stops in the wintry middle of nowhere to watch the snow come down. (Can one fail to sense by now that the dark and the snowfall symbolize a death wish, however momentary, i.e., that hunger for final rest and surrender that a man may feel, but not a beast?)

So by the end of scene two the performance has given dramatic force to three elements that work upon the man. There is his relation to the world of the owner. There is his relation to the brute world of the horse. And there is also that third presence of the unownable world, the movement of the all-engulfing snow across all the orders of life, the man's, the owners, and the horse's — with the difference that the man knows of that second dark-within-the-dark of which the horse cannot, and the owner will not, know.

The man ends scene two with all these forces working upon him simultaneously. He feels himself moved to a decision. And he feels a last call from the darkness: "the sweep / Of easy wind and downy flake." It would be so easy and so downy to go into the woods and let himself be covered over.

But scene three (stanza four) produces a fourth force. This fourth force can be given many names. It is certainly better, in fact, to give it many names than to attempt to limit it to one. It is social obligation, or personal commitment, or duty, or just the realization that a man cannot indulge a mood forever. All of these and more. But, finally, he has a simple decision to make. He may go into the woods and let the darkness and the snow swallow him from the world of beast and man. Or he must move on. And unless he is going to stop here forever, it is time to remember that he has a long way to go and that he had best be getting there. (So there is something to be said for the horse, too.)

Then and only then, his question driven more and more deeply into himself by these cross-forces, does the man venture a comment on what attracted him: "The woods are lovely, dark and deep." His mood lingers over the thought of that lovely dark-and-deep (as do the very syllables in which he phrases the thought), but the final decision is to put off the mood and move on. He has his man's way to go and his man's obligations to tend to before he can yield. He has miles to go before his sleep. He repeats that thought and the performance ends.

But why the repetition? The first time Frost says "And miles to go before I sleep," there can be little doubt that the primary meaning is: "I have a long way to go before I get to bed tonight." The second time he says it, however, "miles to go" and "sleep" are suddenly transformed into symbols. What are those "something-elses" the symbols stand for? Hundreds of people have tried to ask Mr. Frost that question and he has always turned it away. He has turned it away *because he cannot answer it.* He could answer some part of it. But some part is not enough.

For a symbol is like a rock dropped into a pool: it sends out ripples in all directions, and the ripples are in motion. Who can say where the last ripple disappears? One may have a sense that he knows the approximate center point of the ripples, the point at which the stone struck the water. Yet even then he has trouble marking it surely. How does one make a mark on water? Oh very well — the center point of that second "miles to go" is probably approximately in the neighborhood of being close to meaning, perhaps, "the road of life"; and the second "before I sleep" is maybe that close to meaning "before I take my final rest," the rest in darkness that seemed so temptingly dark-and-deep for the moment of the mood. But the ripples continue to move and the light to change on the water, and the longer one watches the more changes he sees. Such shifting-and-being-at-the-same-instant is of the very sparkle and life of poetry. One experiences it as one experiences life, for every time he looks at an experience he sees something new, and he sees it change as he watches it. And that sense of continuity in fluidity is one of the primary kinds of knowledge, one of man's basic ways of knowing, and one that only the arts can teach, poetry foremost among them.

Frost himself certainly did not ask what that repeated last line meant. It came to him and he received it. He "felt right" about it. And what he "felt right" about was in no sense a "meaning" that, say, an essay could apprehend, but an act of experience that could be fully presented only by the dramatic enactment of forces which is the performance of the poem.

Now look at the poem in another way. Did Frost know what he was going to do when he began? Considering the poem simply as an act of skill, as a piece of juggling, one cannot fail to respond to the magnificent turn at the end where, with one flip, seven of the simplest words in the language suddenly dazzle full of never-ending waves of thought and feeling. Or, more precisely, of felt-thought. Certainly an equivalent stunt by a juggler — could there be an equivalent — would bring the house down. Was it to cap his performance with that grand stunt that Frost wrote the poem?

Far from it. The obvious fact is that *Frost could not have known he was going to write those lines until he wrote them.* Then a second fact must be registered: *he wrote them because, for the fun of it, he had got himself into trouble.*

Frost, like every good poet, began by playing a game with himself. The most usual way of writing a four-line stanza with four feet to the line is to rhyme the third line with the first, and the fourth line with the second. Even that much rhyme is so difficult in English that many poets and almost all of the anonymous ballad makers do not bother to rhyme the first and third lines at all, settling for two rhymes in four lines as good enough. For English is a rhyme-poor language. In Italian and in French, for example, so many words end with the same sounds that rhyming is relatively easy — so easy that many modern French and Italian poets do not bother to rhyme at all. English, being a more agglomerate language, has far more final sounds, hence fewer of them rhyme. When an Italian poet writes a line ending with "vita" (life) he has literally hundreds of rhyme choices available. When an English poet writes "life" at the end of a line he can summon "strife, wife, knife, fife, rife," and then he is in trouble. Now "life-strife" and "life-rife" and "life-wife" seem to offer a combination of possible ideas that can be related by more than just the rhyme. Inevitably, therefore, the poets have had to work and rework these combinations until the sparkle has gone out of them. The reader is normally tired of such rhyme-led associations. When he encounters "life-strife" he is certainly entitled to suspect that the poet did not really want to say "strife" — that had there been in English such a word as, say, "hife," meaning "infinite peace and harmony," the poet would as gladly have used that word instead of "strife." Thus, the reader feels that the writing is haphazard, that the rhyme is making the poet say things he does not really feel, and which, therefore, the reader does not feel except as boredom. One likes to see the rhymes fall into place, but he must end with the belief that it is the poet who is deciding what is said and not the rhyme scheme that is forcing the saying.

So rhyme is a kind of game, and an especially difficult one in English. As in every game, the fun of the rhyme is to set one's difficulties high and then to meet them skilfully. As Frost himself once defined it, freedom consists of "moving easy in harness."

In "Stopping by Woods on a Snowy Evening" Frost took a chance. He decided to rhyme not two lines in each stanza, but three. Not even Frost could have sustained that much rhyme in a long poem (as Dante, for example, with the advantage of writing in Italian, sustained triple rhyme for thousands of lines in *The Divine Comedy*). Frost would have known instantly, therefore, when he took the original chance, that he was going to write a short poem. He would have had that much foretaste of it.

So the first stanza emerged a-a-b-a. And with the sure sense that this was to be a short poem, Frost decided to take an additional chance and to redouble: in English three rhymes in four lines is more than enough; there is no need to rhyme the fourth line. For the fun of it, however, Frost set himself to pick up that loose rhyme and to weave it into the pattern, thereby accepting the all but impossible burden of quadruple rhyme.

The miracle is that it worked. Despite the enormous freight of rhyme, the poem not only came out as a neat pattern, but managed to do so with no sense of strain. Every word and every rhyme falls into place as naturally and as inevitably as if there were no rhyme restricting the poet's choices.

That ease-in-difficulty is certainly inseparable from the success of the poem's performance. One watches the skill-man juggle three balls, then four, then five, and every addition makes the trick more wonderful. But unless he makes the hard trick seem as easy as an easy trick, then all is lost.

The real point, however, is not only that Frost took on a hard rhyme-trick and made it seem easy. It is rather as if the juggler, carried away, had tossed up one more ball than he could really handle, and then amazed himself by actually handling it. So with the real triumph of this poem. Frost could not have known what a stunning effect his repetition of the last line was going to produce. He could not even know he was going to repeat the line. He simply found himself up against a difficulty he almost certainly had not foreseen and he had to improvise to meet it. For in picking up the rhyme from the third line of stanza one and carrying it over into stanza two, he had created an endless chain-link form within which each stanza left a hook sticking out for the next stanza to hang on. So by stanza four, feeling the poem rounding to its end, Frost had to do something about that extra rhyme.

He might have tucked it back into a third line rhyming with the *know-though-snow* of stanza one. He could thus have rounded the poem out to the mathematical symmetry of using each rhyme four times. But though such a device might be defensible in theory, a rhyme repeated after eleven lines is so far from its original rhyme sound that its feeling as rhyme must certainly be lost. And what good is theory if the reader is not moved by the writing?

It must have been in some such quandary that the final repetition suggested itself — a suggestion born of the very difficulties the poet had let himself in for. So there is that point beyond mere ease in handling a hard thing, the point at which the very difficulty offers the poet the opportunity to do better than he knew he could. What, aside from having that happen to oneself, could be more self-delighting than to participate in its happening by one's reader-identification with the poem?

And by now a further point will have suggested itself: that the human insight of the poem and the technicalities of its poetic artifice are inseparable. Each feeds the other. That interplay is the poem's meaning, a matter not of WHAT DOES IT MEAN, for no one can ever say entirely what a good poem means, but of HOW DOES IT MEAN, a process one can come much closer to discussing.

There is a necessary epilogue. Mr. Frost has often discussed this poem on the platform, or more usually in the course of a long evening after a talk. Time and again I have heard him say that he just wrote it off, that it just came to him, and that he set it down as it came.

Once at Bread Loaf, however, I heard him add one very essential piece to the discussion of how it "just came." One night, he said, he had sat down after supper to work at a long piece of blank verse. The piece never worked out, but Mr. Frost found himself so absorbed in it that, when next he looked up, dawn was at his window. He rose, crossed to the window, stood looking out for a few minutes, and *then* it was that "Stopping by Woods" suddenly "just came," so that all he had to do was cross the room and write it down.

Robert Frost is the sort of artist who hides his traces. I know of no Frost work sheets anywhere. If someone has raided his wastebasket in secret, it is possible that such work sheets exist somewhere, but Frost would not willingly allow anything but the finished product to leave him. Almost certainly, therefore, no one will ever know what was in that piece of unsuccessful blank verse he had been working at with such concentration, but I for one would stake my life that could that work sheet be uncovered, it would be found to contain the germinal stuff of "Stopping by Woods"; that what was a-simmer in him all night without finding its proper form, suddenly, when he let his still-occupied mind look away, came at him from a different direction, offered itself in a different form, and that finding that form exactly right the impulse proceeded to marry itself to the new shape in one of the most miraculous performances of English lyricism.

And that, too — whether or not one can accept so hypothetical a discussion — is part of HOW the poem means. It means that marriage to the perfect form, the poet's shapen declaration of itself, its moment's monument fixed beyond all possibility of change. And thus, finally, in every truly good poem, "How does it mean?" must always be answered "Triumphantly." Whatever the poem "is about," *how* it means is always how Genesis means: the word become a form, and the form become a thing, and — when the becoming is true — the thing become a part of the knowledge and experience of the race forever.

6

FILM

This chapter offers a few comments about the nature of film, a few definitions of some indispensable technical terms, a few suggestions about topics, a good sample essay, and, finally, some questions that an essayist may want to ask himself as he begins to think about writing on a film.

Perhaps one's first thought is that a film (excluding cartoons, documentaries, newsreels, and so on) is rather like a play: a story is presented by means of actors. The film, of course, regularly uses some techniques not possible in the playhouse, such as close-ups and rapid changes of scene, but even these techniques can usually be approximated in the playhouse, for example by means of lighting. It may seem, then, that one can write about a film as though it were a photographic record of a play. And indeed some films are nothing more than film records of plays.

There are, however, crucial distinctions between film and drama. First, though drama makes use of visual matters, such as gestures, tableaux effects, and scenery, the plays that we value most highly are *literature*: the word dominates, the visual component is subordinate. One need not be one of those film fanatics who believe that the invention of the sound track was an impediment to film to believe that a film is more a matter of pictures than of words. The camera usually roves, giving us crowded streets, empty skies, rainy nights, or close-ups of filled ashtrays and chipped coffee cups.* Some of the greatest

---

* Films made for television, however, in contrast to the films under discussion, are, for the most part, close to drama. They are usually in essence a play recorded on film, showing people talking and moving on a stage but conveying no sense of a large world and no sense of details, offering nothing to look at.

sequences in cinema, such as the battle scene in Orson Welles's *Falstaff*, have no dialogue. In short, the speaker in a film does not usually dominate. In a play the spectator normally focuses his attention on the speaker, but in a film when a character speaks the camera often gives us a **reaction shot,** focusing on the face or gestures of a character who is affected by the speech, thus giving the spectator a visual interpretation of the words. Even when the camera does focus on the speaker, it is likely to offer an interpretation. An extreme example is a scene from *Brief Encounter:* a gossip is talking, and the camera gives us a close-up of her jabbering mouth which monstrously fills the screen. This distance between film and drama can be put in another way: a film is more like a novel than a play, the action being presented not directly by actors but by a camera, which, like a novelist's point of view, comments on the story while telling it. Even the choice of the kind of emulsion-coated celluloid is part of the comment. A highly sensitive or "fast" film requires less light to catch an image than a "slow" film does, but it is usually grainier. Perhaps because newsreels commonly use fast film a grainy quality is often associated with realism. Moreover, because fast film shows less subtle gradations from black to white than slow film does, its harshness makes it especially suitable for *The Battle of Algiers* but unsuitable for musical comedies or romantic historical subjects where color film is a more likely choice. The medium, as everyone knows, is part of the message; Laurence Olivier made Shakespeare's *Henry* V in color but *Hamlet* in black and white because these media say different things. But of course a film-maker, though he resembles a novelist in offering pervasive indirect comment, is not a novelist any more than he is a playwright or director of a play; his medium has its own techniques, and he works with them, not with the novel's or the drama's. The wife who came out of the movie theater saying to her husband "What a disappointment; it was exactly like the book" knew what a film ought to be.

Below is a brief grammar and dictionary of film, explaining the cinematic devices that help film-makers embody their vision in a work of art. An essay on a film will probably use some of them, but there is no merit in mechanically trotting them all out.

A **shot** (very rarely a fraction of a second, and usually not more than fifteen or so seconds) is what is recorded between the time a camera starts and the time it stops, i.e. between the director's call for "Action" and his call to "Cut." Perhaps the average shot is about ten seconds. Three common shots are: (1) a **long shot** or **establishing shot,** showing the main object at a considerable distance from the camera and thus presenting it in relation to its general surroundings (for example, captured soldiers, seen across a prison yard, entering the yard); (2) a **medium shot,** showing the object in relation to its immediate surroundings (a couple of soldiers, from the knees up, with the yard's wall behind them); (3) a **close-up,** showing only the main object, or, more often, only a part of it (a soldier's face, or his bleeding feet). The close-up, a way of getting emphasis, has been heavily used in recent years, not always successfully. As Dwight Macdonald said of *Midnight Cowboy* and *Getting Straight,* "a movie told in close-ups is like a comic book, or like a novel composed in punchy one-sentence paragraphs and set throughout in large caps. How refreshing is a long or middle shot, a glimpse of the real world, so lovely and so *far away,* in the midst of those interminable processions of [a] hairy ogre face."

While taking a shot, the camera can move: it can swing to the right or left while its base remains fixed (a **pan shot**), up or down while fixed on its axis (a **tilt shot**), forward or backward (a **traveling shot**), or in and out and up and down fastened to a crane (a **crane shot**). The fairly recent invention of the zoom lens enables the camera to change its focus fluidly, so it can approach a detail — as a traveling shot does — while remaining fixed in place. Much will depend on the angle (high or low) from which the shots are made. If the camera is high (a **high angle shot**), looking down on the men, it will dwarf them, perhaps even reduce them to crawling insects, making them pitiful or contemptible; if the camera is low (a **low angle shot**), close to the ground and looking up toward the men, thereby showing them against the sky, it probably will give them added dignity. But these are not invariable principles. A low angle shot, for example, does not always add dignity: films in which children play important parts often have lots of low angle shots, showing adults as menacing giants. In short, by its distance from the subject, its height from the ground, and its angle of elevation, the camera comments on or interprets what happens. It seems to record reality, but it offers its own version. It is only a slight exaggeration to say that the camera always lies.

A group of related scenes — such as the three scenes of soldiers mentioned in the previous paragraph — is a **sequence,** though a sequence is more likely to have thirty scenes than three. Moreover, within a sequence there may be an **intercut,** a switch to another action that, for example, provides an ironic comment on the main action of the sequence. If intercuts are so abundant in a sequence that, in effect, two or more sequences are going at once (e.g., shots of the villain about to ravish the heroine alternating with shots of the hero riding to her rescue), we have a **cross-cut.** In the example just given, probably the tempo would increase, the shots being progressively shorter as we get to the rescue. Though often a sequence will early have an establishing shot, it need not. Sometimes an establishing shot is especially effective if delayed, as in Dreyer's *Day of Wrath*, where scenes of a witch tied to the top rungs of a ladder lead to a long shot of the context: the witch has been tied to the top of a tall ladder near a great heap of burning faggots. Still at a distance, the next shot shows the soldiers tilt the ladder up into the air and onto the pyre.

Within a sequence, the transitions normally are made by **straight cuts** — a strip of film is spliced to another, resulting in an instantaneous transfer from one scene to the next. Two older and now rather unfashionable sorts of transition are sometimes still employed, usually between sequences rather than within a sequence. These are the **dissolve** (the scene dissolves while a new scene appears to emerge from beneath it, there being a moment when we get a blur of both scenes), and the **fade** (in the **fade-out** the screen grows darker until black, in the **fade-in** the screen grows lighter until the new scene is fully visible). In effect the camera is saying "Let us now leave X and turn to Y," or "Two weeks later." In *2001* a pre-historic ape-like creature discovers that he can use a bone as a tool, and he destroys a skeleton with it. Then he throws the bone triumphantly into the air, where it dissolves into a spaceship of the year 2001. The point is that the spaceship is the latest of man's weapons and progress is linked with destructiveness. Two older methods, even less in favor today than the dissolve and the fade but used in many excellent old films and in some modern films that seek an archaic effect are the **iris** (the new scene first appears in the center of the previous scene and then expands until it fills the screen, or the new scene first appears along the perimeter and then closes in on the previous scene) and the **wipe** (a sort of windshield wiper crosses the screen, wiping off the first scene and revealing the next). In Kurosawa's *High and Low* a wipe is used with no archaic effect: an industrialist, trying to decide whether to pay an enormous ransom to free a child, has been told to toss the money from a train; the scene showing him arriving at his decision in his luxurious home is wiped off by a train that rushes across the screen. He has decided to pay.

Mastery of terminology does not make anyone a perceptive film critic, but it helps a writer to communicate his perceptions to his reader. Probably an essay on a film will not be primarily about the use of establishing shots or of wipes, or of any such matters, but rather it will be about some of the reasons why a particular film pleases or displeases, succeeds or fails, seems significant or insignificant, and in discussing these large matters it is sometimes necessary (or at least economical) to use the commonest technical terms. Large matters are often determined in part by such seemingly small matters as the distance of the camera from its subject, or the way in which transitions are made, and one may as well use the conventional terms. But it is also true that a film-maker's technique and technology alone cannot make a first-rate film. There has to be an idea, a personal vision, a theme (see pp. 91–93) that is embodied in all that is flashed on the screen.

Printed below is a student's essay on a film. Because it is on a version of *Macbeth*, it is in some degree a comparison between a film and a play, but it does not keep shifting back and forth nor does it make the obvious point that there are many differences. Rather, it fairly quickly announces that it will be concerned with one kind of difference — the use of visual symbols that the camera can effectively render — and it then examines four such symbols.

Here is the skeleton of the essay, "A Japanese *Macbeth*," paragraph by paragraph:

The Japanese film of *Macbeth* is not a film of a stage-performance; it is a cinematic version.

The film sometimes changes Shakespeare's plot, but this essay will be concerned only with the changes that are visual symbols: the fog, the castle, the forest, the horses.

The fog, the castle, and the forest can be treated briefly. The fog shows nature blinding man; the castle shows man's brief attempt to impose his will on the natural landscape; the forest shows nature entrapping man.

The nervous, active horses — which could not be actually shown on the Elizabethan stage — suggest man's fierce, destructive passions.

The film though literally false to the play is artistically true.

This is a solid organization: the title, though not especially interesting, gives a good idea of the general topic; the first paragraph introduces a significant point, and the second narrows it and announces precisely what the essay will cover. The third paragraph studies three of the four symbols announced in the second paragraph, and the fourth paragraph studies the fourth, more complicated symbol. The concluding paragraph in a way reaffirms the opening paragraph, but it does so now in the light of concrete evidence that has been offered. Organizing the essay, of course, is only part of the job. The writer of this essay has done more than work out an acceptable organization; he has some perceptions to offer, and he has found the right details and provided neat transitions so that the reader can move through the essay with pleasure.

A Japanese Macbeth

A Japanese movie-version of Macbeth sounds like a bad
idea--until one sees Kurosawa's film, Throne of Blood, in
which Toshiro Mifune plays Macbeth. It is a much more satisfying film than, say, Olivier's Othello, largely because
it is not merely a filmed version of a play as it might be
performed on a stage, but rather it is a freely re-created
version that is designed for the camera. The very fact that
it is in Japanese is probably a great help to Westerners.
If it were in English, we would be upset at the way some
speeches are cut, but because it is in Japanese, we do not
compare the words to Shakespeare's, and we concentrate on
the visual aspects of the film.

There are several differences in the plots of the two
works. Among the alterations are such things as these:
Shakespeare's three witches are reduced to one; Lady Macbeth
has a miscarriage; Macbeth is killed by his own troops and
not by Macduff. But this paper will discuss another sort of
change, the introduction of visual symbols, which the camera
is adept at rendering, and which play an important part in
the film. The four chief visual symbols are the fog, the
castle, the forest, and the horses.

The fog, the castle, and the forest, though highly
effective, can be dealt with rather briefly. When the film
begins we get a slow panoramic view of the ruined castle
seen through the fog. The film ends with a similar pano-

ramic view. These two scenes end with a dissolve, though
almost all of the other scenes end abruptly with sharp cuts,
so the effect is that of lingering sorrow at the transience
of human creations, and awe at the permanence of the mysterious natural world, whose mist slowly drifts across what
once was a mighty castle built by a great chief. The castle
itself, when we come to see it in its original condition, is
not a particularly graceful Japanese building. Rather, it
is a low, strong building, appropriate for an energetic
warrior. The interior scenes show low, oppressive ceilings,
with great exposed beams that almost seem to crush the
people within the rooms. It represents man's achievement in
the center of the misty tangled forest of the mysterious
world, but it also suggests, despite its strength, how stifling that achievement is, in comparison with the floating
mists and endless woods. The woods, rainy and misty, consist of curiously gnarled trees and vines, and suggest a
labyrinth that has entrapped man, even though for a while
man thinks he is secure in his castle. Early in the film we
see Macbeth riding through the woods, in and out of mists,
and behind a maze of twisted trees that periodically hide
him from our sight. Maybe it is not too fanciful to suggest
that the branches through which we glimpse him blindly
riding in the fog are a sort of net that entangles him. The
trees and the mist are the vast unfathomable universe; man
can build his castle, can make his plans, but he cannot
subdue nature for long. He cannot have his way forever;

death will ultimately catch him, despite his strength. One later scene of the forest must be mentioned. Near the end of the film, when the forest moves (the soldiers are holding up leafy boughs to camouflage themselves), we get a spectacular shot; Shakespeare talks of the forest moving, but in the film we see it. Suddenly the forest seems to give a shudder and to be alive, crawling as though it is a vast horde of ants. Nature is seen to rise up against Macbeth's crimes.

Shakespeare's stage could do very little about such an effect as the fog, though his poetry can call it to mind, and it could do even less about the forest. Kurosawa did not feel bound to the text of the play: he made a movie, and he took advantage of the camera's ability to present impressive and significant scenic effects. Similarly, he made much use of horses, which, though mentioned in Shakespeare's play, could not be shown on the Elizabethan stage. In fact, in <u>Macbeth</u> (III.iii.12-13) Shakespeare more or less apologizes for the absence of horses when one murderer explains to the other that when horsemen approach the palace it is customary for them to leave their horses and to walk the rest of the way. But the film gives us plenty of horses, not only at the start, when Macbeth is galloping in the terrifying forest, but throughout the film, and they are used to suggest the terror of existence, and the evil passions in Macbeth's heart. Shakespeare provided a hint.

After King Duncan is murdered, Shakespeare tells us that
Duncan's horses "Turned wild in nature, broke their stalls,"
and even that they ate each other (II.iv.16-18). In the
film, when Macbeth and his wife plot the murder of their
lord, we see the panic-struck horses running around the
courtyard of the castle--a sort of parallel to the scene of
Macbeth chaotically riding in and out of the fog near the
beginning of the movie. The horses in the courtyard apparently have sensed man's villainous plots, or perhaps they
are visual equivalents of the fierce emotions in the minds
of Macbeth and his wife. Later, when Macbeth is planning to
murder Banquo, we see Banquo's white horse kicking at his
attendants. Banquo saddles the horse, preparing to ride
into the hands of his assassins. Then Kurosawa cuts to a
long shot of the courtyard at night, where Banquo's attendants are nervously waiting for him to return. Then we hear
the sound of a galloping horse, and suddenly the white horse
comes running in, riderless. Yet another use of this motif
is when we cut to a wild horse, after Macbeth's wife has
said that she is pregnant. In the film the wife has a miscarriage, and here again the horse is a visual symbol of the
disorder engendered within her (the child would be the heir
to the usurped throne), as the other horses were symbols for
the disorder in her mind and in Macbeth's. All of these
cuts to the horses are abrupt, contributing to the sense of
violence that the unrestrained horses themselves embody.

Moreover, almost the only close-ups in the film are some shots of horses, seen from a low angle, emphasizing their powerful, oppressive brutality.

Throne of Blood is not Shakespeare's Macbeth--but even a filmed version of a staged version of the play would not be Shakespeare's Macbeth either, for the effect of a film is simply not identical with the effect of a play with live actors on the stage. But Throne of Blood is a fine translation of Macbeth into an approximate equivalent. Despite its lack of faithfulness to the literal text, it is in a higher way faithful. It is a work of art, like its original.

CONCLUDING REMARKS ON WRITING ABOUT FILM

These questions may help to bring impressions out into the open, and may with some reworking provide topics for essays.

1. If the film is adapted from fiction or drama, does it slavishly follow its original and neglect the potentialities of the camera? If visual symbols are used, are they used effectively?

2. If the film is adapted from fiction or drama, does it do violence to the theme of the original? Is the film better than its source? Are the additions or omissions due to the medium or to a crude or faulty interpretation of the original? (In Sillitoe's story, "The Loneliness of the Long Distance Runner," the central character is a tough anarchic kid in a reform school. He rejects everything, including love. But in the film, based on a script that Sillitoe himself provided, the boy is a sensitive proletarian hero who rejects bourgeois and upper-class authority and is loyal to his own class and has a nice girl. For some reason Sillitoe chose to sentimentalize his own story.)

3. Can film deal as effectively with inner action — mental processes — as with external, physical action? In a given film, how is the inner action conveyed?

4. Are shots and sequences adequately developed or do they seem jerky? (Sometimes, of course, jerkiness may be desirable.)

5. Are the characters believable?

6. Are the actors appropriately cast? (Wasn't it a mistake to cast Gregory Peck as Captain Ahab?)

7. Is the music appropriate and functional? (Among other things, music may imitate natural sounds, may give a sense of locale, may suggest states of mind, may provide ironic commentary, may — by repeated melodies — help to establish connections.) If there are electronic sounds, are they functional?

8. All works of art are contrivances, of course, but (as a Roman saying puts it) the art is to conceal art. Does the film seem arty, a mere *tour de force*, or does it have the effect of inevitability, the effect of rightness, conveying a sense that a vision has been honestly conveyed? Are characters or scenes clumsily dragged in? Are unusual effects significant? Does the whole add up to something? Do we get scenes or characters or techniques that at first hold us by their novelty but then have nothing further to offer?

9. Is the title significant? Are the newspaper or television advertisements appropriate?

Some final advice:

Early in the essay it is usually desirable to sketch enough of the plot to give the reader an idea of what happens. (In the essay printed above, the student does not sketch the plot, but he says it is a version of *Macbeth*, and thus he gives the necessary information.) But do not try to recount everything that happens: it can't be done, and the attempt is boring. Once you introduce the main characters and devote a few sentences to the plot, thus giving the reader a comfortable seat, get down to the job of convincing him that you have something interesting to say about the film — that the plot is trivial, or that the hero is not really cool but cruel, or that the plot and characters are fine achievements but the camera-work is sometimes needlessly tricky, or that all is well.

Sample Essays

These two essays are better characterized as reviews than as critical essays. A critical essay normally aims at helping a reader to understand better a work with which he is already familiar, though it usually assumes that his familiarity is a bit faded and therefore it briefly reminds him of the plot, relationships between characters, and so forth. But a **review** normally aims at describing and evaluating a work so that the reader can decide whether or not he wishes to know it at first hand.

Gregg Kilday, writing about a film that was adapted from a novel, assumes the reader has some familiarity with the novel but not with the film. He unobtrusively reminds us of the gist of the novel, but he correctly assumes that it is not his job to go into much detail about it, except in so far as discussion of the novel helps to reveal the special qualities of the film. The essay is not really a comparison of two works, but a review of a new film, and the reader finishes it with a sense that the film need not be seen. One other point: because Kilday's review was published in a college newspaper it is somewhat more colloquial than the other essays in this book. Kilday, a student talking to students, knows the degree to which he can adopt a relaxed tone.

Stanley Kauffmann's review of Ingmar Bergman's *Wild Strawberries* begins by devoting the first four brief paragraphs to three of Bergman's earlier films, thus helping the reader (who probably has seen at least one of them) to adjust to what will be a discussion of a new and therefore unfamiliar work. Because the title of the review, and the first paragraph, tell the reader what the review will be chiefly about, the reader understands that the first four rather skimpy paragraphs are providing a context. The first paragraph that is devoted fully to *Wild Strawberries* (the fifth) tells the plot, giving the reader the help he needs in reading about a new work. Most of the remainder of the first half of the review is devoted to discussing the strengths of the film and then the weaknesses. Next, Kauffmann speaks more generally about Bergman and goes on to conjecture (on the basis of the films thus far discussed) what Bergman's future films may be like. Finally, in a paragraph that is only loosely related to its predecessor, Kauffmann talks about the chief actor in *Wild Strawberries*. The transition is weak, but it is not so weak that the reader is puzzled by the sudden introduction of a new topic. Kauffmann clearly gives a signal: "This notice would be unfinished without mention of. . . ." Two additional paragraphs, labeled "Postscript," were not part of the original review but were appended some years later when Kauffmann collected his reviews into a book. Unfortunately, most of us do not have several years in which to revise our essays.

The Moviegoer: *Women in Love*

"The older I get, the less I like Lawrence. There is something so adolescent about his work. He becomes so, . . . so tedious." Well, perhaps. After all, it is a common complaint voiced against Lawrence by his critics — not the first-rate scholars, mind you, but the rank and file of literary nitpickers that prey on literary reputations. It might very well be, however, that the temptation to indulge in such criticism is a function of increasing age; at present, to achieve such dubious critical acumen at the expense of surrendering the remaining shreds of one's adolescence seems to me a rather uninviting proposition.

Conveniently, Ken Russell's current film of Lawrence's *Women in Love* solves the problem quite neatly. Thanks to Larry Kramer's screenplay, which closely follows the plot of the novel, and thanks to Alan Bates's amusing but rather lightweight portrayal of Rupert Birken, Lawrence's protagonist and spokesman, the film turns poor old D.H. into the adolescent's adolescent. (Incidentally, someone along the assembly line was indiscreet enough to have Bates/Birken wear a beard cut exactly like Lawrence's own. They seem to be daring us to make the connection.) And since (cautionary baritone) *this film has been rated R* — which only means that even an orphan can get in if he looks old enough to be bar mitzvahed — those of us who still have a few days of adolescence left to savor are not to be denied a chance to see Lawrence exposed *for what*, as some would have it, *he really is*.

Essentially, *Women in Love*, the novel, is a partially dramatized dialectic on the meaning of sex, love, and marriage. Lawrence's characters — Gerald, a machine-driven industrialist (played by Oliver Reed in the movie); Gudrun (Glenda Jackson), a willful, aspiring artist; Ursula (Jennie Linden), her simpler, more sensual, sister; and, of course, Birken — tramp about their country homes in the English countryside circa 1910 while strenuously debating the finer points of their relationships. Eventually they pair off and work out their respective destinies. For the movie version, Kramer has saved great chunks of their conversation in an almost suicidal attempt to remain faithful to the book. Unfortunately, his fidelity goes unrewarded. One never really quite believes the way Lawrence manipulates dialogue for his own didactic purposes. In the novel that doesn't really matter, because in his semi-mystic descriptions of nature, his hypersymbolic dramatic vignettes, his sometimes fumbling but mostly honest attempts to define sexuality, Lawrence gives us so much else to bolster his argument. His dialogue is only a part of a most imposing whole, and so we forgive it its deficiencies. When Kramer's screenplay captures the dialogue, but neglects those elements of the novel that support it, it is like cutting off the visible peak of an iceberg, thinking you've preserved the entire thing whole. What results is rather more silly than imposing.

In any case, audiences aren't likely to devote a great deal of attention to the running debates between Birken and his friends. It is in the nature of movies that actions speak louder than words — particularly when the words are as diffuse as those in *Women in Love*. Conceivably, Russell could have saved his actors from adolescent soul-searching by providing proper dramatic channels for the novel's ideas. But here again, Russell's *Women in Love* lacks the depth of the original. Take the sex scenes, for example. Sex for Lawrence is something of a double-edged sword. (Metaphorically speaking, one assumes.) It frees man to flow with larger forces of nature and life, while at the same time it condemns him to struggle over positions of subservience and dominance with other men. The novel's sexual encounters are the arena on which this complex of issues is unraveled. Russell, though, shows us only the physical side of sex, not its psychological or spiritual dimensions. He does so with an intensity that is often quite unsettling. Every time Gudrun begins to bare a breast, the soundtrack pours it on as if to invite us to spend a Night on Bald Mountain. And once the sex begins the camera tumbles about so that one can only assume the cameraman himself is joining the two lovers in some kind of kinky *ménage à trois*. Sex in Russell's movie is hot, harried, and sweating. It is adolescent sex. All that is needed is the back seat of a car to make it complete. To some extent, of course, that is the way Lawrence knew and hated sex. But then Lawrence was struggling for something better, and for him to have gotten so far so consciously was something of an achievement. The real point of Lawrence's novel is that he meant to go much further, but the movie — except for the interminable conversations which no one is going to listen to anyway — gives no indication of the dimensions of the quest.

If there is a common denominator of failure in the film, it is a certain earthbound literalness that prevents us from taking the meaning of the characters' actions at anything but face value. In re-creating Edwardian England, Russell has gone to a great degree of bother. The end product, however, is simply too much detail. When Russell attempts an outdoor scene, it looks more like he's constructed a horizonless hot-house. Consequently, in key sequences — as when Birken abandons the intellectual Hermione (Eleanor Bron) in order to submerge himself in nature — one never makes the necessary leap from physical facts to their metaphoric meanings. Why Birken isn't tearing himself apart with prickly burrs as he rolls naked in the ferns and bushes is a more absorbing question than why he stripped in the first place.

The few images that do work suggest the direction the film should have taken. The first few shots of a nude wrestling match between Birken and Gerald, deep, low-angle, lit by a darkly golden fire, are quite eerie in their implications. (Although the inevitable pulsing soundtrack and tumultuous camerawork mar the development of the sequence.) A shot of a drowned girl, entwined in the arms of her dead lover as they are washed up onto a muddy shore, is equally effective. (Although it is mistakenly intercut with shots of Birken and Ursula making love. Properly, the omen is directed at Gerald of whose fears it is much more illustrative.) One of the film's concluding images comes closest to suggesting the metaphoric associations flowing beneath Lawrence's narrative. Gerald, after breaking from Gudrun in a scene that parallels Birken's rupture with Hermione, wanders off, exhausted and spent, into the snow. (The two are, at the time, on an outing in the Swiss Alps.) In such circumstances, nature does not offer Gerald the salvation it provided Birken: the landscape into which Gerald wanders is barren and frigid. He collapses, curls up like a tiny fetus dwarfed by a field of greyish white, his darker footsteps trailing offscreen like an endless umbilical cord. The actual physical setting of Gerald's death is overshadowed by its implication of loneliness and sterility. Compared to the cluttered literalness of most of the film, those few, tentative steps toward approaching a sparser, more abstract method of story-telling are much more suggestive of the grandeur of Lawrence's design.

Both in comparison with the novel on which it was based, and on its own transcendent internal elements, Russell's *Women in Love* is something less than adequate. Even taken as the simpler story of four individuals in and out of love, it is far from satisfactory. Audiences fresh from the carnival of casual sex that is *Woodstock* aren't likely to have much patience with the difficult, struggling sex of *Women in Love*; Russell's film is ungrounded in any larger pattern of significance that could make a consideration of such sexuality important.

The relationship between Birken and Gerald should also prove something of a stumbling block for movie audiences just learning to accept male homosexuality as a valid means of exploring love and sex. Birken's desire to achieve a mystic yet sensual union with another man must be seen in reaction to his fears of Hermione and Ursula. Birken hates women for their sex at the same time that he is drawn to them; he associates the demands of the two women with those of motherhood and death, forces that limit and frustrate his lofty aspirations for freedom. But since the movie caricatures Hermione to the point of foolishness and eliminates the sensuality in Ursula that would make her Lawrence's earth mother, it presents no compelling force to drive Birken toward Gerald. His interest appears ambiguous, if not entirely incomprehensible, as is the central wrestling match itself. Given such ambiguity, audiences conditioned to accepting homosexual pairings as either platonic or sexual, but not as a more realistic combination of both, don't quite know what to think except to wonder why in the world the whole thing is called *Women in Love* at all.

All of which points toward the fact that while Russell's movie looks a good deal like Lawrence, it offers little of the Lawrence feel. And when you can no longer feel the force and logic behind Lawrence's work, the mere plots and characters on which his work is built *do* look quite foolish, peopled as they are with serious little adolescents not yet fully capable of critical self-awareness. But it is unfair to blame Lawrence when the fault lies in Russell's lack of feeling for his material. During one scene in the novel — interestingly enough, a scene absent from the movie — Birken decries the emptiness of modern life and art. "I'm sure," he says, "life is all wrong because it has become much too visual — we can neither hear nor feel nor understand, we can only see." That's about how you feel after seeing Russell's version of *Women in Love*. And, as Lawrence might have added, seeing ain't necessarily believing.

STANLEY KAUFFMANN

Wild Strawberries

Ingmar Bergman, the Swedish director who writes his own scripts, is one of the most interesting and irritating film artists alive. There is no one making full-length pictures today (as distinct from experimental shorts) who is more aware of the poetic potentialities of the film. Yet of the four Bergman pictures I have seen, one is dreadful, one pretentious, one moderately good, and the latest, *Wild Strawberries*, teeters on the edge of complete realization.

(With foreign pictures, sequence of American release is not necessarily sequence of creation, nor do we always see all of a man's work. We get films as and if they filter through import channels.)

Even the inferior picture, *Three Strange Loves*, was distinguished by an investigation of emotional relationships far below the surface of most movies. His pretentious film, *The Seventh Seal*, was, to me, symbolically opaque and allegorically illogical; yet obviously it is the work of a man to whom the camera is a lyric instrument, who has large imagination and superb techniques.

Smiles of a Summer Night was a wry, rueful sex comedy, a Victorian period piece. A friend of mine said it would have been a fine picture if a Frenchman had made it, and indeed it is worried by an un-Gallic laboring of points and an obvious load of philosophical baggage. Yet here again is a film by a man with a sympathy for arresting themes, with an eye for the possibilities of the human face, with a power to make the very form of his film serve his theme.

Wild Strawberries deals with a seventy-six-year-old doctor on the day he is to receive an honorary degree. He wakes from a dream of his own death, and drives from Stockholm to the university town of Lund with his daughter-in-law. She is to rejoin the doctor's son who teaches at the university and from whom she has been estranged by his coldness. On the way she tells the old man that his son has inherited his coldness from him. They visit a house where his family used to summer when he was young and where he picked wild strawberries with a girl he loved and lost; he visits his mother, ninety-six, who is encased in the egotism of the ancient; he picks up several hitchhikers who represent various elements in modern life. At the end of the day, after the ceremony, he goes to bed in his son's house, honored and sadder.

There is much in this film that is extraordinarily beautiful. The dream sequence at the beginning is a blend of Caligari and Kafka. The old man's reminiscences of his youth at the country place are done with a warm sense of family fun that makes one yearn to have been part of it. Bergman's touch in establishing period feeling is swift and sure — we see a young man seated in a tree reading a book, dressed in white trousers, white shirt, tie, and straw boater, and we know at once where we are. He has a gift for eccentric characterizations, like the neurotic couple to whom the doctor gives a lift and who shortly cram the interior of the car with their almost palpable unhappiness. And his basic concept — a day's ride, a life's journey — is a sound one.

Yet despite the jewels he has strung on this thread, the picture does not satisfy: precisely because they are separate jewels, not architectural blocks in a structure. The film is a series of events which do not relate or accrete strongly enough. For example, the opening dream — in itself haunting — is full of symbols which we feel are being established for later use. But only one of them — the watch without hands — is fulfilled later; the others are just vivid images that seem to have occurred to Bergman.

Without growth, the picture does not fulfill a fundamental requirement of drama: the protagonist is unchanged at the end. We are *told* he is different, he utters a few lines to that effect, but they seem appended, not a convincing development. At best, the immense symbolic apparatus of the picture has produced a very small result. This criticism is not academic; it is arrived at by the viewer's solar plexus which is knotted with impatience at the sight of all these good materials left unfused.

Bergman has had extensive theatrical training and experience and has recently been appointed director of the Royal Dramatic Theatre in Stockholm — at forty-one the youngest in its history. It is possible that, in contrast to the theater, he looks on the film as a free form, an opportunity for rhapsody and for that psychic exploration dear to the Scandinavian spirit and difficult on the stage. In fine imaginative surges, he tries to pry with his camera between close-knit life and death, between eternity and now. His films have an air of quest, of probing, of beating at great doors that he wants to open for himself and us.

Heaven and we know that this ambition is rare and valuable in films. But if my theory is right and Bergman does view the film as a medium liberated from theatrical disciplines, he will, I think, continue to make pictures studded with beautiful episodes which an audience conditioned to form and resolution must attempt to finish for him. His scripts have a certain resemblance to the plays of the late Ugo Betti; they paddle around on great, timeless, heartaching seas. We can be grateful for the glimpses thus afforded but, although we do not expect final answers from mere fellow men, we are left dissatisfied by the errant voyagings.

This notice would be unfinished without mention of the excellent performance in the leading role by Victor Sjöström, who as Seastrom directed in Hollywood from 1923 to 1931 and has since been acting in Sweden. Some old actors' faces have an odd childlike purity; it radiates from Sjöström. Of his many moving scenes one moment stands out particularly. In a dream sequence, his parents, as they were when he was a child, are sitting on a rock while Father fishes. They see him, as he was then, and wave to him. We see the old man as he is now, and, with all the sadness of time past and passing, his eyes fill at the sight of them. It is lovely.

POSTSCRIPT. Although several subsequent viewings clarify the use of more of the symbolism, they do not alter much of the criticism above. Nevertheless they put the picture in a higher place. With increased familiarity, its texture seems increasingly exquisite, its technique more magical, the articulation of the dream scenes more tartly imaginative. Also, Victor Sjöström has died since the above was written, and, for me, that extrinsic fact colors the film; it has become that admirable man's valedictory.

Still the picture is unsatisfying, mainly because of its virtues. They raise expectations — in themselves and in the large issues they touch — that are not fulfilled. *Wild Strawberries* deals superbly with some familiar contrasts: of past and present, of the differing blindnesses and egotisms of youth and age, men and women, of the sound of the passage of time on even the happiest days. Bergman handles these matters without sentimentality and with unfailing effect, but finally one feels that the apparatus of potentially profound drama has been confined to a plateau of pathos.

APPENDIX

WILLIAM FAULKNER

A Rose for Emily

I

When Miss Emily Grierson died, our whole town went to her funeral: the men through a sort of respectful affection for a fallen monument, the women mostly out of curiosity to see the inside of her house, which no one save an old manservant — a combined gardener and cook — had seen in at least ten years.

It was a big, squarish frame house that had once been white, decorated with cupolas and spires and scrolled balconies in the heavily lightsome style of the seventies, set on what had once been our most select street. But garages and cotton gins had encroached and obliterated even the august names of that neighborhood; only Miss Emily's house was left, lifting its stubborn and coquettish decay above the cotton wagons and the gasoline pumps — an eyesore among eyesores. And now Miss Emily had gone to join the representatives of those august names where they lay in the cedar-bemused cemetery among the ranked and anonymous graves of Union and Confederate soldiers who fell at the battle of Jefferson.

Alive, Miss Emily had been a tradition, a duty, and a care; a sort of hereditary obligation upon the town, dating from that day in 1894 when Colonel Sartoris, the mayor — he who fathered the edict that no Negro woman should appear on the streets without an apron — remitted her taxes, the dispensation dating from the death of her father on into perpetuity. Not that Miss Emily would have accepted charity. Colonel Sartoris invented an involved tale to the effect that Miss Emily's father had loaned money to the town, which the town, as a matter of business, preferred this way of repaying. Only a man of Colonel Sartoris' generation and thought could have invented it, and only a woman could have believed it.

When the next generation, with its more modern ideas, became mayors and aldermen, this arrangement created some little dissatisfaction. On the first of the year they mailed her a tax notice. February came, and there was no reply. They wrote her a formal letter, asking her to call at the sheriff's office at her convenience. A week later the mayor wrote her himself, offering to call or to send his car for her, and received in reply a note on paper of an archaic shape, in a thin, flowing calligraphy in faded ink, to the effect that she no longer went out at all. The tax notice was also enclosed, without comment.

They called a special meeting of the Board of Aldermen. A deputation waited upon her, knocked at the door through which no visitor had passed since she ceased giving china-painting lessons eight or ten years earlier. They were admitted by the old Negro into a dim hall from which a staircase mounted into still more shadow. It smelled of dust and disuse — a close, dank smell. The Negro led them into the parlor. It was furnished in heavy, leather-covered furniture. When the Negro opened the blinds of one window, a faint dust rose sluggishly about their thighs, spinning with slow motes in the single sunray. On a tarnished gilt easel before the fireplace stood a crayon portrait of Miss Emily's father.

They rose when she entered — a small, fat woman in black, with a thin gold chain descending to her waist and vanishing into her belt, leaning on an ebony cane with a tarnished gold head. Her skeleton was small and spare; perhaps that was why what would have been merely plumpness in another was obesity in her. She looked bloated, like a body long submerged in motionless water, and of that pallid hue. Her eyes, lost in the fatty ridges of her face, looked like two small pieces of coal pressed into a lump of dough as they moved from one face to another while the visitors stated their errand.

She did not ask them to sit. She just stood in the door and listened quietly until the spokesman came to a stumbling halt. Then they could hear the invisible watch ticking at the end of the gold chain.

Her voice was dry and cold. "I have no taxes in Jefferson. Colonel Sartoris explained it to me. Perhaps one of you can gain access to the city records and satisfy yourselves."

"But we have. We are the city authorities, Miss Emily. Didn't you get a notice from the sheriff, signed by him?"

"I received a paper, yes," Miss Emily said. "Perhaps he considers himself the sheriff. . . . I have no taxes in Jefferson."

"But there is nothing on the books to show that, you see. We must go by the — "

"See Colonel Sartoris. I have no taxes in Jefferson."

"But, Miss Emily — "

"See Colonel Sartoris." (Colonel Sartoris had been dead almost ten years.) "I have no taxes in Jefferson. Tobe!" The Negro appeared. "Show these gentlemen out."

II

So she vanquished them, horse and foot, just as she had vanquished their fathers thirty years before about the smell. That was two years after her father's death and a short time after her sweetheart — the one we believed would marry her — had deserted her. After her father's death she went out very little; after her sweetheart went away, people hardly saw her at all. A few of the ladies had the temerity to call, but were not received, and the only sign of life about the place was the Negro man — a young man then — going in and out with a market basket.

"Just as if a man — any man — could keep a kitchen properly," the ladies said; so they were not surprised when the smell developed. It was another link between the gross, teeming world and the high and mighty Griersons.

A neighbor, a woman, complained to the mayor, Judge Stevens, eighty years old.

"But what will you have me do about it, madam?" he said.

"Why, send her word to stop it," the woman said. "Isn't there a law?"

"I'm sure that won't be necessary," Judge Stevens said. "It's probably just a snake or a rat that nigger of hers killed in the yard. I'll speak to him about it."

The next day he received two more complaints, one from a man who came in diffident deprecation. "We really must do something about it, Judge. I'd be the last one in the world to bother Miss Emily, but we've got to do something." That night the Board of Aldermen met — three gray-beards and one younger man, a member of the rising generation.

"It's simple enough," he said. "Send her word to have her place cleaned up. Give her a certain time to do it in, and if she don't . . ."

"Dammit, sir," Judge Stevens said, "will you accuse a lady to her face of smelling bad?"

So the next night, after midnight, four men crossed Miss Emily's lawn and slunk about the house like burglars, sniffing along the base of the brickwork and at the cellar openings while one of them performed a regular sowing motion with his hand out of a sack slung from his shoulder. They broke open the cellar door and sprinkled lime there, and in all the out-buildings. As they recrossed the lawn, a window that had been dark was lighted and Miss Emily sat in it, the light behind her, and her upright torso motionless as that of an idol. They crept quietly across the lawn and into the shadow of the locusts that lined the street. After a week or two the smell went away.

That was when people had begun to feel really sorry for her. People in our town remembering how old lady Wyatt, her great-aunt, had gone completely crazy at last, believed that the Griersons held themselves a little too high for what they really were. None of the young men were quite good enough for Miss Emily and such. We had long thought of them as a tableau; Miss Emily a slender figure in white in the background, her father a spraddled silhouette in the foreground, his back to her and clutching a horsewhip, the two of them framed by the back-flung front door. So when she got to be thirty and was still single, we were not pleased exactly, but vindicated; even with insanity in the family she wouldn't have turned down all of her chances if they had really materialized.

When her father died, it got about that the house was all that was left to her; and in a way, people were glad. At last they could pity Miss Emily. Being left alone, and a pauper, she had become humanized. Now she too would know the old thrill and the old despair of a penny more or less.

The day after his death all the ladies prepared to call at the house and offer condolence and aid, as is our custom. Miss Emily met them at the door, dressed as usual and with no trace of grief on her face. She told them that her father was not dead. She did that for three days, with the ministers calling on her, and the doctors, trying to persuade her to let them dispose of the body. Just as they were about to resort to law and force, she broke down, and they buried her father quickly.

We did not say she was crazy then. We believed she had to do that. We remembered all the young men her father had driven away, and we knew that with nothing left, she would have to cling to that which had robbed her, as people will.

III

She was sick for a long time. When we saw her again, her hair was cut short, making her look like a girl, with a vague resemblance to those angels in colored church windows — sort of tragic and serene.

The town had just let the contracts for paving the sidewalks, and in the summer after her father's death they began to work. The construction company came with niggers and mules and machinery, and a foreman named Homer Barron, a Yankee — a big, dark, ready man, with a big voice and eyes lighter than his face. The little boys would follow in groups to hear him cuss the niggers, and the niggers singing in time to the rise and fall of picks. Pretty soon he knew everybody in town. Whenever you heard a lot of laughing anywhere about the square, Homer Barron would be in the center of the group. Presently we began to see him and Miss Emily on Sunday afternoons driving in the yellow-wheeled buggy and the matched team of bays from the livery stable.

At first we were glad that Miss Emily would have an interest, because the ladies all said, "Of course a Grierson would not think seriously of a Northerner, a day laborer." But there were still others, older people, who said that even grief could not cause a real lady to forget *noblesse oblige* — without calling it *noblesse oblige.* They just said, "Poor Emily. Her kinsfolk should come to her." She had some kin in Alabama; but years ago her father had fallen out with them over the estate of old lady Wyatt, the crazy woman, and there was no communication between the two families. They had not even been represented at the funeral.

And as soon as the old people said, "Poor Emily," the whispering began. "Do you suppose it's really so?" they said to one another. "Of course it is. What else could . . ." This behind their hands; rustling of craned silk and satin behind jalousies closed upon the sun of Sunday afternoon as the thin, swift clop-clop-clop of the matched team passed: "Poor Emily."

She carried her head high enough — even when we believed that she was fallen. It was as if she demanded more than ever the recognition of her dignity as the last Grierson; as if it had wanted that touch of earthiness to reaffirm her imperviousness. Like when she bought the rat poison, the arsenic. That was over a year after they had begun to say "Poor Emily," and while the two female cousins were visiting her.

"I want some poison," she said to the druggist. She was over thirty then, still a slight woman, though thinner than usual, with cold, haughty black eyes in a face the flesh of which was strained across the temples and about the eyesockets as you imagine a lighthouse-keeper's face ought to look. "I want some poison," she said.

"Yes, Miss Emily. What kind? For rats and such? I'd recom — "

"I want the best you have. I don't care what kind."

The druggist named several. "They'll kill anything up to an elephant. But what you want is — "

"Arsenic," Miss Emily said. "Is that a good one?"

"Is . . . arsenic? Yes ma'am. But what you want — "

"I want arsenic."

The druggist looked down at her. She looked back at him, erect, her face like a strained flag. "Why, of course," the druggist said. "If that's what you want. But the law requires you to tell what you are going to use it for."

Miss Emily just stared at him, her head tilted back in order to look him eye for eye, until he looked away and went and got the arsenic and wrapped it up. The Negro delivery boy brought her the package; the druggist didn't come back. When she opened the package at home there was written on the box, under the skull and bones: "For rats."

IV

So the next day we all said, "She will kill herself"; and we said it would be the best thing. When she had first begun to be seen with Homer Barron, we had said, "She will marry him." Then we said, "She will persuade him yet," because Homer himself had remarked — he liked men, and it was known that he drank with the younger men in the Elk's Club — that he was not a marrying man. Later we said, "Poor Emily," behind the jalousies as they passed on Sunday afternoon in the glittering buggy, Miss Emily with her head high and Homer Barron with his hat cocked and a cigar in his teeth, reins and whip in a yellow glove.

Then some of the ladies began to say that it was a disgrace to the town and a bad example to the young people. The men did not want to interfere, but at last the ladies forced the Baptist minister — Miss Emily's people were Episcopal — to call upon her. He would never divulge what happened during that interview, but he refused to go back again. The next Sunday they again drove about the streets, and the following day the minister's wife wrote to Miss Emily's relations in Alabama.

So she had blood-kin under her roof again and we sat back to watch developments. At first nothing happened. Then we were sure that they were to be married. We learned that Miss Emily had been to the jeweler's and ordered a man's toilet set in silver, with the letters H.B. on each piece. Two days later we learned that she had bought a complete outfit of men's clothing, including a nightshirt, and we said, "They are married." We were really glad. We were glad because the two female cousins were even more Grierson than Miss Emily had ever been.

So we were surprised when Homer Barron — the streets had been finished some time since — was gone. We were a little disappointed that there was not a public blowing-off, but we believed that he had gone on to prepare for Miss Emily's coming, or to give a chance to get rid of the cousins. (By that time it was a cabal, and we were all

Miss Emily's allies to help circumvent the cousins.) Sure enough, after another week they departed. And, as we had expected all along, within three days Homer Barron was back in town. A neighbor saw the Negro man admit him at the kitchen door at dusk one evening.

And that was the last we saw of Homer Barron. And of Miss Emily for some time. The Negro man went in and out with the market basket, but the front door remained closed. Now and then we would see her at a window for a moment, as the men did that night when they sprinkled the lime, but for almost six months she did not appear on the streets. Then we knew that this was to be expected too; as if that quality of her father which had thwarted her woman's life so many times had been too virulent and too furious to die.

When we next saw Miss Emily, she had grown fat and her hair was turning gray. During the next few years it grew grayer and grayer until it attained an even pepper-and-salt iron-gray, when it ceased turning. Up to the day of her death at seventy-four it was still that vigorous iron-gray, like the hair of an active man.

From that time on her front door remained closed, save for a period of six or seven years, when she was about forty, during which she gave lessons in china-painting. She fitted up a studio in one of the downstairs rooms, where the daughters and granddaughters of Colonel Sartoris' contemporaries were sent to her with the same regularity and in the same spirit that they were sent on Sundays with a twenty-five cent piece for the collection plate. Meanwhile her taxes had been remitted.

Then the newer generation became the backbone and the spirit of the town, and the painting pupils grew up and fell away and did not send their children to her with boxes of color and tedious brushes and pictures cut from the ladies' magazines. The front door closed upon the last one and remained closed for good. When the town got free postal delivery Miss Emily alone refused to let them fasten the metal numbers above her door and attach a mailbox to it. She would not listen to them.

Daily, monthly, yearly we watched the Negro grow grayer and more stooped, going in and out with the market basket. Each December we sent her a tax notice, which would be returned by the post office a week later, unclaimed. Now and then we would see her in one of the downstairs windows — she had evidently shut up the top floor of the house — like the carven torso of an idol in a niche, looking or not looking at us, we could never tell which. Thus she passed from generation to generation — dear, inescapable, impervious, tranquil, and perverse.

And so she died. Fell ill in the house filled with dust and shadows, with only a doddering Negro man to wait on her. We did not even know she was sick; we had long since given up trying to get any information from the Negro. He talked to no one, probably not even to her, for his voice had grown harsh and rusty, as if from disuse.

She died in one of the downstairs rooms, in a heavy walnut bed with a curtain, her gray head propped on a pillow yellow and moldy with age and lack of sunlight.

V

The Negro met the first of the ladies at the front door and let them in, with their hushed, sibilant voices and their quick, curious glances, and then he disappeared. He walked right through the house and out the back and was not seen again.

The two female cousins came at once. They held the funeral on the second day, with the town coming to look at Miss Emily beneath a mass of bought flowers, with the crayon face of her father musing profoundly above the bier and the ladies sibilant and macabre; and the very old men — some in their brushed Confederate uniforms — on the porch and the lawn, talking of Miss Emily as if she had been a contemporary of theirs, believing that they had danced with her and courted her perhaps, confusing time with its mathematical progression, as the old do, to whom all the past is not a diminishing road, but, instead, a huge meadow which no winter ever quite touches, divided from them now by the narrow bottleneck of the most recent decade of years.

Already we knew that there was one room in that region above stairs which no one had seen in forty years, and which would have to be forced. They waited until Miss Emily was decently in the ground before they opened it.

The violence of breaking down the door seemed to fill this room with pervading dust. A thin, acrid pall as of the tomb seemed to lie everywhere upon this room decked and furnished as for a bridal: upon the valance curtains of faded rose color, upon the rose-shaded lights, upon the dressing table, upon the delicate array of crystal and the man's toilet things backed with tarnished silver, silver so tarnished that the monogram was obscured. Among them lay a collar and tie, as if they had just been removed, which, lifted, left upon the surface a pale crescent in the dust. Upon a chair hung the suit, carefully folded; beneath it the two mute shoes and the discarded socks.

The man himself lay in the bed.

For a long while we just stood there, looking down at the profound and fleshless grin. The body had apparently once lain in the attitude of an embrace, but now the long sleep that outlasts love, that conquers even the grimace of love, had cuckolded him. What was left of him, rotted beneath what was left of the nightshirt, had become inextricable from the bed in which he lay; and upon him and upon the pillow beside him lay that even coating of the patient and biding dust.

Then we noticed that in the second pillow was the indentation of a head. One of us lifted something from it, and leaning forward, that faint and invisible dust dry and acrid in the nostrils, we saw a long strand of iron-gray hair.

INDEX